Palgrave Execut

MW00626519

Today's complex and changing business environment brings with it a number of pressing challenges. To be successful, business professionals are increasingly required to leverage and spot future trends, be masters of strategy, all while leading responsibly, inspiring others, mastering financial techniques and driving innovation.

Palgrave Executive Essentials empowers you to take your skills to the next level. Offering a suite of resources to support you on your executive journey and written by renowned experts from top business schools, the series is designed to support professionals as they embark on executive education courses, but it is equally applicable to practicing leaders and managers. Each book brings you in-depth case studies, accompanying video resources, reflective questions, practical tools and core concepts that can be easily applied to your organization, all written in an engaging, easy to read style.

More information about this series at
https://link.springer.com/bookseries/16879

Shardul S. Phadnis · Yossi Sheffi · Chris Caplice

Strategic Planning for Dynamic Supply Chains

Preparing for Uncertainty Using Scenarios

palgrave
macmillan

Shardul S. Phadnis
Asia School of Business
Kuala Lumpur, Malaysia

Yossi Sheffi
Massachusetts Institute of Technology
Cambridge, MA, USA

Chris Caplice
Massachusetts Institute of Technology
Cambridge, MA, USA

ISSN 2731-5614   ISSN 2731-5622   (electronic)
Palgrave Executive Essentials
ISBN 978-3-030-91812-5   ISBN 978-3-030-91810-1   (eBook)
https://doi.org/10.1007/978-3-030-91810-1

To Aaji *(who enterprisingly debut-authored in her 70s) and* Aaba *(whose devoted service earned him the moniker "poor people's doctor")—my paragons of purposeful living in an uncertain world for* Fiona *and* Ashwin.
—Shardul S. Phadnis

To Anat.
—Yossi Sheffi

To Kristin.
—Chris Caplice

Preface

The research presented in this book has its roots in the early 2000s. In 2004, the MIT Center for Transportation & Logistics (CTL) launched *Supply Chain 2020*, a project to identify the principles underlying supply chain excellence and preparedness. From there, the project expanded to include fundamental questions about the structure of supply chain strategy, the nature of strategic alignment, and the logic of future visioning exercises.

In keeping with MIT's spirit of *mens et manus* (mind and hand), the project involved collaborations between CTL and several companies for formulating supply chain strategies, as well as government agencies interested in long-range transportation planning. These engagements centered around questions such as: "What should a national pharmaceuticals distribution network look like (circa 2010) if the Affordable Care Act adds up to 30 million Americans to the healthcare system?" or "What supply chain capabilities does a beverage manufacturer need to serve consumers increasingly influenced by social media?" Or "Which transportation asset should a state invest in to promote regional competitiveness in a dynamic trade environment?"

While such questions came from the public and private sectors, they had several qualities in common. First, they had no easy answers. Even more importantly, it was often not clear what the right questions were in the first place. For example, should the Vice President of Supply Chain aim to adapt his brewer's supply chain strategy to the growing influence of social media on its consumers? If yes, how? Second, when one did come up with relevant questions, their answers typically depended on ambiguous factors and were difficult to justify logically. For the brewer it meant understanding whether the adoption of social media meant consumers would be sharing pictures of a group of friends drinking a bucket of beers of a microbrewer's seasonal ale or a global blockbuster lager (affecting demand for the respective products), or having a photo of the friend whose 21st birthday was being celebrated on beer bottles (affecting the brewer's packaging). Third, all these questions required looking deep into the future. Their answers would lead to investments in assets with lifespans measured in years and decades. Forecasting such a long-term future was difficult in the stable 1960s, but it became even more challenging in the turbulent twenty-first century.

Recognizing these challenges made a few things clear, though. One, these questions were of strategic importance: decisions based on the answers would affect competitive advantages or involve judicious use of taxpayer dollars invested by public-sector organizations. Two, it was evident that the traditional supply chain planning methods—such as demand forecasting, inventory models, stochastic network optimization, risk management—were inadequate for answering these questions. It became necessary to have a methodology that could handle unpredictability about the future and ambiguity of the factors involved. Three, such a methodology would also need to harness the wisdom of a collection of experts in various domains connected to the supply chain.

This led the MIT CTL researchers to *scenario planning*, a method used since the 1950s to make strategic decisions while managing the ambiguity and unpredictability inherent in such decision contexts. Initial explorations of scenario planning involved creation of scenarios for specific industry cases and their discussions in CTL's executive education programs. Their purpose was educational; the CTL team did not use the scenarios to formulate actual supply chain strategies. A session in 2006 even explored a scenario of an outbreak of a deadly virus that could turn into a global pandemic![1] While this was a useful academic exercise (after all, no such event had happened for over 80 years), the CTL researchers learned about the efficacy of the scenario method just as much as the program participants did.

One of the first major breaks for CTL's scenario planning application came in 2010, with the Future Freight Flows project. The project, launched as a part of the National Cooperative Highway Research Program (NCHRP), was primarily concerned with improving how freight infrastructure investment decisions were made. The project aimed to provide federal, state, and local

---

[1] We thank our CTL colleague and friend Jim Rice for sharing this with us.

planners with a better method for strategic planning of freight infrastructure investments. The CTL team developed multiple scenarios and test-applied them in various workshops across the US. The workshops also allowed the CTL team to understand how scenario immersion changed the judgment of the experts invited to the workshops.

Around the same time, a US-based pharmaceuticals distributor (Medford, a pseudonym) engaged with CTL to capture and assess its as-is supply chain strategy and to develop scenarios to guide its strategy development. The insights from this project deepened the researchers' appreciation for scenario planning as a decision-making process that could influence senior managers' thoughts about the organization's emerging future.

Between 2010 and 2014, the CTL team conducted scenario planning exercises in dozens of organizations—a chemical firm, a convenience store chain, a food and beverage producer, and even a department of the United Nations—in the Americas, Europe, and Asia. These projects informed and shaped the supply chain strategies of organizations and were often integral to their strategy formulation process. For example, a large chemical firm's supply chain strategy for Asia-Pacific was developed using scenarios created collaboratively by the CTL team and the company's supply chain strategy group.

The lessons learned from these projects have been published in several scholarly papers, managerial articles, and policy documents. However, their full stories remain untold. Given the nature of those publications, none of them narrate from start to finish what challenges an organization faced, how the scope of a project was defined to tackle those challenges, what information was gathered (and from which sources) to create the scenarios (and why), how the scenarios were subsequently synthesized, and how they were applied to make strategic choices.

This is what motivated the authors to write this book. This book aims to give a visceral view of the MIT CTL scenario planning projects used for developing strategies. By sharing the ground-level details, the authors hope that readers will relate to the cases and, possibly, see the challenges in their own organizations more clearly using the perspective presented in this book.

Kuala Lumpur, Malaysia   Shardul S. Phadnis
Cambridge, USA   Yossi Sheffi
Cambridge, USA   Chris Caplice

Acknowledgments

Several individuals have contributed to various parts of the projects described in this book. We thank a notable few for their contributions to the foundation of this book. Jim Rice and Roberto Perez-Franco were among the first to get involved in the scenario planning activity at CTL. We have brainstormed projects with them and facilitated several scenario workshops together. Larry Lapide and Mahender Singh were the first two directors to lead the *Supply Chain 2020* project; they laid the foundation for CTL's scenario planning activity. Edgar Blanco, Jarrod Goentzel, Loic Lagarde, Luis Blackaller, Miguel Sanchez, and Paco Alonso were involved in scenario creation, collateral development, workshop facilitation, or post-workshop analysis in various projects.

Just as important are our partners in the public and private sectors who sponsored the projects and hosted the workshops. Tony Furst, Barbara Ivanov, and Bill Rogers championed the Future Freight Flows (FFF) project. Ted Dahlburg was an early enthusiastic adopter to host FFF's inaugural workshop at the Delaware Valley Regional Planning Commission. His team also developed the artwork that would become affiliated with the FFF project over time. Supply chain leaders at three organizations—Hoppy Brew, Medford, and Chemica (pseudonyms to maintain anonymity)—strongly believed in the scenario planning methodology and adopted it to formulate supply chain strategies. We are immensely thankful to them and their colleagues who participated in the engagements, which lasted several months. We have learned a lot from our colleagues and friends in the industry and academia.

Our collaborations and exchanges with Jonathan Byrnes, Emmanuel Coucke, Charlie Fine, Dan Frey, John Gray, Srihari Iyer, Nitin Joglekar, Subu Nemmara, and Steve Raetz have helped add more nuance to the writing. We are particularly grateful for the collaborations with Paul Schoemaker—the guiding light for our dispassionate, scientific inquiry of scenario planning—which have enriched our understanding of scenario planning and made us realize that there is a lot more to learn about its practice.

Publications based on CTL's scenario planning projects benefited from thoughtful critique and suggestions for improvements from many. Our special thanks go to Ken Cottrill and Dan McCool of CTL, as well as Andrea and Dana Meyer of Working Knowledge. Jack Louis's work on earlier versions of this manuscript helped us structure and sharpen the book's message. Aalap Trivedi of DraftEd helped refine its composition.

Finally, and most importantly, we are grateful for the support of our families. Shardul is blessed to have Charlotte's support and her seamless management of kids' activities and umpteen expat social gatherings, allowing him to write. Bonds with his parents, brother, and other family members, nurtured remotely, eased the two-plus years of pandemic-enforced isolation that coincided with the writing of this book. Yossi and Chris appreciate the love and support of their wives, Anat and Kristin, respectively.

About This Book

The book covers three in-depth cases. These cases are purposefully chosen from the projects the CTL team completed to highlight different perspectives on strategic supply chain planning and frameworks for scenario creation and application. Cases are presented in conjunction with the scenario frameworks such that the theoretical material is followed by illustrative cases woven longitudinally throughout the book. The book is intended for practitioners—leaders and managers operating supply chain functions in a variety of private- and public-sector organizations—as well as professors and students in business schools and graduate programs interested in strategic supply chain planning, urban planning, and infrastructure development. It explains how corporate supply chain executives, leaders of freight carriers, and managers of regional/urban planning organizations should make decisions about long-lived supply chain assets and freight infrastructure in dynamic and unpredictable business environments.

Praise for *Strategic Planning for Dynamic Supply Chains*

"Imagining the unthinkable! This book is an essential contribution to all supply chain professionals in times of unprecedented events and turbulent markets that challenge every supply chain and demand for higher capabilities by preparing for the unknown."
—Ralf Busche, *Senior Vice President European Site Logistics Operations BASF, Ludwigshafen am Rhein, Germany*

"Once again, the MIT team from the Center for Transportation and Logistics have broken new ground. The use of scenario planning, whilst widely used elsewhere, has rarely been deployed in the development of supply chain strategies. Now, this timely book provides a valuable guide to help organisations re-shape their supply chains to cope with the challenges of an uncertain future."
—Martin Christopher, *Emeritus Professor of Marketing and Logistics, Cranfield School of Management, UK and author of* Logistics & Supply Chain Management

"Scenario planning is conceptually straightforward but can be challenging to implement. This work clearly unfolds, explains and makes accessible what it takes to utilize scenario planning to support strategic decision-making in an uncertain environment."
—Tony Furst, *Former Director, Office of Freight Management & Operations Federal Highway Administration, Washington, DC, USA*

"The authors powerfully explain how storytelling, via scenario planning, gives insights in a roaring, uncertain future. Many assume that transportation investments in the US are made from top down, however hundreds of agencies act more like islands than a hierarchy. Here's a practical path for multiple actors to set priorities."

—Barbara Ivanov, *Former Director Freight Systems Division Washington State Department of Transportation, USA*

"Practical and case-based, this innovative book utilizes scenario planning as a method to anticipate changes and challenges in supply-chain infrastructure. Well-written and accessible, the focus is on improving decision making and organizational learning in the face of an unpredictable future."

—George Wright, *Professor of Management Science, University of Strathclyde, UK, author of* The Sixth Sense: Accelerating Organizational Learning with Scenarios *and Founding Editor in Chief of* Futures & Foresight Science

Contents

About the Authors

Shardul S. Phadnis is an Associate Professor of Operations and Supply Chain Management at the Asia School of Business. Previously, he served as the Associate Professor and Director of Research at MIT Supply Chain and Logistics Excellence (SCALE) Network's Malaysia Institute for Supply Chain Innovation. His research explores the intersection of supply chains and strategic management: how organizations create value by orchestrating supply chain operations, and how strategy processes influence the adaptability of supply chain structures and processes. He received the *Giarratani Rising Star Award* from the Industry Studies Association for his research in apparel supply chains in 2015. He is a member of the editorial board of Futures & Foresight Science. Dr. Phadnis holds a Ph.D. in Engineering Systems from the Massachusetts Institute of Technology.

Yossi Sheffi is the Elisha Gray II Professor of Engineering Systems and Director of the MIT Center for Transportation and Logistics (CTL). He is the author of a textbook and six award-winning management books that were translated into numerous languages. He is also a multiple entrepreneur, having founded five successful companies, all acquired by larger enterprises. His research areas include supply chain risk management, sustainability, and network structure. Under his leadership, the MIT CTL has launched many educational, research, and industry–government outreach programs. These include the MIT Master of Engineering in Logistics and the MITx Micro-Masters program in supply chain management. Prof. Sheffi launched an international expansion of MIT CTL, establishing academic supply chain management centers in Latin America, Europe, and Asia, known as the SCALE global network.

Dr. Sheffi has been recognized in numerous ways in academic and industry forums, including the 1997 Distinguished Service Award given by the Council of Supply Chain Management Professionals, the Salzberg Life Time Award, the Franz Edelman Award, the Eccles medal, and many others. He was awarded an honorary doctorate at the University of Zaragoza, Spain, and is a life fellow of Cambridge University's Clare Hall College.

Chris Caplice serves as the Executive Director of the MIT Center for Transportation & Logistics (CTL), where he is responsible for the planning and management of research, education, and corporate outreach programs. He is the creator and currently the Director of the MITx MicroMasters Program in Supply Chain Management, the very first MicroMasters credential ever offered. In the first five years, more than 447,000 students from 196 different countries have participated in these online courses, and more than 36,000 Verified Certificates have been awarded. A total of 3435 MicroMasters credentials have been awarded to date. In 2018, he was awarded the MITx Prize for Teaching and Learning, the Irwin Sizer Award for the Most Significant Improvement to MIT Education, and the MIT Teaching with Digital Technology Award. In 2016, Dr. Caplice was selected as the first Silver Family Research Fellow in recognition of his contribution to supply chain education and research. Also in 2016, he received the Council of Supply Chain Management Professionals (CSCMP) Distinguished Service Award.

List of Figures

List of Tables

1

Introduction

It would be banal to begin a book about supply chain uncertainty written in 2021 by citing the COVID-19 pandemic as an example of unanticipated events unleashing unprecedented disruptions in global supply chains, including a massive toll on human life. Nevertheless, one of the most illuminating examples of preparing for unpredictable supply chain disruptions comes from this pandemic. After the pandemic ravaged businesses in most industries in the previous year, 2021 saw a boom in demand for all products, including automobiles. Yet, most global automakers—with the exception of one—failed to capitalize on that surge in demand and ended up cutting their production targets. The exception was Toyota Motor Company. The reason it stood out was even more exceptional.

Global automakers were forced to cut production targets in 2021 because of massive supply shortages in automotive semiconductor chips. These chips are used in an increasing array of automotive applications—ignition control, steering, safety systems, on-board entertainment—as cars get "smart" and "connected."[1] When the pandemic forced stay-at-home and work-from-home regimes in 2020, the demand for computer tablets and laptops skyrocketed. This led to a surge in demand for semiconductor chips from computer equipment manufacturers, pushing the semiconductor foundries to operate near full capacity and with little excess capacity to cater to the swell in automakers' demand. The problem was so severe that the US and German governments lobbied, on behalf of their automakers, their counterparts in

Taiwan to influence the world's largest chipmaker, Taiwan Semiconductor Manufacturing Co. Ltd. (TSMC),[2] to give preference to the automotive industry. Toyota, on the other hand, needed no such pampering. According to its Chief Financial Officer, Kenta Kon, Toyota had stockpiled several months' worth of chips to prepare for a potential shortage.[3] As a result, Toyota raised its earnings forecast by 50% for the first quarter of 2021, when all other major automakers were lowering theirs. In the second quarter of 2021, Toyota surpassed GM for the first time in terms of number of cars sold, a record performance that continued throughout 2021.[4] What is extraordinary is that Toyota did this by violating the central tenet of its eponymous Toyota Production System's lean inventory policy—a policy imitated by organizations in various industries all over the world for over four decades, which, ironically, may have contributed to other automakers' semiconductor shortages!

What prompted Toyota to take such an unexpected action? Allegedly, it was in response to Toyota's experience of nearly six months of chip shortage a decade earlier, when another unpredictable event—a tsunami triggered by the Fukushima earthquake on March 11, 2011—incapacitated the main plant of its major chip supplier, Renesas Electronics, for several months. That experience made Toyota executives aware of the long lead times in the semiconductor supply chains and the supply risk of managing chip inventories using the principles of lean manufacturing.

Is prior experience of a supply chain disaster necessary for learning lessons that may prompt actions that seem almost prophetic in hindsight? Or, can companies envision such events systematically, and with conviction, to take bold strategic actions—actions that may even go against their core philosophy? A method to facilitate such learning would help firms to not only choose operational policies to prepare supply chains for unpredictable environments but also make judicious selections of long-lived, rigid supply chain assets—such as warehouses, factories, or specialized machinery—that have planned lives of a decade or longer.

This book introduces one such method that has been widely used at the highest levels of organizational hierarchies to prepare for unpredictable environments for over 50 years: scenario planning. It provides guidelines for various types of organizations for using scenario planning to prepare their supply chains for unpredictable events. These guidelines have been developed and refined through application in several real-world projects conducted with corporations and government planning entities by researchers at the MIT Center for Transportation & Logistics. This book focuses on three cases, intertwining the guidelines with their application.

The rest of this chapter provides a brief overview of supply chains, highlighting the major developments shaping them in the twenty-first century.

Supply Chains: A Brief Primer

August is the "Back to School" shopping month in America. A mother in Massachusetts may decide to take advantage of the local retailers' special promotional offers to buy clothes for her children's new school year. These clothes may have been sewn in garment factories in Bangladesh, quite likely by mothers like her. The fabric used for making these garments may have been woven at highly automated textile mills in China, using yarn spun from cotton grown in Indian farms. Connecting a mother shopping at a Massachusetts clothing retailer to a group of women in Bangladesh or cotton farmers in India is a series of companies that extract resources from nature, transform them into various forms, and store and transport them from one site to the next.

The term "supply chain" refers to a figurative chain of organizations and activities linked together in extracting commodities from nature (e.g., crude oil, ores, animals, plants), transporting them via different modes (e.g., air, road, rail, water) through a series of manufacturing processes, with intermediate storage in warehouses and distribution centers, into final consumer products and industrial goods. Supply chains of most products can be traced back to companies that extract resources from nature, either by harvesting agricultural crops (as in cotton farms in the garment supply chains), mining minerals from the earth, or raising animals as sources of food and other products. Such end-to-end supply chains also typically cross multiple industries (such as cotton farming, textile mills, apparel manufacturing, and retail) through an array of intermediary companies and service providers that move and store physical materials, track the money, and maintain and analyze the data essential to plan and execute a supply chain's operations.

Rather than being linear in structure, supply chains are complex multitiered networks, extending upstream from a focal manufacturer through its immediate suppliers (Tier-1), their suppliers (Tier-2), and so on, all the way upstream to the commodity suppliers. Supply chains also extend downstream from the manufacturer to distributors to either industrial customers or consumers via retailers. Modern supply chains are also concerned with reverse logistics: recycling and responsible disposition.

Lowering trade barriers in the late twentieth century, coupled with the Internet-enabled global connectivity, has allowed supply chains to stretch across the globe to access the desired materials, expertise, and goods. These developments followed advances in transportation technology in the late nineteenth and early twentieth centuries, including the development of refrigeration and electricity. A key development that ushered in the era of global supply chains was the commercialization of the use of standard shipping containers across both maritime and land movements. Malcolm McLean converted the World War II T-2 tanker, the *SS IdealX*, into a container ship that, in April 1956, sailed from Port Newark-Elizabeth Marine Terminal for the Port of Houston, carrying 58 containers. Legend has it that among the 100 dignitaries in attendance in Newark was Freddy Fields, a top official of the International Longshoremen's Association, who understood the implications of containerization on the number of union workers in every port. When asked about what he thought of the newly fitted container ship, he replied, "I'd like to sink that son of a bitch."[5]

An Illustrative Example: Nestlé's Palm Oil Supply Chain

Like most other commercial buyers of palm oil, Nestlé buys the raw material from distributors, who procure it from refiners, who acquire crude palm oil from mills, who source palm fruit from brokers, who buy the fruit from hundreds of small farmers and large plantations in Indonesia and Malaysia. Well over a third of the palm oil comes from small farms.[6] Hundreds of thousands of palm fruit producers transport the fresh fruit bunches to local palm oil mills, which extract the reddish palm oil and the pale-yellow palm kernel oil. Palm oil refineries then remove impurities and separate various fatty acids from the raw oil for different applications. The Palm Oil Refiners Association of Malaysia defines 14 different standardized palm oil products.[7] The refined palm oil products then go to ingredient makers that produce edible oils and fats, saponified oils for soap, esterified oils for biodiesel, and dozens of other derivative products. Thus, any one of the wide range of consumer goods that uses palm oil is based on a very complex, multi-tiered, and opaque supply chain.

Many other raw materials (e.g., fossil fuels, wood products, minerals, ores, natural fibers, grains, tea, coffee, and cocoa) follow similar paths of aggregation from natural sources, purification, and separation as they end up in different products. They all feature a similarly complex, interlinked supply network of contributing intermediary companies that include the miners, growers, suppliers, manufacturers, transportation carriers, warehouses providers, distributors, retailers, and the myriad other supporting organizations involved in the design, procurement, selling, tracking, payments, customs clearance, and servicing of goods.

Geographic and Organizational Spread of Supply Chains

The geographic and organizational spread of these activities can vary between supply chains. For example, at Ford's River Rouge complex during the early twentieth century, most of these activities were controlled by Ford and collocated in proximity to one another. In the second half of the twentieth century, companies started outsourcing the manufacturing of certain components, and even complete products, to specialized suppliers. Companies also decided to relocate factories in countries with low labor costs.

Such outsourcing and geographic spread enable companies to access the highest-quality components and materials from specialized suppliers who offer economies of scale and expertise, as well as cheaper factors of production than those available in home markets. The result has been a lengthening of the supply chains, which span multiple organizations, geographies, levels of technological sophistication, as well as a variety of regulatory regimes, political forces, and social norms.

This lengthening of supply chains is a double-edged sword, though. On the one hand, it allows companies to focus on their core competencies and enables flexibility in choosing suppliers to meet changing volume, technology, and service requirements. Companies can choose suppliers who, due to their focused expertise and scale, could incorporate advanced technologies in their components and subassemblies, enabling a faster introduction of the latest technology. They can also divide their production needs among qualified suppliers, thereby gaining greater flexibility to adjust to specific product demands. Technology giants like Apple, Cisco, and Microsoft exemplify both these trends—they outsource manufacturing to concentrate on product design, marketing, sales, and management of their respective supply chains.[8]

On the other hand, as the distance—geographic and organizational—between the linked companies increases, the supply chain gets exposed to potentially more heterogeneous socioeconomic, cultural, and regulatory environments. Lengthening the supply chain in space, time, or number of intermediaries increases the potential for mishaps, as the chain can only be as robust as its most vulnerable link. Thus, companies need to be able to adapt their operations to changing conditions and unexpected events. For a supply chain to continue to perform well over time, the choices of assets, capabilities, and organizational relationships need to be such that they perform well in a wide range of potential business environments (exhibiting "robustness") or can be adjusted relatively easily (possessing "strategic agility") when needed.

Recognizing the Strategic Importance of Supply Chains

Supply chain management has evolved as a result of lengthening supply chains. From a siloed, internally facing function focused on reducing operational costs of transportation and warehousing, it has become a strategic function influencing revenue through its impact on customer service. Effective supply chain management promotes product availability and delivery speed; it also ensures business continuity in an uncertain business landscape.

Because of the function's strategic importance, most manufacturing, retail, and distribution companies now have Chief Supply Chain Officers (CSCOs), responsible for a holistic supply chain view, reporting to the CEO. In many companies, the supply chain function encompasses procurement, inbound and outbound transportation, inventory management, and distribution. It often includes manufacturing, warranties and repairs, and processing of returned goods. CSCOs often control more than 50% of the company's annual spending and lead over two-thirds of the company's total workforce.[9]

In several firms, the leaders of their supply chain organizations go on to become CEOs. A famous example of this is Tim Cook, who succeeded Steve Jobs to become the CEO of Apple. Before he was the CEO, Mr. Cook was the company's Chief Operations Officer and led its supply chain function. Mary Barra led General Motors' Supply Chain, Purchasing, and Product Development before being named the company's CEO in 2014. Brian Krzanich served as Intel's Chief Operations Officer before being named its CEO in 2013. The list continues to grow. A background in operations, along with finance and sales & marketing, has accounted for nearly one in five CEO appointments in S&P500 companies since the early 1990s. Operations leaders are being tapped for the CEO role with increasing frequency in the twenty-first century.[10]

Twenty-First Century Supply Chains

Supply chains of the twenty-first century in nearly all industries are being shaped by four major drivers. They are *global* in scope, becoming more *digital* in various ways, face stakeholders that demand greater accountability on *environmental, social, and corporate governance (ESG)*, and increasingly serve informed and *demanding customers*. These drivers pose major challenges to the strategic planning of supply chains.

Global Scope

The COVID-19 pandemic put the global nature of supply chains under the spotlight. Many of the life-saving vaccines that would eventually pull the world out of the pandemic were developed through multinational collaborations among firms such as Pfizer (US) and BioNTech (Germany); or the Oxford University, Anglo-Swedish AstraZeneca, and the Serum Institute of India. AstraZeneca's production network of the COVID-19 vaccine, one of the world's most extensive, included 25 firms in 15 countries.[11] The main factor limiting the number of countries involved was the difficulty of replicating specialized knowledge of vaccine production. However, the 200-plus components used for vaccine production—including glass vials, filters, resins, tubing—were produced all over the world. This has been the case even for companies that produced the vaccine independently, such as Moderna.

National governments got involved in the vaccine supply chains as well. Israel led the world in vaccinating its population primarily because of its "Real-world Epidemiological Evidence Collaboration Agreement" with Pfizer, allowing the company to collect epidemiological and population-level vaccine effectiveness data in exchange for assuring vaccine supply.[12] The Biden administration loosened restrictions placed under the Defense Production Act on the export of raw materials needed for producing the vaccines, so the Serum Institute of India could accelerate vaccine production during India's second devastating wave of the pandemic.[13] The governments were also demanding customers: the European Union took AstraZeneca to court when the company could deliver only a third of its promised 90 million doses by March 2021.[14]

This global scope is by no means limited to the vaccine supply chains. Some of the world's largest industries generate a significant portion of their revenue from exports. For example, in 2019,[15] 26% (of $3 trillion) and 19% ($2.2 trillion) of revenues, respectively, of the global car & automobile manufacturing industry and the auto parts & accessories manufacturing industry—two of the world's three largest industries delivering physical goods—were generated from exports. For the third-largest industry, oil & gas production (which is location-dependent on fossil energy sources), exports contributed 65% of its $2.9 trillion revenue. The exports-to-revenue ratios for some other major industries were 24% (of $1.4 trillion) for consumer electronics manufacturing, 43% (of $1.3 trillion) for pharmaceuticals &

medicine manufacturing, 20% ($0.84 trillion) for semiconductor & electronic parts manufacturing, and 61% (of $0.82 trillion) for apparel manufacturing. Naturally, these numbers tell only a partial tale: export of finished goods. They do not include the inbound importation of parts and material used in these industries.

Overall, world trade as a fraction of global GDP has increased from about 27% in 1970 to over 59% in 2018. This fraction has barely budged from its all-time high of 60.8% in 2008 despite the protectionist rhetoric and actual trade barriers of Brexit and the Trump administration between 2016 and 2020.[16]

That protectionist trend, however, has created uncertainty about how the global trade may change in different industries in the future. This poses significant challenges for the strategic planning of supply chains. Companies need to decide whether they should contract with overseas suppliers, have a global production footprint, or limit their production and supply sources to their home markets. Such decisions determine the design of their distribution network and logistics partners. They need to decide whether they can license a foreign technology for its products or service networks. Similar uncertainty is experienced on the market side. Questions about a feasible form of foreign market entry, where to produce for the foreign market, and so on, need to be answered for strategic supply chain planning while in the fog of uncertainty.

Increasingly Digital

Advances in digitization have been shaping manufacturing and supply chains since the 1950s, with the advent of programmable logic controllers, the development of Material Requirements Planning, and the progress of robotics. The transformative potential of digital tools surfacing in the twenty-first century is just as revolutionary. For instance, the introduction of smartphones has ushered in a new era of retail. With an Internet-connected phone in hand, a shopper can examine a product (e.g., book, television, or washing machine) at a physical retail store and check prices of the same model at other retailers, including online-only ones. This phenomenon is termed "showrooming" as it effectively turns physical stores into showrooms where people inspect the product but buy it elsewhere. It was at least partly responsible for the bankruptcies of dozens of retailers, including some iconic ones such as RadioShack, Sears, and Toys "R" Us. Even luxury fashion is not spared.[17]

However, there has been a reverse effect as well. Consumers could also "web-room" to check online if a particular product is available at a store locally and then buy the product online only to pick it up at the physical store instead of waiting for it to be delivered. These developments have blurred the line between online and physical stores, ushering in the "omnichannel" world. The question for the retailer is where to fulfill the order from—a distribution center or another store. To do this effectively, the retailer has to first have an omniscient view of all its inventory regardless of its location. Note that omnichannel arose with the increased use of smartphones after 2010. Few imagined before then the need to respond anytime, anywhere, or anyhow to orders; retailers were making investments in long-lived assets, many of which became obsolete within a few years.

A bevy of digital advances started emerging in the second decade of the twenty-first century. Many observers believe that digital advances like the Internet of Things, augmented reality, blockchain, Big Data analytics, 3D printing, and automation will revolutionize supply chains. At the time of writing, the jury is still out regarding which of these technologies will have a lasting impact and which may turn out to have only niche applications. Individually, these digital advances have been creating several novel applications. For example, in April 2015, GE Aviation's GE90 engine—used on Boeing 777 aircraft—became the first aircraft engine to use a part ("T25 sensor housing") produced using 3D printing after the part was certified by the US Federal Aviation Administration.[18] 3D printing allows the creation of highly complex geometries that can be impossible to produce with subtractive manufacturing methods. GE would go on to replace 300 parts in its GE9X engine with just seven 3D-printed components.[19] 3D printing has the potential to reduce the complexity of the associated supply chain, in terms of the number of parts handled, and conceivably speed up the production of highly complex parts. However, the technology is still slow and is consequently used mainly for prototype and one-of-a-kind manufacturing. These include medical applications (such as implants and prosthetics), concept models, custom jewelry, and out-of-production spare parts.

However, the transformative potential of these technologies lies not in what they can do individually, but in the range of possibilities they create in conjunction with other technologies. As a result, these technologies are lumped together under the umbrella of the "Fourth Industrial Revolution" (also called Industrial Internet of Things or Industry 4.0). It is difficult, and conceivably impossible, to predict what supply chain applications and supply chain structures would emerge as part of the Fourth Industrial Revolution. The number and scope of the applications are limited only by the creativity of entrepreneurs.[20]

However, increasing digitization also has a dark side. As companies increasingly rely on computer networks to manage their sprawling supply chains, the vulnerability of these networks becomes their Achilles' Heel. In 2020 and 2021, high-profile cyberattacks derailed operations of major supply chains. In November 2020, a ransomware attack forced Americold,[21] a major US provider of cold-chain distribution, to halt its operations, leading not only to a loss of immediate capacity but also raising concerns about future attacks disrupting the distribution of COVID-19 vaccines that many Americans (and the world) were eagerly waiting for. A few months later, another ransomware attack forced Colonial to shut down the oil pipeline supplying fuel from Texas to as far north as New York, causing fuel shortages and panic buying in several states in between.

The use of personal data for commercial purposes and artificial intelligence (AI)-based algorithms processing voluminous data has been receiving increasing public and regulatory scrutiny in the twenty-first century. The Facebook–Cambridge Analytica data scandal,[22] in which the consulting firm Cambridge Analytica, collected personal data belonging to millions of Facebook users without their consent and later used it for political advertising, shone a spotlight on the commercial use of personal data. AI algorithms, it is feared, could embody personal biases and social norms and propagate social injustices. Proposals for regulating such AI and machine learning applications started emerging in the US[23] and the European Union[24] after the Facebook–Cambridge Analytica scandal. The Big Tech companies in China[25] have experienced a much more heavy-handed response. As Big Data applications and AI are increasingly used in supply chain applications, strategic planners of supply chains need to be cognizant of the pros and cons of these technologies, as well as any potential uncertainties in their future development. While companies try to stay abreast of and make sense of existing digital technologies, technologies continue to evolve and new ones emerge.

Increasing Focus on Environmental, Social, and Corporate Governance (ESG)

Another trend evident in many supply chains is an increasing emphasis on ESG. Non-profit organizations such as Greenpeace and the World Wide Fund for Nature have been campaigning for many years to raise awareness about the harm caused to the natural environment by economic activity. This resulted in several concrete actions. For instance, by mid-2020, 69 countries in the world had passed regulations imposing either a ban on plastic bags or a fee for their use.[26] This included China, which pledged to ban non-compostable plastic bags entirely by the end of 2022. Without federal regulation, several US states, such as California and New York, have enacted bans on single-use plastics. In Europe, extended producer responsibility regulations put the onus on manufacturers to reduce the end-of-life environmental costs of their products, leading to the development of reuse, buyback, or recycling programs for many products.

The impetus also goes the other way. Facing sustainability-conscious consumers at home, many European companies in China have indicated to regional government officials that they will find it difficult to expand or open new production sites if local power is generated from the burning of coal (as of 2021, 60% of China's energy came from burning coal).[27] In January 2021, Black Rock, the world's largest asset manager, announced that it will ask companies to disclose their plans to achieve net-zero greenhouse gas emissions. The company was concerned that global warming as well as a lack of effective regulation would result in financial losses for companies.

Among consumers, millennials are likely to push for more environmentally sustainable business activity. A 2019 Gallup poll[28] found that 67% of people aged 18–29 and 49% of those aged 30–49 say that global warming is real, man-made, and a serious threat. This was also the first time that a majority of Americans were "concerned believers" who thought that global warming will pose a serious threat in their lifetime.

ESG issues are not limited to clean energy and the natural environment; they also include concerns such as declining biodiversity, slavery and indentured labor, and racial inequity. As seen from the environmental movement, companies can expect to be held responsible for violations of ethical ESG practices not just within their own operations but also in their extended supply chains. For most companies, visibility into the supply chain typically ends at their immediate, Tier-1 suppliers (the ones they pay directly for material and parts). As supply chains get stretched across the globe and pass through multiple levels of companies, it becomes exponentially difficult for manufacturers to even know which organizations are parts of their supply chains, let alone have any way of knowing their operating practices. Yet, companies may need to build visibility into the deep tiers of their supply chains so they can monitor compliance with ESG throughout.

A Deep-Tier Supplier Problem

After years of unsafe automobile wheel hub polishing practices, a massive dust explosion killed 75 workers and injured another 185 at Kunshan Zhongrong Metal Production Company on August 2, 2014 in China's eastern province of Jiangsu. Chinese officials blamed the chairperson of the factory and local regulators for the severe safety lapses.[29] Yet China Labor Watch, an NGO dedicated to workers' causes, also blamed GM, because the automaker used car wheel maker Citic Dicastal Wheel Manufacturing Co., the world's biggest aluminum alloy wheel hub producer, and Citic Dicastal used Zhongrong.

In response to the accident, GM president Dan Ammann offered his condolences but also said, "Our tier-one suppliers on a global basis are required to make sure that they are sourcing from suppliers that are implementing the right safety standards."[30] China Labor Watch took issue with GM's efforts to distance itself from unsafe deep-tier suppliers, saying that GM "has a duty to ensure safe production in its supply chain, and it shares responsibility for this deadly explosion."

In addition to the criticism, the event created physical disruptions in GM's supply chain. GM had to find alternative suppliers and incurred significant added expenses due to unconsolidated purchases from multiple alternative suppliers and expedited shipments to avoid disrupted production of cars. Deliveries were further threatened when Chinese authorities closed some 268 factories without warning as part of a crackdown on dust-related safety lapses.[31]

The challenge GM faced was familiar to many other companies—a failure by a small, deep-tier supplier in a distant developing country can tarnish the original equipment manufacturer's (OEM's) global brand. On the surface, Citic Dicastal has been a good Tier-1 supplier to GM since 2003.[32] Citic Dicastal had even won a *Supplier of the Year* award from GM in 2010.[33] "Citic Dicastal's own factories are clean and well-organized," said a middleman who had done business with the company, but who also noted, "Their external suppliers are small businesses with awful working conditions."[34] Monitoring such deep-tier suppliers is difficult. Zhongrong had been inspected by the government, but Liu Fuwen, a worker at Zhongrong, said, "If government officials came to inspect the factory, management would ask the workers to clean the dust before they arrived."[35]

Demanding Consumers

As if these issues were not challenging enough, consumers' expectations for high levels of service have increased dramatically. A 2019 Nielsen global survey of consumer loyalty found that only eight percent of people consider themselves loyal to a brand.[36] Value for money (39% of respondents) is the most important factor influencing their purchase, followed by superior quality (34%), price (32%), and convenience (31%)—all factors directly influenced by the product's supply chain. The demanding nature of consumers is quite evident in e-commerce. In major cities in the US and

China, an e-commerce shopper can receive many items ordered online within two hours. For most products, Amazon promises two-day free delivery. These offerings have created high service expectations that, in turn, induce high-stakes strategic decisions for any retailers regarding how to serve customers.

Another example is the aforementioned omnichannel supply chains, wherein retailers give consumers an option of not only buying an item from a physical store, online, or by phone, but also of receiving the item where they want: at their residence, at their office, or picking it up at a particular store or locker location. The items have to be readily available lest the consumer defects to a competitor's store. To compete, retailers must have multiple stocking locations, including fulfillment centers and stores situated in proximity to the consumer's location. Even with a very large number of locations, many traditional retailers cannot stock the expansive numbers of items that can be displayed on an e-commerce retailer's website.

This behavior is not limited to consumers alone; business buyers can also be demanding. A global survey of over 15,000 consumers and business buyers conducted by Salesforce in 2020–21 found that 80% of respondents consider the buying experience a company provides to be just as important as its products and services, with 71% acknowledging that they have made a purchase decision based on the quality of that experience.[37] A majority (52%) of consumers expected their suppliers' offers to be always personalized. Overall, the survey found that customers expected their suppliers to understand their business needs and goals, with 84% of business buyers acknowledging that they are more likely to buy products from the sales representatives who showed such understanding.

Strategic Supply Chain Planning: Preparing for Unpredictable Environments

These drivers, shaping nearly all twenty-first-century supply chains, create challenges for strategic supply chain planning. Strategic planning often involves making decisions about long-lived capital investments such as building a factory, installing a particular information technology (IT) system, or creating an organizational unit to develop and implement custom AI and Big Data applications. Planners must assess the benefits of different investment options over the lifespans of the assets involved, that may be measured in years or decades, based on factors that are beyond the company's control.

Naturally, there is a lot of uncertainty about how mega drivers might shape these factors. Global supply chains are fraught with uncertainty about trade relationships between nations, which exposes them to uncertainties prevalent at local levels in different countries. Rapid evolution of digital solutions requires companies to understand developments and separate the hype from reality. Many ESG issues are too complex to tackle and often require coordination with a host of organizations—non-profits, community groups, and other businesses—to find impactful solutions. Changing consumer preferences and expectations continue to challenge predictions.

Predicting the future has always been a challenge, and it is almost a fool's errand to predict the twenty-first century's mercurial global business environment more than a few months ahead. Dealing with uncertainty is a central challenge not just for businesses but across virtually all disciplines, from medicine to physics to information sciences. Businesses, however, face a more difficult forecasting predicament than, say, natural scientists. In games of chance, for example, an honest die neither changes its possible outcomes (1 through 6) nor the probability of these outcomes (1/6 each) before each roll. Similarly, natural scientists trying to measure physical constants can use Bernoulli's law of large numbers[38] to accumulate data over years and decades, to obtain ever better estimates of some physical property. However, the statistical forecasting models of gamblers and scientists all come with the same basic underlying assumption that the future will be like the past. In other words, the measure of uncertainty in the future would be the same as in the past.

Whereas the rolls of dice and orbits of planets follow unchanging laws, demands for goods and the desired particulars of their delivery tend to shift unpredictably with capricious whims of customers, demographic trends, strategic actions of competitors, environmental events, and regulatory actions. Technological advances sprout new products and product categories. New supply bases become available, often because of public policy initiatives in emerging countries to invest in certain industries and/or logistics infrastructure. New business models emerge. Such changes are equivalent to someone secretly chiseling away the die surfaces to create new facets and repainting its dots before each roll. Thus, a business forecast model based on past experiences can be very wrong owing to changes in the relationships between the underlying factors and the element one tries to forecast.

In fact, strategic planning for twenty-first-century supply chains does not need a high-powered forecasting methodology that generates predictions of the complex world over planning horizons stretching a few years to decades into the future. Such an effort is likely to be fruitless. Instead, companies need a process that allows them to comprehend the numerous drivers shaping their supply chains, understand their implications, assess what may be reasonably

predictable and what is truly uncertain, and use that information to make
living strategic plans. Such plans will have, by necessity, certain committed
components, yet retain flexibility where needed. Companies need to learn
about the dynamic business environment to support strategic planning. Such
a process can create the type of learning exhibited by Toyota in our opening
example.

Organization of the Book

This book presents scenario planning as the organizational learning process
for strategic supply chain planning. It begins with a closer look at the different
roles organizations play in their supply chains (Chapter 2). It highlights three
distinct roles, wherein each role forces different questions about strategic
supply chain planning. A vignette illustrating each role is presented.

Chapter 3 introduces scenario planning, beginning with a brief historical
overview. It emphasizes that scenario planning is a method for _foresight_, not
forecasting. This distinction may be particularly important for supply chain
practitioners, who generally are well versed in various forecasting techniques
but may wrongly assume that scenario planning is one of these techniques.
This chapter concludes with the example of United Parcel Service (UPS),
an iconic supply chain company that has been an exemplary practitioner of
scenario planning for strategic planning.

The next four chapters include in-depth descriptions of the practice of
scenario planning for supply chains. Chapter 4 presents a systematic, generic
process for developing scenarios for strategic planning. Chapter 5 illustrates how this process can be applied in the organizations playing the three
different roles in their supply chains introduced in the preceding chapter.
Chapter 6 depicts a generic scenario application process, while Chapter 7
presents the application of this process in the three different types of organizations. These four chapters form the heart of the book's central topic of
scenario-based strategic supply chain planning.

Chapter 8 concludes the book with a discussion of learning from scenarios.
It highlights the lessons learned from the cases presented in the book. This
chapter also discusses how a scenario planning intervention may be evaluated
to answer the question "does it work?".

Notes

1. These microcontroller units control applications like ignition, combustion, acceleration, braking, steering, etc. See https://www.bloomberg.com/news/articles/2021-04-07/how-toyota-s-supply-chain-helped-it-weather-the-chip-shortage.
2. https://www.reuters.com/article/us-autos-semiconductors-taiwan-idU SKBN2AK04S.
3. https://www.bloomberg.com/opinion/articles/2021-02-15/toyota-broke-its-just-in-time-rule-just-in-time-for-the-chip-shortage. Phadnis, S., Schoemaker, P. 2022. "Visibility Isn't Enough—Supply Chains Also Need Vigilance." *Management and Business Review.*
4. Sheffi, Y. 2021 (October 25). "What Everyone Gets Wrong About the Never-Ending COVID-19 Supply Chain Crisis." *Sloan Management Review.*
5. https://www.pbs.org/wgbh/theymadeamerica/whomade/mclean_hi.html.
6. http://www.undp.org/content/undp/en/home/presscenter/pressreleases/2015/03/11/indonesia-government-addresses-deforestation-challenges-in-its-aim-to-double-palm-oil-production-by-2020.html.
7. Ibid.
8. Sheffi, Y. 2015. *The Power of Resilience.* Cambridge, MA: MIT Press, pp. 18–19.
9. https://www.forbes.com/sites/kevinomarah/2016/04/21/supply-chain-leader-as-ceo/?sh=2c5441069207.
10. Nearly 20% of all CEOs appointed at S&P500 companies between 1992 and 2005 had operations background (another 20% came from sales and marketing; 22% came from finance) and CEOs appointed more recently were more likely to have operations background. See: Koyunku, B., Firfiray, S., Claes, B., Hamori, M. 2010. "CEOs with Functional Background in Operations: Reviewing Their Performance and Prevalence in the Top Post." *Human Resource Management*, 49(5), 869–882.
11. https://www.nature.com/articles/d41586-021-00727-3.
12. https://govextra.gov.il/media/30806/11221-moh-pfizer-collaboration-agreement-redacted.pdf.
13. https://www.pri.org/stories/2021-04-26/us-loosens-export-restrictions-help-indias-full-blown-coronavirus-crisis.
14. https://www.bbc.com/news/56483766.
15. All industry statistics are reported from the respective IBISWorld Industry Research reports published in 2021.

16. https://www.macrotrends.net/countries/WLD/world/trade-gdp-ratio#:~:text=Trade%20is%20the%20sum%20of,a%201.87%25%20increase%20from%202016.

17. https://www.wsj.com/articles/showrooming-hits-luxury-fashion-1397088388.

18. http://additivemanufacturing.com/2015/04/16/ge-aviations-first-additive-manufactured-part-takes-off-on-a-ge90-engine/.

19. https://www.ge.com/news/reports/the-next-generation-this-team-of-young-engineers-helped-bring-3d-printing-inside-the-worlds-largest-jet-engine.

20. Phadnis, S. 2018. "Internet of Things and Supply Chains: A Framework for Identifying Opportunities for Improvement and Its Application." In S. Loo, S. Raman (Eds.), *Emerging Technologies for Supply Chain Management* (pp. 7–24). Penang, Malaysia: WOU Press.

21. https://www.wired.com/story/hackers-targeting-covid-19-vaccine-cold-chain/.

22. https://www.businessinsider.com/cambridge-analytica-whistleblower-christopher-wylie-facebook-data-2019-10.

23. In April 2021, the U.S. Federal Trade Commission presented guidelines for "truth, fairness, and equity in your company's use of AI." See details at: https://www.ftc.gov/news-events/blogs/business-blog/2021/04/aiming-truth-fairness-equity-your-companys-use-ai.

24. In April 2021, European Commission publications a proposal lying down harmonized rules on Artificial Intelligence, known as the "Artificial Intelligence Act." See details at https://eur-lex.europa.eu/legal-content/EN/TXT/?qid=1623335154975&uri=CELEX%3A52021PC0206.

25. https://www.economist.com/business/2021/04/08/chinas-rulers-want-more-control-of-big-tech.

26. https://www.statista.com/chart/14120/the-countries-banning-plastic-bags/.

27. https://www.economist.com/china/2021/06/17/chinas-climate-sincerity-is-being-put-to-the-test.

28. https://news.gallup.com/poll/248027/americans-concerned-ever-global-warming.aspx.

29. http://www.autonews.com/article/20140803/GLOBAL02/140809957/gm-looks-for-alternative-supplies-in-china-after-deadly-factory-blast.

30. Murphy, C., White, J., Watts, J. 2014 (August 5). "GM Doesn't Plan to Change Supply-Chain Safety Process." *Wall Street Journal*.

31. http://asq.org/qualitynews/qnt/execute/displaySetup?newsID=18877.

32. http://www.dicastal.com/en/index_mnewlook_t12_i16.html.

33. http://media.gm.com/media/us/en/gm/news.detail.html/content/Pages/news/us/en/2011/Mar/0311_soy.html.
34. http://english.caixin.com/2014-08-26/100721484.html.
35. http://www.bjreview.com.cn/nation/txt/2014-08/11/content_633994.htm.
36. https://www.nielsen.com/eu/en/press-releases/2019/consumer-disloyalty-is-the-new-normal/.
37. https://www.salesforce.com/resources/articles/customer-expectations/.
38. https://pdfs.semanticscholar.org/4613/275174cdf6bce4008207214dc08f257e1ba5.pdf.

2

Managing Supply Chains: Three Organizational Roles

The scope of strategic planning varies significantly with the role organizations play in global supply chains. The diversity of organizational roles in supply chains became evident during the COVID-19 pandemic. For vaccine manufacturers (as well as manufacturers of gloves, cars, or computers), critical supply chain issues revolved around the availability of raw materials and access to production and transportation capacity. Equally important was the ability to distribute the vaccines, where it was critical to maintain vaccines in frigid temperatures (as low as -80 degrees Celsius for the Pfizer-BioNTech vaccine) throughout the supply chain from production sites to patients. A specific challenge was to meet the demand for vaccines, given the prevalent supply shortages, vaccine hesitancy, and equity considerations at the time. Government policy shaped supply chains as well. A data-sharing agreement with Pfizer helped Israel secure vaccine supply and lead the world in vaccinating its population; loosening restrictions on essential raw materials under the US Defense Production Act helped boost the vaccine production in India.

This chapter highlights three distinct roles organizations play in supply chains—roles that are relevant for strategic planning. The book illustrates each role with a vignette of an organization and the project carried out by the MIT CTL research team working with the organization's strategic supply chain planning teams.

© The Author(s), under exclusive license to Springer Nature
Switzerland AG 2022
S. S. Phadnis et al., *Strategic Planning for Dynamic Supply Chains*,
Palgrave Executive Essentials,
https://doi.org/10.1007/978-3-030-91810-1_2

Different Organizational Roles That Shape Supply Chains

At a high level, organizations play three archetypical roles in any supply chain: functional, business model, or infrastructural. The context of strategic supply chain planning depends on the role an organization plays in the supply chain. Accordingly, the challenges of strategic planning should be confronted with these roles in mind.

In the *functional* role, the goal of managing the supply chain is to align with and support the parent organization's overarching business strategy. Such a role is prevalent in three types of companies. First, in companies whose customers gain value by consuming or using the products engineered and/or produced by the parent company (such as automakers, drug manufacturers, producers of consumer packaged goods and appliances, electronics and computer manufacturers, producers of industrial goods, chemical firms), the organizational role is to deliver products to customers in a way that aligns with the company's business strategy. Thus, a producer of basic chemicals would aim to deliver the chemicals at the lowest possible cost, whereas a patented high-margin pharmaceuticals producer would aim for an expedited response to customer need (with business qualifiers such as quality, safety, etc. being common to both). Second, in retail organizations (brick-and-mortar and e-commerce merchants), the organizational role is to support the retailer's strategy, be it everyday low-cost, high-level of service or the buying experience. Third, in service organizations—in industries such as healthcare (clinics, hospitals), entertainment (amusements parts, movie halls), and hospitality (hotels, restaurants)—the organizational role is to ensure availability of goods required for delivering the service. In the context of these examples, the term "supply chain strategy" for all three types of companies refers to long-term choices regarding supply chain assets, capabilities, and organizational design to align them with the company's business strategy.

In the *business model* role, the organization's goal is to create value for its customers (who are beneficial owners of the items) by providing them with logistics services. In this case, the main identity of the organization is not an internal "Supply Chain" function that subordinates itself to the parent organization; rather, managing certain aspects of customers' supply chains is the company's business. Companies operating in a business model role include transportation carriers, warehouse operators, third-party logistics (3PL) service providers, supply chain software providers, and e-commerce platform operators. For example, they include garment wholesalers that buy clothes in bulk and sell to small and medium-sized retailers; pharmaceutical distributors that acquire drugs produced by pharma companies and deliver them to hospitals, clinics, and pharmacies; or international freight forwarders that plan and oversee the shipment of goods, ensuring compliance with import–export requirements, from manufacturing sites to customers or market locations. These organizations may not have a "supply chain strategy" per se that is distinct from their business strategy; they generate value for their customers by effectively managing their customers' supply chain activities, either in part or entirely.

Finally, in the *infrastructural role*, the organizational goal is to create and/or manage the infrastructure needed to support the supply chain activities of other companies. The scope of their work is typically confined to a specific geographic region. This category includes organizations that build and maintain highways, railroads, ocean ports, airports, and intermodal terminals. They are often governmental organizations, but such infrastructural services may also be provided by private companies. For example, railroad infrastructure in most countries is built and maintained by the national or regional governments and used by passenger and freight rail carriers, which may be either public or private organizations. In contrast, freight rail transport in the United States is provided by private organizations, which are responsible for building and maintaining their own rail infrastructure, in addition to operating goods transport. Similarly, airports around the world are run by both private companies and public-sector organizations. Ports are usually owned and operated by a combination of public and private ownership; a government entity may own the land while private companies own and operate port terminals.

Naturally, the boundaries between these roles are ambiguous. A company like UPS may manage other companies' supply chains, playing the business model role while also having a supply chain function that procures vehicles and parts for the parent organization, and an infrastructural role in that it builds its own terminals and distribution centers. Similarly, American railroads play the infrastructural role, as they create and maintain their own railroad infrastructure, as well as the business model role as their business revolves around providing supply chain services to companies whose goods they carry. For example, the American railroad BNSF Railway would play the infrastructural role when contemplating decisions about expanding, maintaining, or discontinuing parts of its railroad infrastructure, and play the business model role when making decisions about exploiting its existing railroad infrastructure to generate business.

Functional Role: Integrated Supply Chain Management

The adage that a chain is only as strong as its weakest link is certainly true for supply chains, but it offers little explanatory insight into what a supply chain is, what it does, or how well it functions. The fundamental metric of supply chain performance is "perfect delivery" or "perfect order." It means that a complete customer order was delivered on time, damage-free, and with all the required documentation. Internal company metrics of the various elements of supply chain performance leading to a high rate of perfect orders can vary across time and from one organization to another. However, failure can occur anywhere at any time and for any reason. With so much of a business's competitive advantage, profitability, or even long-range viability at stake, supply chain management has become an important competence in many organizations.

Many companies build a competitive advantage by focusing research and development on product innovation or manufacturing technology (such as patented branded drugs, semiconductor chips, and high-tech electronics). Owing to the ease of copying products and the spread of engineering talent around the world, these companies have begun appreciating the strategic value of their supply chain activities. This is often reflected in the presence of Chief Supply Chain Officers (CSCOs) on the company's executive teams and their promotions as the CEOs in many companies.

Companies in which the supply chain is managed as a functional role may operate in a variety of industries—agriculture, pharmaceuticals, apparel, computers, and electronics—all of which depend on their supply chain functions to deliver products. These include procurement, transportation of raw materials to factories, production, transportation of finished goods to customers, and after-sales customer service. In these companies, the challenge is to align the functional goals with the company's business strategy. In addition, the companies may also recognize the importance of aligning their suppliers' and customers' goals to their own functional goals and to the overall business objectives of the company. They seek to coordinate suppliers' and customers' actions and operations using approaches such as sharing of forecasts and sales information; collaborative planning, forecasting, and replenishment; risk sharing through supply contracts; joint product development.

Perhaps the central challenge facing the senior supply chain executives in these companies is formulating a supply chain strategy such that the supply chain assets and capabilities are governed using performance metrics that align with the overall objectives of the company's core strategy.[1] As with the company's core strategy, the supply chain strategy is broad in scope and purpose. It occupies a top-down position just below that of the company's core strategy. It mandates specific objectives, as well as decisions to achieve them, through the implementation of specific operational practices. It also integrates several potentially unique resources that define a company's identity. In sum, the supply chain strategy links the overall corporate strategy to the supply chain operational practices, enabled by the company's resources such as assets, culture, and capabilities.

Vignette: Enabling Beer Delivery at Hoppy Brew

Beer, one of the oldest man-made drinks, dates back to at least the fifth millennium BC in Persia.[2] The art of fermenting malted barley, and less commonly other grains, to convert the starch in the grains into sugars and then into alcohol, still carries a charm. Thousands of microbreweries blossomed in the United States in the early twenty-first century, arguably in response to the disillusionment with mass-produced beers and, possibly, as part of the general trend for customization of many products and services to individual needs and wants. In addition, tens of thousands of home-brewers create their own concoctions based on their preferred tastes, aromas, and colors.

Given the allure of the (al)chemists conjuring a combination of compounds to produce this potion—from the Trappist monks of the seventeenth century to the brew masters ruling over the mass production of ale in their twenty-first-century breweries—one could easily be forgiven for discounting the more mundane activities in this business. The supply chain function oversees procurement of raw materials to running the breweries to delivering the beer to the alehouses, bars, clubs, and taverns. It is the supply chain that ensures consistent sourcing of the right quantities and qualities of barley and hops (amid changing agricultural patterns and demands for fair-trade and sustainable farm produce), secures the supply of water for the brewing process (increasingly important as water becomes a scarce commodity), buys the required bottles, cans, or kegs, and delivers the right quantities and packaging of fresh beer to satisfy an increasingly demanding consumer base with a broad palate, while complying with a slew of regulations that constrain its distribution, retailing, and consumption.[3] After all, beer (and its alcoholic brethren) is the only product whose production, transportation, and sale induced two amendments to the Constitution of the United States: the Eighteenth Amendment banning alcoholic beverages in 1917 and the Twenty-First Amendment lifting the ban in 1933.

Fast forward to the autumn of 2013, the supply chain executives of Hoppy Brew (pseudonym)—one of the world's leading producers of beers, spirits, and soft drinks—were contemplating the changes in the business environment and how those changes would affect the company. The changes were not as drastic as constitutional amendments but could not be shrugged off as inconsequential either. Consumers, increasingly armed with ubiquitous smartphones, were beginning to realize that companies might be willing to meet their demands for what they wanted, where, and when. Would that force Hoppy Brew to adopt new packaging formats and methods, changing from its current model of delivering beer in identical-looking branded bottles and faceless kegs? What should Hoppy Brew do to inject more variety into its beer line-up, if the mercurial consumer were to start appreciating the varying seasonal tastes of microbreweries more than the stable know-what-you-are-going-to-get taste of one of Hoppy Brew's mass-produced beers?

The executives pondered other changes, too. How might global climate change redraw the world map of barley and hops growing, and what should the company do to adapt? How could the plethora of regulations that govern the end-to-end beer supply chain—from the use of genetically modified organisms (GMOs) in crops to licensing requirements for beer distribution to punishments for drunk-driving—change the brewing business? What changes would such regulations force on the supply chain? Would legalization of marijuana have any effect on beer sales?

These and other changes in the business environment had made the supply chain executives of Hoppy Brew wonder, "Do we have the right supply chain to support the business in this changing yet unpredictable environment?" Chapter 5 outlines the development of scenarios for the company grappling with such uncertainties.

Business Model Role: Value Creation by Managing Supply Chains

In the business model role, a company's value proposition is to operate and/or manage the supply chain(s) of customer businesses. Logistics service providers, such as UPS and DHL, are the best examples of organizations playing this role. There is little distinction between business strategy and supply chain strategy for these companies. The business strategy of such a company includes the supply chain assets, capabilities, and organization needed to operate the supply chains of their customers. Any failure of this supply chain hurts the operations of the customer companies and could even jeopardize their future viability. Such companies do not just recognize the importance of managing supply chains effectively, they live it! Supply chain excellence is their core competence.

A prime example of a company in this category, besides the more familiar ones cited above, is C.H. Robinson. This Eden Prairie, Minnesota-based company notes that "optimizing supply chains is at the core of all that we do."[4] It boasts a roster of more than 100,000 active customers, which the company serves by providing surface, ocean, and air freight transportation, as well as intermodal services, to seamlessly transfer cargo from one freight mode to another (such as from long-haul rail to truck for last-mile deliveries). The company also provides customs-related services and specialized services such as consulting on issues related to cross-border trade policies, project logistics, or managed procurement services. For some customers, it manages the entire supply chain. What makes C.H. Robinson different from trucking companies or warehouse operators is that it facilitates these logistics-related services without owning any trucks, trains, ships, or airplanes. It leases warehouses and leverages the use of transportation assets that it does not own. This business model, widely known as third-party logistics or 3PL, relies on a company's ability to build relationships with owners and operators of logistics assets and to link them together to create supply chains to serve the needs of its customer companies. At the core of C.H. Robinson's capabilities is its cherished asset: the multimodal Transportation Management System that allows it to orchestrate a network of over 70,000 contract carriers to manage over $21 billion in freight expenditure annually. While the company does not own hard assets (trucks or distribution centers), it is subject to fierce competition from a crop of digital freight brokers who put pressure on its margins. Consequently, a strategic decision for the company could be about the kind of information and communications system to invest in, possibly developing its own or acquiring one, or developing a combination of commercial software with its existing system. Other strategic decisions may include international expansion or targeting specific industries to serve.

Some of the supply chain engagements of 3PLs may last a few years—for example, during a given automobile model—while others may live to serve just one project. A 3PL like C.H. Robinson creates value by enabling its customers to focus on their core competence by outsourcing the management of parts of their supply chain. Hundreds of 3PL companies exist, from small, one-person truck brokerages to global 3PLs employing hundreds of thousands of people. For such companies, strategic decisions focus on building a set of supply chain assets and capabilities (including hard assets, IT systems, and networks of relationships) that can be assembled to meet the specific supply chain needs of their customers. As customers' needs change, the potential of given assets, capabilities, and relationships to generate value also changes. Therefore, companies that manage supply chains as their primary business need to continuously evaluate how their assets and capabilities can be adapted and leveraged.

Vignette: Pharmaceutical Distribution by Medford

Every day, hundreds of thousands of healthcare provider locations in the United States receive essential, potentially life-saving medicines and other healthcare products. These items are manufactured and shipped from thousands of factories across the globe. The distribution of the COVID-19 vaccines in the United States brought supply chains to the attention of the public. Until then, the mind-boggling logistics involved in servicing the vast network of retail pharmacy stores and hospitals, as well as an array of outpatient outlets, including long-term care facilities, urgent care centers, community clinics, physician offices, and diagnostic labs, remained largely hidden. Pharmaceutical distributors form the backbone of this supply chain, moving medicines from points of production to points of consumption. Distributors are unlike other supply chain participants in that they do not manufacture, prescribe, or dispense medications. Instead, they are exclusively a conduit for secure, reliable, and efficient drug delivery.

Rather than attempt to procure all those different products from multiple manufacturers, healthcare providers place orders with a small number of distributors. In turn, distributors maintain distribution centers stocked with thousands of stock-keeping units (SKUs) of medicines, ancillary medical supply kits, and medical devices that their healthcare provider customers may need. This includes carrying a full line of products from every pharmaceutical manufacturer and many over-the-counter consumer and durable goods that pharmacies often sell. For instance, the median number of prescription drug SKUs alone stocked by a US distributor in 2008 was 17,559. This number rose to 45,673 when considering all non-prescription drugs, other healthcare products, and general merchandise.[5] Distributors also provide financial credit, pharmacy management systems, and in-store retail support to pharmacies. To provide this comprehensive inventory of products, distributors maintain relationships with manufacturers of every branded, generic, and specialty drug and with manufacturers of over-the-counter (OTC) and consumer products. Just as the healthcare providers prefer using a distributor to avoid managing thousands of relationships with—and daily small shipments from—individual manufacturers, the manufacturers prefer selling products through a distributor to avoid managing hundreds of thousands of relationships with—and small shipments to—individual healthcare providers.

In the United States, three pharmaceutical distributors—also called "wholesalers" because of their older business model—dominate the industry: AmerisourceBergen, Cardinal Health, and McKesson. The market share of the Big Three distributors grew from 87% in 2013 to 95% in 2018,[6] with much of the growth coming from acquisitions and mergers. The Big Three dominate the pharmaceutical distribution industry and are giants compared to other healthcare companies. For instance, in 2020,[7] McKesson, AmerisourceBergen, and Cardinal Health earned revenues of $231 billion, $190 billion, and $153 billion, respectively, making them the seventh, eighth, and 14th largest companies in the United States.[8] Yet, their names remained unknown to most Americans (until the US opioid epidemic and the resulting lawsuits that brought pharmaceutical supply chains to the mainstream news). By comparison, brands of smaller companies in the healthcare sector are better known. These include Johnson & Johnson and Pfizer, with 2020 revenues of $83 and $42 billion, respectively. Such relative obscurity[9] despite the large revenue they earn is quintessential of a company adopting the supply chain business model, unless it also serves consumers directly, such as UPS. This is because these companies, by and large, serve other businesses (such as pharmaceutical producers, who pay the distributors for the service of delivering the medicines) and interact only with businesses, such as pharmacies and hospitals (to whom the distributors deliver the medicines), rather than consumers. In addition, the businesses these companies serve rely on their brand and prefer it not be confused with their suppliers' and business providers' brands.

Medford (pseudonym) is one such US-based pharmaceuticals distributor.[10] In 2010, its executives questioned if the company had the right distribution network and associated services for delivering pharmaceuticals. This question was triggered by the passage of President Barack Obama's signature Patient Protection and Affordable Care Act ("PPACA") on March 23, 2010. In 2009, 45 million Americans under the age of 64 lacked health insurance.[11] The *individual mandate* of PPACA, which required all Americans to obtain health insurance or pay a penalty, had the potential to increase the volume of healthcare services by a sixth. If this had happened, the increase in the volume of drugs carried by the pharma distributors would require investments in supply chain infrastructure to support the growth. However, the estimates of this growth varied widely. Furthermore, PPACA was being challenged in the courts, precisely due to questions about the constitutionality of the *individual mandate*, casting doubt on the possibility of such growth.

The degree of uncertainty surrounding the constitutionality of PPACA in 2010 is perhaps best exemplified by the fact that the US Supreme Court upheld the *individual mandate* by the slimmest 5–4 majority, and that majority was provided by the surprising vote of Chief Justice John Roberts, appointed by President George W. Bush, a Republican, whose party vehemently opposed the PPACA.

The razor-thin profit margins of the distribution business complicated Medford's executives' decisions about whether and how to prepare for a potential flood of medicines flowing through their supply chain. If Medford under-invested in additional capacity, it would lose business to competitors due to capacity constraints. If Medford over-invested in additional capacity, it may lose business to competitors due to higher costs and non-competitive prices. In 2009, the average profit margin in the industry hovered around one percent. Even the Big Three distributors' profit margins were no larger. Comparing this to other industries in the US healthcare sector demonstrates how thin these margins are. Diagnostic laboratories, for example, had roughly one-ninth of the revenues of distributors ($50 billion) yet more than six times the profit margins. Medical supplies distributors had 30% of the revenues ($135 billion) yet more than four times the profit margins. The contrast was even starker considering distributors' supply chain partners. On the downstream, nursing care facilities and emergency care centers, for example, had roughly 20% of the revenues and yet 4.5 and 8 times (respectively) the distributors' profit margins. Such profit margins were common in specialty hospitals, which had only five percent of the distributors' revenues. The picture was remarkably similar on the upstream. Alongside Medicare and other government programs, private healthcare insurers, prime payers into the pharmaceutical supply chain, had some 25% of the revenues but four times the profit margins. Pharmaceutical manufacturers had half the revenue of distributors, roughly $250 billion, yet enjoyed eight times the distributors' profit margins.

Furthermore, several other issues were weighing on Medford executives' minds. In May and October 2008, two of the Big Three—McKesson and Cardinal Health—had been fined a record-setting total of $47.25 million by the US Drug Enforcement Administration (DEA) for their alleged failure to detect and report suspicious sales of controlled substances such as prescription narcotics. The two distributors were accused of shipping unusually large amounts of prescription narcotics to Internet pharmacies, who were then filling online orders from individuals without legitimate prescriptions.[12] In addition to paying the fine, both McKesson and Cardinal Health had also agreed to implement enhanced controls at 56 distribution centers to prevent the diversion of controlled medicines for illegitimate purposes. This meant that Medford needed to spend money on similar enhanced controls at its distribution centers, further dipping into Medford's shallow profit margins.

At the same time, the drug distributors were also investing in compliance with a set of drug *pedigree* regulations. A pedigree is a document listing each step in a drug's journey along the supply chain from its production to its administration to a patient. The pedigree requirements were originally established by the federal Prescription Drug Marketing Act of 1987 but were delayed by legal challenges.[13] Noting the importance of pedigree in deterring counterfeit drugs from entering the supply chains, California and Florida had developed their pedigree regulations[14] to fill the void left by the absence of a federal standard. California's Pedigree Law required a drug manufacturer to start an electronic pedigree document with a unique serial number for each drug package and record each change in ownership of that specific package as it passed through the supply chain. In contrast, Florida's Pedigree Law[15] required the first distributor (not the manufacturer) who bought drugs from the manufacturer to start a paper-based (not electronic) pedigree but without requiring serialization at the level of individual drug packages. Several other states were considering their own pedigree laws, which could exacerbate the complexity arising from diverse standards. Medford executives wondered what kind of pedigree solution (i.e., IT system with supporting business processes) they should develop to comply with the different, and possibly conflicting, requirements of different states.

While mulling over these challenges, Medford's executives were also aware that the US healthcare sector was undergoing several technological changes. The very nature of drugs was changing. High-margin drugs with patent protection were being replaced by low-margin generic drugs, putting more pressure on distributors' revenues. The volumes of biologic drugs (which need to be maintained in a controlled two-to-eight degrees Celsius) and personalized medicines (which are delivered directly to the patient or their doctor's office, instead of a pharmacy) were growing, prompting investments in new distribution capabilities. Further, advances in information technologies were creating solutions that were enabling doctors to diagnose patients remotely and provide electronic prescriptions, which could then be filled by an online pharmacy and obviate the need to go to a physical pharmacy. Such capabilities were likely to put cost pressure on the traditional large customers of the pharmaceutical distributors. Finally, these events were taking place during 2008–2009, when the country was in the midst of its worst recession since the Great Depression of the 1930s.

These developments in the business environment had made Medford's executives wonder if they had the right supply chain capabilities and organization to support drug delivery in the United States. They also wondered what other capabilities they would need to remain competitive while continuing to operate on razor-thin margins.

Infrastructural Role: Creating Infrastructure for Supply Chain Excellence

Organizations taking the infrastructural role create the logistics infrastructure that other businesses, in various industries, use to operate their supply chains. Such logistics infrastructure includes highways and railroads, cargo air and water ports, intermodal facilities, border crossings, logistics parks, and warehouses and distribution centers. Typically, such infrastructure is developed either directly by government agencies, such as the Department of Transportation or Regional Planning Commissions, or by private businesses through projects tendered by government agencies through initiatives such as build-operate-and-transfer. The development and enhancement of such infrastructure are generally guided by long-range plans of the regional government bodies. A country's logistics performance—measured in terms of the cost, time, and complexity to perform import and export activities— depends on such infrastructure, which affects its global trade as well as local economic growth.[16] Recognizing its importance, many national and regional governments invest heavily in their logistics infrastructure.

One of the best-known examples of such investment is the city-state of Singapore. The country became a sovereign state on August 9, 1965, after separating from Malaysia. Starting as a "fishing village" in 1965, Singapore has undergone dazzling growth to become one of the world's major international transport hubs. Fueled by business-friendly policies and infrastructure investments, the Port of Singapore went on to become the busiest port in the world, a spot it lost to Shanghai only in 2010. Between 1965 and 2018, Singapore's per capita GDP grew 125-fold in constant-dollar terms, from $516.5 of a low-income country to $64,582 (both in 2018 USD), ranking it among the 10 richest countries in the world, above the United States. This growth rate is twice that of the second steepest growth experienced by another country in Southeast Asia, Thailand, which grew more than 50-fold from $137.9 to $7,273.6 per capita (in 2018 USD) over the same period.

Singapore was ranked first in the world in 2007 and 2012 for its logistics performance by the World Bank and is the only country to be ranked among the top seven in every year of this survey besides Germany and the

Netherlands. Singapore's Changi Airport has been one of the 15 busiest cargo airports in the world (in terms of tons of freight) every year for the first two decades of the twenty-first century.[17]

Singapore's transformation was enabled by its long-term view of infrastructure development. With a population of fewer than six million people and a land area one-quarter the size of the US state Rhode Island, domestic demand in Singapore was not sufficient to support its growth plans. Instead, Singapore relied on creating logistics connectivity with the rest of the world to enable entrepôt trade to fuel its growth. A combination of dozens of free-trade agreements, efficient import–export–transshipment enabled by a novel IT system, TradeNet, and a world-class logistics infrastructure developed with the Urban Redevelopment Authority (URA) and the Singapore Economic Development Board (EDB) has allowed Singapore to overcome its land and population constraints to become a leading player in the facilitation of global trade. A common thread among the planning processes of the URA, the EDB, the Port Authority of Singapore, Changi Airport, and other government agencies is the use of long-range planning processes enabled by advanced foresight techniques.

For organizations playing the infrastructural role in supply chains, strategic decisions involve the creation, extension, modification, and maintenance of physical, informational, financial, and regulatory infrastructure to support economic growth. The customers of this infrastructure are usually businesses (of both the functional and business model categories) that decide to base their operations in or route freight flows through a particular region with good infrastructure. As consumer markets, production bases, and sources of raw materials evolve, the infrastructural needs of these businesses change. Therefore, the authorities involved in creating and managing the infrastructure need to evaluate how the infrastructure assets need to change over time.

Vignette: Future Freight Flows in the US

"Port to Pantry: Infrastructure Brings You Breakfast!"[18] That is the heading of a graphic in the Infrastructure Report Card by the American Society of Civil Engineers (ASCE) intended to raise awareness of the role of America's infrastructure in the daily lives of average Americans. The graphic accompanied the 2017 edition of the report card[19] that gave America's infrastructure a poor grade of D+. Excluding the grade of B earned by the railroad industry, the grades for all other elements of the transportation infrastructure were consistently abysmal: Roads (D), Bridges (C+), Ports (C+), Inland Waterways

(D), and Aviation (D). The Report Card[20] estimated that the country needed to invest $4.59 trillion over 10 years to improve its infrastructure. Although this includes funding for all types of infrastructure (excluding broadband)—energy; dams and levees; solid waste, wastewater, and hazardous waste; public parks; and schools—transportation constitutes a significant component of the sum.

Citizens tend to care about transportation infrastructure because it affects their daily commute, shopping runs, and family travels in terms of the quality and time spent in travel. However, freight transportation infrastructure remains invisible to most consumers. It consists of not only roads and bridges that cargo trucks share with passenger cars but also the freight train network, ocean and river ports, cargo airports, pipelines, intermodal transshipment facilities, and customs ports of entry where goods enter (and exit) the country. Furthermore, what matters is not just the individual components of this infrastructure, but also the linkages among different components that enable the seamless flow of goods along the end-to-end supply chains. Moreover, every piece of infrastructure needs to be the right size, neither too large (and costly) nor too small (and congested). This challenge is made more acute by demand for transportation, which changes over time with seasons and with growth in population and trade activities. Yet, the quality and capacity of the freight transportation infrastructure determine the performance of supply chains and the competitiveness of the country's businesses. This reality came to the fore during 2021, when product shortages and high prices resulted from increased demand for products that could not be accommodated efficiently by the US logistics infrastructure.

Builders of freight transportation infrastructure face several challenges. Starting with the obvious, it takes time, often years and sometimes decades, to build these assets. Also, the process of planning, addressing the concerns of numerous stakeholders, and obtaining environmental clearance, can take from several months to several years. For example, one highly successful freight infrastructure project was the 20-mile-long Alameda Corridor, which links the ports of Long Beach and Los Angeles to the transcontinental rail lines near Los Angeles. Whereas the initial planning of the Alameda Corridor began in 1981, approval took until 1994, construction began in 1997, and the final opening for traffic did not happen until 2002. Despite the two-decade gestation, the Alameda Corridor is considered a very successful project.

Adding to the difficulties and the crucial need to get things right is the high cost of building transportation infrastructure in the US Due to various regulations, corruption, and "not in my backyard" attitudes, the costs of an underground rail line in San Francisco and Los Angeles is about $1 billion. It is $2.6 billion in New York. Underground lines and extensions built in Sweden cost $220 million for an underwater extension in Nacka and up to $400 million under the Stockholm city center. French light rail urban lines cost between $40 million and $100 million per mile.[21]

Once built, the transportation infrastructure elements are expected to remain in service for a few decades. This requires planners to envision ever-changing demand patterns many years into the future. Factors such as changes in consumer tastes; evolution of residential, commercial, and industrial areas; shifts in global trade flows; and advances in information and production technologies can shift the demand for any given element of freight infrastructure. For example, the growth of e-commerce has led to a continual increase in parcel deliveries to consumer homes. The implications of this trend on transportation infrastructure are felt particularly acutely in urban areas like New York City, where the average number of daily deliveries to households tripled between 2009 and 2017 to more than 1.1 million. These deliveries create congestion along city streets. While it is generally impractical to widen or build new roads in dense urban areas, the resulting infrastructure challenge includes the management of transportation infrastructure assets. To tackle this, actions may include the imposition of night-time deliveries, encouraging unattended deliveries in off-hours, using urban consolidation centers, or developing innovative parking and curb-use pricing. Furthermore, various groups of stakeholders—farmers, manufacturers, truckers, rail companies, shipping lines—may differ in their needs for transportation infrastructure services. Planners need to consider all these variables.

The ASCE's dismal report card in 2017 on America's decrepit infrastructure was not the country's first year of poor grades for infrastructure. ASCE first published the Infrastructure Report Card in 1988 and has done so about every four years since then. America's infrastructure has always been graded a D or D+ over these years. As local, regional, and federal transportation planning agencies seek to improve the quality of this economic enabler, they grapple with the challenges of transportation infrastructure investment planning.

In 2009–2010, the American Association of State Highway and Transportation Officials (AASHTO) established the Project 20–83 research series of the National Cooperative Highway Research Program (NCHRP)[22] to examine global and domestic long-term shifts in cargo flows and their implications. The intent was to help state departments of transportation (DOTs) deal with challenges and opportunities created over the following

30–40 years. It acknowledged that new developments in the future would dramatically reshape transportation priorities and needs.[23] The research program set two specific goals: anticipate potential issues to prepare transportation agencies to respond to new and emerging challenges, and explore visions of what the future could look like to enable transportation agencies to help shape the future through their decision-making.

Under NCHRP Project 20-83(01), MIT CTL was asked to "provide decision makers with a critical analysis of the driving forces behind high-impact economic changes and business sourcing patterns that may affect the US freight transportation system."[24]

Strategic Planning in Supply Chains

Planning is a central activity in most management functions and in supply chain management in particular owing to the complexity of the underlying system. In all three supply chain roles discussed previously, planners and managers must make provisions for satisfactory customer service in the future. For instance, managers allocate an adequate stock of goods in retail stores to meet demand, manufacture a sufficiently large quantity of product in a particular campaign to satisfy the demand until the next production campaign, route trucks to minimize travel time while satisfying customer delivery windows, schedule maintenance of transportation infrastructure to minimize travel, and so on. Such planning decisions seek to optimize the use of an organization's existing assets and are called *operational decisions*. The decisions are important because they attempt to make effective use of the organization's extant assets, and they often consume a large portion of supply chain planners' and managers' attention.

However, these operational or tactical planning decisions are markedly different from the more *strategic decisions* discussed in this book. The strategic decisions in the supply chain have nothing to do with the efficient use of current assets in the short term, but rather with the development of an asset base that can effectively serve the organization's mission in the long term. A company's capability to design or reformulate supply chain strategy has been heralded as the "ultimate core competency of an organization."[25] To illustrate strategic planning for supply chains organizations in each of the three roles introduced earlier, consider the summary in Table 2.1.

Table 2.1 Key features of strategic planning in supply chains

	Functional role	Business model role	Infrastructural role
Key decision	Capabilities and objectives of supply chain functions to serve the company's business goals	Which customers to serve, markets to compete in, and supply chain services to offer	Infrastructure elements to add, enhance, maintain, or discontinue
Objective for strategic decision	Align functional strategy with business strategy	Maximize profits, generate growth, and build competitive advantage (by understanding customers' supply chains, creating long-lasting customer relationships, etc.)	Develop logistics infrastructure to support the region's economic growth
Local factors likely to affect the key decision	• Company's business strategy • Other functional strategies • Nature of relationship with customers and suppliers (such as logistics service providers, contract manufacturers)	• Logistics needs of chosen customers and markets • Competitive dynamics of logistics services industry • Regulations of logistics service providers in chosen markets	• Regional goods flow (direction, volume, value density) • Demand for various transportation modes • Condition of transport infrastructure (e.g., road, rail, ports) operated by the third party
Decision-making team	• Company's CSCO • Supply chain executives	• CEO • Company's senior executives in sales, marketing, operations, finance, HR	• Director of the regional transportation planning commission • Managers and planners of transport infrastructure

(continued)

Table 2.1 (continued)

	Functional role	Business model role	Infrastructural role
Stakeholders relevant for strategic decision-making	• CEO and board of directors • Senior company executives of other functions not involved in the supply chain organization • Customers and suppliers • Industry regulators	• Supply chain executives in customers' companies • Organizations in the infrastructure role • Transportation and trade regulators	• Shippers and carriers based in the region • Other infrastructure planning agencies relevant for the region • Environmental groups • Citizens of the region • Public planning agencies

Strategic Planning in the Functional Role

Strategic planning in the *functional role* of supply chains pertains to the formulation of an integrated supply chain strategy as a contributor to a business unit or a corporation. The goal of strategic planning is to specify the capabilities required in the company's supply chain functions and the objectives needed to guide the functions' activities. The intent is to have the strategies and goals of different supply chain functions aligned with the business strategy and complement each other. The strategic planning in this role is likely to be led by the company's CSCO and supported by its supply chain executives.

The choices made about supply chain strategy are determined by the company's business strategy (which the supply chain needs to support) but are also affected by the strategies of other functions that are not in the purview of the supply chain organization (such as marketing, sales, human resources, finance, legal). In addition, other stakeholders affecting the strategy include the company's current and potential customers and suppliers, as well as regulatory agencies governing the procurement, shipment, handling, and distribution of the company's products and ingredient raw materials.

Strategic Planning in the Business Model Role

Strategic planning in companies in the *business model* role focuses on formu lating the company's business strategy. The goal of strategic planning is to specify the customer segments to serve, the markets to operate in, and the supply chain products and services to offer in the chosen markets. This leads to the creation of the company's portfolio of logistics services that it sells to customers. The strategic planning in this type of company is likely to be led by the company's CEO and supported by senior executives in all func- tional areas such as marketing, finance, human resources, and operations. The strategic planning activity aims to deepen and expand the relationships with customer companies, creating "stickiness" while increasing revenues. Many companies in this role have grown and prospered by following their customers into new businesses and new geographies.

Choices made in strategic planning are affected by the supply chain requirements of existing and potential customers, logistics services provided by competitors in the market, and any industry-specific regulations. Thus, the stakeholders relevant for strategic planning in a company in the *busi- ness model* role are in large part external to the company, such as customer companies, providers of logistics infrastructure, and the agencies regulating transportation and trade activities. This contrasts with the companies in the *functional* role, where the company's non-supply chain functions are important stakeholders.

Strategic Planning in the Infrastructural Role

Strategic planning in organizations playing the *infrastructural role* pertains to the long-range planning of logistics infrastructure in a particular region. Often, such projects are undertaken by government agencies that seek to attract businesses to the region. The plans may stipulate adding new elements to the region's logistics infrastructure (e.g., building a new highway or a new cargo airport, constructing a new pipeline), enhancing the capacity or effec- tiveness of the existing infrastructure elements (e.g., adding new lanes to an existing highway, electrifying a rail line, replacing toll booths with free-flow tolling), managing existing infrastructure elements by changing pricing and other operational rules of usage and maintaining such infrastructure elements (e.g., road repairs, updating of traffic signs and signals). The strategic plan- ning in this role is typically led by senior executives in charge of infrastructure planning in the region's planning agency, working closely with the region's elected officials.

ade in this strategic planning process are affected by the
sired) flows of goods transported within and through the
volume of cargo transported, demands on various modes
nd conditions of logistics assets operated by third parties.
ng agency must consider the relevant stakeholders, such as
cargo owners such as manufacturers, retailers, and distri-
-,, carriers operating in the region, other relevant planning agencies
in the region, and citizens and environmental groups. The process typically
includes various regulatory agencies and, in many cases (in the US), the
courts.

Difficulty in Strategic Planning in Supply Chains

Despite its importance, strategic planning in supply chains remains a challenge for three reasons related to the underlying difficult decision-making
context. The combination of uncertainty in long planning horizons and
complexity introduced by a multitude of factors and diverse stakeholders
affecting the decision make any business strategic planning a "wicked
problem."[26] This term is used to refer to cases where defining the problem
itself is a non-trivial task, let alone the difficulty in finding a solution.
Such a difficult decision context is further exacerbated by two attributes
of the decision-making process: operational focus in many organizations
and inappropriateness of the extant (operational) planning tools for strategic
planning.

"Wicked" Decision-Making Context

The strategic planning problems in all three supply chain perspectives require
decision makers to consider a long planning horizon, measured in years or
even decades. As a result, planners need to envision the future environment
in which the invested assets will operate. This contrasts with operational planning, where the manager is making decisions in the current environment
with mostly known conditions. Predicting the future over multiple years or
even decades with any reasonable accuracy is almost impossible. Niels Bohr,
the Nobel laureate in Physics and father of the atomic model, once said,
"Prediction is very difficult, especially if it's about the future!".

To appreciate this, imagine driving a car in 2007, the year the first iPhone
was introduced. Drivers in 2007 planned their routes and traveled along
the planned route regardless of the traffic conditions. Fast forward 10 years,

almost every driver has a smartphone that provides real-time traffic updates and even reroutes a driver in the event of unexpected congestion. In fact, drivers can now outsource personal transportation, because hailing a car with an app such as Uber® or Lyft® is literally at one's fingertips, eliminating the need for owning a car, obtaining driving directions, navigating the traffic, and looking for parking.

Understanding the direct impacts of technological innovations is difficult; predicting the second- and third-order impacts accurately is generally intractable. The difficulty in prediction is compounded by the fact that strategic planning in supply chains requires the decision makers to first identify the numerous factors and stakeholders relevant to the strategic decision. Following this, they need to consider how these factors may affect the possible outcomes of their potential decisions and what actions different stakeholders might take. None of these can be assessed with certainty. Even if the factors could be evaluated accurately in isolation, their combined effects on the strategic supply chain decision are difficult to ascertain. As a result, long-range planning problems are considered "wicked problems," and strategic planning in supply chains is no exception.

Myopic Operational Focus

The second factor that complicates strategic decision-making in supply chains is that most organizations focus on short-term, operational issues. Efforts to improve their current operations and extract the most value out of their existing resources and relationships dominate most organizations in all three supply chain perspectives. A director of logistics at a brewery may try to optimize the allocation of trucks and their routes to complete day-to-day deliveries at the lowest cost while meeting all customers' delivery requirements (functional role). A vice president at a 3PL overseeing sales of supply chain services may explore more ways to serve existing customers to generate more revenue (business model role). A manager of a region's road infrastructure may look for short-term solutions to reduce congestion on the region's major highways (infrastructural role).

Such an operational focus is necessary for an organization to satisfy its mission on a day-to-day basis, and is managed and monitored through key performance indicators, which themselves may be chosen during the strategic planning process. Managers' objectives may directly stipulate a certain level of performance in their operational duties, such as reducing transportation spending (functional), increasing revenue from a particular customer account (business model), or supporting greater traffic volume without increasing average travel time on a particular highway (infrastructural). For most companies, the short-term, quarter-by-quarter focus of analysts and investors drives management to make short-term improvements, which may be reflected in the next quarter's performance.

However, the single-minded pursuit of operational excellence can distract organizations from forward-looking explorations of impending changes in the business environments. It can divert the organizational members' focus on fine-tuning their current operational performance, so much so that they forget to ask whether the organization's environment is changing and if the operational goals are still relevant. To be efficient operationally, supply chain organizations must be tightly structured and pay attention to details to perform consistently at low cost, with good reliability, and at high speed. To be effective strategically, supply chains must develop flexibility and adapt quickly to the changing conditions. This tension between short-term operational focus and long-term strategic goals goes to the heart of the challenge in strategic planning in supply chains.

Absence of Decision-Making Processes for Dealing with Systemic Uncertainty

The third challenge in strategic planning in supply chains is the general absence of rigorous decision-making processes that account for systemic uncertainty in most supply chain organizations. Operational problems in supply chains can typically be described and solved analytically, often using objective, quantitative, historical data. For example, information about a manufacturing company's current production capacity and distribution network efficiency and estimates about next quarter's product demand and logistics costs can be used to determine optimal allocations of its products to factories and distribution centers and to calculate the cost of distribution (functional role). Actual data about the previous year's revenue generated by selling transportation services to a customer could be used by a 3PL service provider for setting revenue targets for the following year (business model role). Statistical models can detect patterns in historical changes in traffic to predict the following year's demand on road capacity (infrastructural role). Supply chain managers and planners are often trained to use such models and are adept in their application.

However, the same numerical models are woefully inadequate for dealing with strategic planning problems. For example, distribution network optimization methods are not equipped to anticipate structural shifts in the business environment, such as those resulting from changes in taxes and tariffs, changes in regulations about freight transport, or zoning laws affecting factory operations. In most business applications, the accuracy of forecasts developed using traditional time-series forecasting methods decreases sharply as the planning horizon exceeds a few months. It is difficult to quantify the effects of a complex interaction of factors and stakeholders' actions on a company's outcomes following any strategic decision. Thus, the tools that are effective at, and hence widely used for, operational and tactical planning are generally inadequate for strategic planning in supply chains.

Due to its lack of amenability to quantitative analytical methods, strategic decision-making typically requires the use of managerial judgment. However, executives that have risen through the ranks by excelling in short-term, operational responsibilities may not possess the judgment necessary to make long-term, strategic decisions unless trained otherwise. Making decisions on issues demanding long-term orientation requires executives to go beyond the immediate situation to envision what may be missing, based on their own experiences and the organization's collective knowledge. The executives' attention may still be consumed by immediate issues relevant in the short term that may be more familiar to them. Or they may consider long-term issues but interpret them using analogies and solutions from their past experience that may not be appropriate for handling the new issues.

Tackling strategic supply chain planning challenged by the confluence of uncertainty and complex interactions in dynamic environments with the mindsets and toolsets honed for excelling on short-term goals requires a holistic methodology to overcome these limitations. Scenario planning is one such method.

Notes

1. Perez-Franco, R., Phadnis, S., Caplice, C., Sheffi, Y. 2016. "Rethinking Supply Chain Strategy as a Conceptual System." *International Journal of Production Economics*, 182, 387–390.
2. https://www.beer100.com/beer-history/ (accessed on September 5, 2019).
3. And several for good reasons, especially due to the ill effects of beer consumption that have led to deaths from drunk driving.
4. https://www.chrobinson.com/en-us/about-us/.
5. Center for Healthcare Supply Chain Research. (2010). 2009–2010 HDMA Factbook (Exhibit 8).

6. https://www.drugchannels.net/2019/10/the-big-three-wholesalers-revenues-and.html.

7. https://fortune.com/fortune500/2021/search/.

8. The only "healthcare" companies to rank above the smallest of the Big Three (Cardinal Health) by 2020 revenues were CVS Health (fourth), the owner of eponymous retail pharmacies and MinuteClinic retail clinics, and two insurance providers: UnitedHealth Group (fifth) and Cigna (thirteenth).

9. UPS and FedEx, with their ubiquitous trucks making parcel deliveries on America's streets (with growth fueled by online commerce) are the exceptions. They appear among America's 50 most popular brands. https://www.rankingthebrands.com/The-Brand-Rankings.aspx?rankingID=423&year=1198.

10. The Medford case is briefly described in Phadnis, S., Schoemaker, P. 2022. "Visibility Isn't Enough—Supply Chains Also Need Vigilance." *Management and Business Review.*

11. https://www.kff.org/uninsured/fact-sheet/key-facts-about-the-uninsured-population/.

12. https://www.dea.gov/sites/default/files/2018-07/2003-2008%20p%20118-153.pdf.

13. https://nabp.pharmacy/newsroom/news/states-fda-pressing-forward-with-pedigree-track-and-trace-rules-and-regulations/.

14. https://www.rxtrace.com/.

15. http://www.leg.state.fl.us/statutes/index.cfm?mode=View%20Statutes&SubMenu=1&App_mode=Display_Statute&Search_String=pedigree&URL=0400-0499/0499/Sections/0499.01212.html.

16. Hausman, W., Lee, H., Subramanian, U. 2013. "The Impact of Logistics Performance on Trade." *Production and Operations Management*, 22(2), 236–252.

17. http://aci-economics.com/.

18. https://www.infrastructurereportcard.org/port-to-pantry/.

19. https://www.infrastructurereportcard.org/.

20. https://www.infrastructurereportcard.org/making-the-grade/report-card-history/.

21. https://www.bloomberg.com/news/articles/2018-01-26/the-u-s-gets-less-subway-for-its-money-than-its-peers.

22. The description of the Future Freight Flows project is based on: Caplice, C., Phadnis, S. 2013. *Strategic Issues Facing Transportation: Scenario Planning for Freight Transportation Infrastructure Investment.* Washington, DC: Transportation Research Board.

23. https://apps.trb.org/cmsfeed/TRBNetProjectDisplay.asp?ProjectID= 2628.
24. Caplice, C., Phadnis, S. 2010. *Strategic Issues Facing Transportation, Volume 1: Scenario Planning for Freight Transportation Infrastructure Investment*. No. Project 20-83 (1).
25. Fine, C. 2000. "Clock Speed Strategies for Supply Chain Design." *Production Operation Management*, 9(3), 213–221.
26. Rittel, H., Webber, M. 1973. "Dilemmas in a General Theory of Planning." *Policy Sciences*, 4(2), 155–169.

3

Scenario Planning: A Tool for Organizational Learning and Foresight

Evolving over half a century, scenario planning methodologies have built on humankind's natural inclinations to make projections about future possibilities and convey their knowledge through storytelling. Just as ancient myths enabled classical cultures to scrutinize life's limitations as imposed by gods, nature, or mortal foes, scenario planning brings imaginative capacities to bear on modern organizations' necessity to make rational decisions under conditions of uncertainty and incomplete information.

"It is often said that all humans are futurists," observed historian James Allen Dator[1] in describing the "distinctive human capacity to imagine, plan, and act to turn imagination into reality. But if humans are futurists," he continues, "then they also are historians." They have beliefs about the past. For most of human existence, the past, present, and future were essentially the same. However, in the modern world of ever-accelerating technological advances and widespread demographic shifts occurring on a global level, the world in the future, even barely a decade hence, will likely differ dramatically from the past and the present. Thus, despite accumulated knowledge of the past and prodigious data on the present, strategic decision-making faces lower predictability of the long-term future than in past eras. Recognizing this important feature of the modern world, scenario planning takes a different approach to decision-making about the future. It draws on an organization's knowledge and educated premises regarding future-relevant forces that may affect the organization in order to develop several possible visions

S. S. Phadnis et al., *Strategic Planning for Dynamic Supply Chains*, Palgrave Executive Essentials, https://doi.org/10.1007/978-3-030-91810-1_3

of the future. In other words, it relies on creating stories: feasible fictions that may become futures or include elements of the future.

It is important to emphasize that scenario planning is not a forecasting methodology. Instead of trying to predict what will happen, scenario planning allows an organization to be better prepared to handle a range of possible futures that *may or may not* materialize. Unlike the pursuit of higher accuracy in quantitative forecasting methods, the objective of scenario planning is to facilitate organizational learning about the evolving environment and influence decision makers to be open to possible shifts in the environment.

What Is Scenario Planning?

As a tool for understanding how the future might unfold and how an organization could prepare for it, scenario planning uses a set of stories—scenarios—each chronicling a different possible vision of the future.[2] Scenarios are described as stories that are "rooted in the future and reference external forces in that context ... [they are] possible and internally plausible while taking the proper form of a story."[3] Typically, a *set* of scenarios created for an organization describes a few markedly distinct, yet realistically plausible, future business environments in terms and features that are specifically relevant to that organization. Different organizations will typically craft different scenarios depending on the time horizon and strategic questions being examined.

Scenario building blends a possible view of the future with a retrospective understanding of the current world from which that future will arise. Each scenario not only maps a vision of the future but also includes a description of how the world evolved to that particular scenario. Inherent in the process of creating multiple scenarios are considerations of interactions among various factors and stakeholders that may result in different scenarios. The long planning horizon in this method forces a long-term perspective. This "long view" is especially beneficial for executives inundated with issues of a short-term nature and provides a systematic approach for strategic conversation and decision-making for the long term.[4]

In particular, the focus in scenario planning is on identifying critical uncertainties in the business environment that, if left unaddressed, could undermine a well-crafted long-term strategic plan. As an exercise intended to grapple with long-term uncertainties, scenario planning avoids tactical decisions based on existing forecasts or status quo thinking. It turns the planning process into a team-based experience aimed at better organizational learning by identifying hidden biases, assumptions, and decision-making processes that inhibit constructive change or undermine flexible plans.

Scenario Planning: Back to the Future

Scenarios have been used as a conceptual tool for almost as long as human societies have grappled with the future—whether it be of society, the body politic, or social institutions.[5] As a means of group understanding as well as communication, such scenarios have often taken the form of essays or novels, dating from Plato's *Republic* to later visionaries like Thomas More or George Orwell.

Modern-day scenario techniques emerged in the post-WWII era based on the influences of nineteenth-century military strategists such as Carl von Clausewitz and Helmuth von Moltke. The complex challenges of the polarizing postwar world of the 1950s led to the emergence of several problem-solving methods that allowed decision makers to think in terms of whole systems operating in multiple dimensions.[6] Scenario planning was one such method.

Scenario planning flourished in the US Air Force and other branches of the military engaged in strategizing for future conflicts. These "sandbox" training exercises continued during the 1950s when the US Department of Defense was selecting weapons systems to tackle the new threat of the Cold War. The challenges multiplied in the face of myriad uncertainties, including the lead times required to develop new weapons systems, the uncertain political environment in which these systems might be deployed, and the unpredictable dynamic inherent in multilateral weapons systems development.[7] This process required a sophisticated new methodology to model future environments and integrate expert knowledge with vastly expanded technical capabilities. Scenario techniques proved a suitable complement to the emergence of systems analysis.

The RAND Corporation, a not-for-profit think tank founded in 1948 as a joint project of the US Air Force and Douglas Aircraft Company, became a pioneer of scenario planning in the 1950s and 1960s. Its work focused almost exclusively on defense-related studies for the US Air Force. Herman Kahn, a leading futurist and civil defense strategist, headed the RAND team that developed provocative scenarios centered on the US military strategy in the thermonuclear age. Kahn, described as a policy intellectual of unquestioned genius who sought to use scenarios to find alternatives to nuclear destruction, expanded the use of scenarios to social forecasting and public policy with his founding of the Hudson Institute.

Kahn's work broadened the methodological foundations for planning and policy analysis. It also influenced the subsequent growth of the field of *futures studies* at the Stanford Research Institute and the California Institute of Technology. Kahn's influence on scenario planning soon migrated to the business world, helping to promulgate the first scenario narratives focused on postwar Japan as an economic powerhouse.

Scenario planning had already attracted a broad swath of early adopters. Beginning in the 1950s, it helped Electrolux spot new consumer markets, Pacific Gas & Electric prepare for a California earthquake, and a leading Austrian insurance company to prepare for the emergence of new markets in central Europe after the fall of the Berlin Wall.[8]

Scenario Planning: Coming of Age

The 1970s introduced the golden age of scenario planning as Royal Dutch Shell developed scenarios around the uncertainty of oil prices following decades of price stability. Beginning in 1967 with a scenario-based study, dubbed "Year 2000," Shell's planners began exploring the possibility of significant oil industry discontinuities. The corporation's divisional and regional businesses were mandated to look two decades ahead, up to 1985, for strategic planning.[9]

A team within the group planning division led by Pierre Wack, a planner at Shell Françoise familiar with Kahn's work,[10] developed two different scenarios. One reflected the conventional view that oil prices would continue to increase by six percent per annum, as they had for decades.[11] The other assumed that the Organization of Petroleum Exporting Countries (OPEC) would exploit US dependence on Middle East oil by withholding supply and driving up prices. Wack's team provided detailed descriptions of the ramifications of an aggressive OPEC, including the possibility of dramatically slower industry growth in the future.

In 1973, OPEC's embargo in the wake of the Fourth Arab–Israeli War sent global oil prices soaring, quadrupling from $2 a barrel to $8 in a matter of a few weeks, leading to the 1973 Oil Crisis and eerily resembling one scenario highlighted by Wack's team. While the embargo caught most of the other oil majors by surprise, Shell's businesses were better prepared to deal with the crisis as a result of their exposure to Wack's team's scenario. Wack's team did not claim the oil crisis would happen; they merely suggested that it *could* happen, which made it a potential future condition that was worth preparing for.

Shortly thereafter, Shell extended scenario planning throughout the company. Conducting scenario analysis in parallel with competitive analysis would start an iterative learning process that helped amplify the original strategic vision.[12] This became a prerequisite for defining strategic options that would be analyzed subsequently. Over the next decade, Shell became one of the most profitable of the seven major oil firms. The awareness of Shell's success with scenario planning popularized this method. By 1980, between 35 and 50% of the Fortune 1000 companies reported using some form of scenario planning for their strategic long-term decision-making.[13]

Over the latter half of the twentieth century, a host of companies, governments, and other organizations used scenario planning to help prepare their leaders and managers to make better long-term decisions. These users include the Australian government, AutoNation, BASF, British Airways, California Teachers Association, Cisco, Corning, Disney, General Electric, JDS Uniphase, KinderCare (a large US chain of daycare centers), Mercedes-Benz, the Singaporean government, UPS, the United States Environmental Protection Agency, and the World Bank.

Intuitive Logics School

Peter Schwartz, Pierre Wack's successor at Shell's planning group, honed his predecessor's method into a dominant approach to scenario planning, which became known as the Intuitive Logics School (ILS). Schwartz maintains that scenario planning does not aim to anticipate an accurate picture of the future, but rather paves a way to better decisions about the future.[14] The ILS scenario planning approach enables organizational *foresight*, rather than *forecasting*. Therefore, ILS scenario studies make no attempt to estimate the likelihoods of different scenarios; instead, they treat each scenario in the set as equally plausible.

Traditional forecasting relies largely on statistical extrapolations that assume the future will be structurally like the past and that long-standing prior trends will continue. This approach naturally constrains the vision of the future to be, structurally, a version of past trajectories. Embodying this assumption, sophisticated forecasting techniques can be used to generate forecasts. However, the folly of such forecasting is generally recognized by managers and economists, who may specify a range of numerical values—instead of a single number—to characterize the uncertainty about a particular variable of the business environment (such as the future price of oil being

$50 or $100 per barrel). Often, in management and economics, planners combine sets of extreme numeric values of multiple relevant uncertain variables to produce "scenarios." However, the ILS calls such combinations of obvious numerical uncertainties "first-generation scenarios." Pierre Wack notes that they are useful as a means for gaining a "better understanding of the situation in order to ask better questions and develop better second-generation scenarios—that is, decision scenarios."[15] The ILS's second-generation scenarios stand out from the first-generation ones because they are developed through a better understanding of the *interplay between different uncertainties and the more predictable elements* of the business environment. It is not just a matter of adding a quantitative range to obvious input or output values, but rather incorporating the underlying qualitative driving forces and their interactions in the process.

Variations of Scenario Planning

Beginning in the 1980s, the growing adoption of scenario planning by US industrial firms began in capital-intensive industries with long strategic planning horizons. However, as the scenario planning spread across a wide variety of industries, from oil companies and vehicle manufacturers to electricity suppliers and transport companies, the method evolved. In fact, by the end of the 1980s, scenario methods had evolved into a complex array of specialized sub-techniques as various industries and companies tried to improve upon the original ideas. ILS, which had grown out of Shell's "Year 2000" scenario project in the 1960s, spawned many variations, some of which included as many as 40 steps.[16] Some practitioners developed branded scenario models while others launched simpler, less resource-intensive approaches focusing on scenario planning as a learning process.

The field of scenario planning evolved with the emergence of quantitative approaches based on time series. Known variously as *Trend-Impact Analysis* (TIA) and *Cross-Impact Analysis* (CIA), these approaches used expert judgments to evaluate the probability of an event's occurrence along with its expected impact. For instance, scenario generation in TIA consists of four steps.[17] The exercise begins with the collection of historical data relevant to the issue in question. In the second step, statistical "curve-fitting" techniques are used to detect patterns in this data, and the patterns are then extrapolated into the future to develop the "surprise-free" scenario. Step three identifies "unprecedented" future events that could cause deviations from the surprise-free future. Finally, experts judge the probability of these unprecedented events, which are then used to adjust the extrapolations.

The CIA method, which was also developed at the RAND Corporation in the 1960s, is similar to TIA, with a fifth additional step. CIA computes conditional probabilities for each pair of future events, based on their a priori estimates by experts, to develop a more refined estimate of the likelihood of resulting scenarios. Thus, in contrast to ILS's emphasis on pure qualitative processes, in which all scenarios are treated as equiprobable, TIA and CIA use quantitative estimates to develop probability-weighted scenarios that can be mathematically processed to estimate likelihoods of various outcomes. Such mathematical precision stands in contrast to the business challenge encountered in strategic supply chain planning, which seldom has such clarity.[18]

Another strain, known as *La Prospective*,[19] originated in France in the late 1970s, focused on the "scientific and political foundations of the future" using scenario techniques. The pioneering scenario work guided public policy and planning and was developed after repeated failures of "classical" forecasting approaches. Influenced by French philosopher Gaston Berger, who founded the Centre d'Études Prospectives (Center for Prospective Studies), and later developed by Michel Godet, the *La Prospective* approach frames normative scenarios that envision positive change in French education, environment, and urbanization. As with TIA and CIA, *La Prospective* also employs quantitative methods to develop scenarios. It first identifies key variables relevant for the study and the actors that affect them. Through interviews with the actors, relationships among all key variables are characterized (e.g., workspace regulations in a region can strongly influence new business investments in the region, but may have only a weak or no effect on the region's social relationships). The matrix of these relationships forms the basis for scenario development. Thus, scenario creation in *La Prospective* is based on the influence that the actions of different actors have on key variables (e.g., regulators affecting work regulations, companies deciding whether to invest in the region), in contrast to extrapolation of historical time-series data in the TIA and CIA.

The common thread for these three approaches is that different future scenarios have different estimated likelihoods. However, the estimation of different probabilities encourages a natural human tendency to focus on the highest probability outcomes. While such a focus may help as a follow-on to a scenario planning initiative, the potential for fixation on the most likely future runs counter to the goal of broadening the decision makers' awareness of uncertainties and the span of possible futures, and on promoting learning about the emerging business environment in general. This book, and the MIT CTL scenario planning projects it describes, follow the ILS approach.

Despite the varied and sometimes confusing methodologies available, the 1990s and early 2000s saw a rapid expansion of the business applications of scenario planning.[20] Between 2000 and 2004, the percentage of business-oriented articles on scenario planning in leading journals multiplied 20-fold over a comparable percentage between 1985 and 1989.

Scenario Planning: A Method for *Foresight*, Not Forecasting

To understand why organizations use scenario planning for making decisions with long time horizons, as well as to assess the efficacy of scenario planning itself, one needs to appreciate the distinction between scenario planning and forecasting methods.

The typical forecasting methods aim to describe the probable future in terms of a single number or trajectory line (e.g., the year-by-year growth of future sales). Some forecasting methods expand the single number into a statistical range of values that bound the value of future outcomes with a certain degree of confidence. These numerical forecasts are then used for developing concrete tactical, operational, and financial plans that often use decision-making formulas. For example, companies may forecast future values such as (i) market demand to develop master production schedules, (ii) volatility of demand to optimize stock levels in retail outlets, or (iii) quarterly revenue to inform the company's shareholders. Forecasts are made by projecting relevant contemporary trends into the future. Therefore, forecasting methods are designed to detect patterns (such as growing or declining trends or seasonal variations) in the present-day operational environment. For short planning horizons—lasting from a few weeks, a quarter, and up to a year—such forecasts can be reasonably accurate and serve their purpose. Indeed, the metric for assessing the quality of a particular forecasting method is its accuracy (or, forecast error), for which several quantitative metrics are available.

In contrast, a scenario planning initiative produces at least two and generally up to five distinctly different narrations of plausible futures. The scenario descriptions are always qualitative and are often written as stories. They may be accompanied by numerical values of key variables if such information is perceived as useful for telling the story more effectively to the intended audience (e.g., "a world in which fuel costs $50 a gallon"). The primary purpose of the scenarios is *not* to forecast, but to help individuals and organizations learn and think about how the future may diverge from the present to become

Table 3.1 Distinction between forecasting and scenario planning

	Forecasting	Scenario planning
Number of projections made	One (possibly with confidence intervals)	Between two and five distinct scenarios
Type of content	Primarily quantitative	Primarily qualitative, stories
Timeline	Short term (a few weeks to a year)	Long term (between two and three years to a few decades)
Purpose	Operational planning	Long-term/strategic planning
Applications	Tactical, operational planning	Strategic decision-making
Method objective	Detect patterns in the present operational environment	Identify forces shaping the operational environment
Assessed by	Forecast accuracy	Change in mindset

structurally different, which in turn can influence strategic decision-making. Therefore, development of scenarios requires identifying forces that shape the long-term business environment. To judge the quality of scenarios, one needs to assess their effect on individual and organizational learning; hence, accuracy is not the correct metric to use. As a result, the metrics used for assessing the quality of a set of scenarios are likely to be more qualitative and not numerical (Table 3.1).

Learning from Scenario Use: Anecdotal Evidence

Pierre Wack, who initiated the scenario planning initiative at Shell in the late 1960s, and his team at Shell believe that "every manager has a mental model of the world in which he or she acts based on experience and knowledge."[21] That belief shaped the goal of their scenario initiative. He noted that the "real target [of Shell's scenario planning efforts] was the microcosms [i.e., the mental models] of our decision makers [...]. We now wanted to design scenarios so that managers would question their own model of reality and change it when necessary, so as to come up with strategic insights beyond their minds' previous reach." Consistent with this, Peter Schwartz, who headed Shell's scenario planning initiative after Pierre Wack's retirement, describes scenario planning as "a tool for ordering one's perceptions about alternative future environments in which one's decisions might be played out."[22]

Anecdotes from other organizations support these arguments. In the UPS case described later, Vern Higberg (Vice President of Corporate Strategy) remarked that UPS "got much richer outcomes than if we had only done competitive analyses, based on trend lines and a view of the world as all about just slugging out for market share. Without scenario planning, you don't see the big changes until they are history."[23]

Management scholars also attest to the learning benefits of scenario planning. Michael Porter, the renowned professor of strategic management at Harvard Business School, advocates the use of scenario planning and notes that "industry scenarios are a useful device for getting a management team involved in thinking about the future systematically, and modifying unrealistic assumptions in a nonthreatening way because scenarios are not intended as forecasts."[24] Professor Kathleen Eisenhardt of Stanford describes scenario planning as one of the "'frame-breaking' tactics that can create alternatives to [decision makers'] obvious points of view."[25]

However, measuring organizational learning or change in its prevailing mindset is considerably more difficult than calculating the accuracy of a forecast by determining the numerical difference between actual and forecasted values. Organizations often measure forecast accuracy, but measurements of learning are less common. As a result, evidence of the effectiveness of scenario planning has largely been anecdotal.

Learning from Scenario Use: Emerging Experimental Evidence

Notwithstanding the endorsements from business leaders and world-renowned scholars, anecdotal evidence lacks the objectivity and rigor provided by scientific inquiries. This has prompted scholarly scrutiny of the effects of scenario planning. Experimental studies have shown that the use of scenarios can affect the participants' confidence in their predictions of uncertain variables.[26] They also show that scenario use has a positive effect on decision quality.[27]

The MIT CTL research team conducted field experiments in the scenario planning workshops in the Future Freight Flows[28] project to test the effect of scenarios on long-range decisions made by field experts. These studies showed that a vast majority of experts changed their judgment about different investments after using scenarios. Furthermore, the use of scenario planning also lowered their preference for investments with low flexibility in favor of those with higher flexibility. Chapter 8 delves more extensively into scenario-based learning.

Overall, emerging experimental studies support the anecdotal claims about the learning benefits of scenario planning's effect on long-term decisions. Thus, scenario planning seems to be a useful tool to help operationally focused executives appreciate a range of possible futures that may evolve over the long term.

Scenario Planning in Supply Chain Management: Case of United Parcel Service (UPS)

Recognizing the challenge of fashioning strategic plans lasting more than a few years, UPS CEO Michael Eskew acknowledged the need for a process that could peer a decade into the future.[29] He asserted, "We are convinced that it is possible and wise, indeed necessary, to develop a set of very long-range scenarios that can lay the foundation for our future strategic plans."[30] Well into its second century in business, UPS has evolved from a parcel service to a full-fledged, multimodal logistics services company.

Six years after borrowing $100 to found American Messenger Service in Seattle in 1907, Jim Casey had a pioneering notion: why not load all the packages for a single area onto a single delivery truck.[31] By 1924, UPS had built the first mechanical sorter and conveyor belt system for package handling. UPS built the world's first air express service in 1929 and grew to become the first intercontinental air service between the US and Europe. In 1975, UPS became the first package-delivery company to serve every address in the continental US and started its expansion outside the US, with service in Ontario, Canada. In 1995, UPS introduced the industry's first guaranteed 8 a.m. overnight delivery service as well as the first same-day service. In 2000, UPS was the first to reach a technology milestone in receiving 6.5 million online tracking requests per day, and in 2007 the company undertook construction of the first-ever US air hub in China. In 2011, UPS launched My Choice, an industry first that provides consumers the ability to control the timing and location of deliveries. In 2013, UPS Store became the first retailer to offer 3D printing. As shown below, its initiatives in the twenty-first century resulted after UPS started practicing scenario planning regularly.

For a company with such a historic number of firsts, the risk of being second remains ever-present—whether missing an opportunity to debut a new service or falling prey to a competitor armed with new technology. Over many decades, the company had earned a hard-won reputation for a relentless focus on operational efficiency and execution. Casey inculcated an operational model to run the company "like a military operation, ordering recruits to be polite at all times and to place speed above all other virtues."[32] Precision in execution was equally valued in modern times, as indicated by the company's reported practice of tracking the frequency with which its drivers shifted gears in the delivery trucks. Such carefully curated work methods, developed by industrial engineers and rooted in time-and-motion studies and other measurement approaches, coupled with well-established business practices and workplace policies, fostered UPS's reputation for consistent customer service.

In addition to a high degree of scrutiny over workplace practices, a loyal workforce had been forged by an enduring policy of internal promotions that produced all of the company's CEOs (until 2020 when UPS chose the first woman and the first outsider to lead the company). In addition, most top executives, industrial engineers, MBAs, and other career professionals had started as part-time package handlers or delivery drivers before rising through the ranks. Thus, a culture obsessed with operational efficiency permeated the organization, from the cabins of package-delivery trucks to the corner offices of the executive suites. As befitting an organization that styles itself after the military, UPS marshaled this operational focus based on a highly centralized, hierarchical organization.

Perhaps one indication of the strong grip of operational execution on the company is that UPS did not possess a formal strategic planning capability until the early 1990s. Around that time, companies like FedEx and government-supported agencies such as Deutsche Post started to challenge UPS's market dominance. Senior leaders became concerned that the company's operational execution mentality was impeding management's ability to see significant changes in the business environment. In 1996, incoming UPS CEO Jim Kelly established the Strategy Advisory Group (SAG) to address these challenges and launched the Corporate Strategy Group (CSG) to develop the strategic planning process that would assist the Management Committee in formulating and tackling key strategic issues.[33] CSG, working with external consultants, developed its own strategic planning process, which included scenario planning, to precede strategy formulation and implementation.

Scenario Planning at UPS Circa 1997[34]

UPS hired Global Business Network (GBN)—the consulting firm formed by Peter Schwartz (of Royal Dutch Shell fame and the author of the seminal book on scenario planning) to guide its scenario planning initiative. Given its pedigree, GBN was arguably the most authoritative consulting firm at the time for a scenario planning project. Using the process led by GBN, UPS developed four scenarios describing the demand environment of the twenty-first century. The scenarios differed along two key dimensions: types of consumers served by UPS and geographic scope of the market as modulated by government policies.

The first scenario, *Global Scale Prevails*, described a global market dominated by traditional consumers and a continuation of the contemporary free-trade trends at the time. Contradicting this "conventional wisdom" scenario on both dimensions was a scenario named *Tangled Paths* consisting of highly competitive business marketplaces, constrained by strong regional and nationalistic governments with regulations restricting cross-national goods flows, and where technology-savvy consumers demanded a high variety of products. The remaining two scenarios—*Regressive World* and *Brave New World*—described another pair of polar opposite worlds: the former consisting of traditional consumers in regional markets defined by strong regulations, and the latter comprising technology-savvy, proactive consumers in a globalized world characterized by seamless cross-border trade.

UPS executives noted that the scenarios provided a common vocabulary.[35] UPS Chairman and CEO Mike Eskew underscored that senior managers started describing different market environments and strategic moves using the scenario names, such as "that seems like a *Regressive World* option" or "that would move us more toward *Global Scale* or *Brave New World*." He also emphasized that scenario usage caused a shift in the mindset of the company's executives. "Left to our own devices," he said, "we would probably have ended up in '*Global Scale Prevails*,' focusing totally on physical assets and missing more virtual opportunities." However, the scenarios made UPS executives aware of the possibility that the future business environment could include elements of different scenarios, and that the company would "have to figure out how to prosper in each one." Indeed, UPS made major strategic moves after the scenario planning exercise.

Strategic Moves After Scenario Exercise

Although the value of scenario planning was debated by the executives of this highly operationally oriented company, many strategic changes that followed were attributed to the practice of scenario planning. For instance, in 1999, UPS changed its corporate charter from a narrow one of "serving the package-delivery needs of our customers" to a much broader one of "enabling global commerce." Apparently, this change acknowledged the potential of a globalizing world of declining trade restrictions and with consumers demanding more specialized services beyond package delivery (as described in the scenario *Brave New World*). It also reflected a need for international cross-border business functions amid an increasingly competitive global economy, and it focused management's attention on end-to-end supply chain operations. Mike Eskew noted that the new charter "served as a springboard for a series of events, starting with the decision to go public in November 1999, and then for the company's five-year strategic plan."[36]

Another strategic initiative was the 2001 acquisition of Mail Boxes Etc.®, a franchisee network providing business services that would extend UPS's market position using the country's dominant, third-party retail shipping operation. The acquisition dramatically changed UPS's footprint[37] to include over 3,000 retail stores in the US (and 900 in 29 countries outside the US) easily accessible to consumers, from its earlier network consisting mostly of package-sorting facilities. Before this acquisition, most UPS facilities were located away from residential and business areas to capitalize on the lower property costs. Face-to-face interaction at a UPS facility was less important for serving business customers. The Mail Boxes Etc.® acquisition reflected the potential scenario of sophisticated consumers of the emerging e-commerce era. The ingenuity of this move is probably evident in the fact that FedEx, UPS's main competitor, acquired the 1,200 retail outlets of copy-store chain Kinko's Inc. nine months later.[38] One difference between the two moves was that UPS paid $191 million for its acquisition of Mail Boxes Etc.®, whereas FedEx had to fork out $2.4 billion for a retail store network of fewer than a third of the retail outlets. It is likely that after UPS's first move, Kinko's realized that the value of its retail store network was considerably higher for FedEx owing to its need to remain competitive with UPS.

After learning from its scenario planning exercises that there was a growing need for solutions that went beyond package delivery, the company unveiled additional services, dubbed *UPS Supply Chain Solutions*, in 2002. This move combined logistics, freight hauling, banking, consulting, and package delivery into a single sales, marketing, and operations team.[39] The unit grew to become a third-party logistics service provider, offering a set of value-added services to manufacturing, retail, and distribution organizations. These include sourcing, finished products distribution, light manufacturing, and repair capabilities—spanning warehousing, planning, distribution, and technology—alongside a suite of professional services. Here was a sophisticated supply chain service fueled by the established precision of package delivery developed over decades.[40] By 2004, the unit had acquired 19 companies and, with 750 operating locations, had become UPS' fastest-growing division.

Scenario Planning at UPS in the Twenty-First Century

Encouraged by the perceived benefits of scenario planning to facilitate the firm's learning about the evolving business environment, UPS followed the 1997 scenario study with a second, more expansive scenario planning project launched in 2004. The new scenario planning project differed from the 1997 exercise in three aspects: UPS drilled down the process to the regions by creating scenarios at the regional level instead of enforcing a single set of global scenarios on the global firm. It conducted interviews with a much wider set of experts and business partners to identify critical environmental factors to weave into its scenarios. It also involved UPS staff from various global business units and lower levels in the hierarchy compared to those involved in the 1997 exercise. Similar to the 1997 exercise, UPS developed four scenarios in 2004, but with added regional scenario descriptions. In addition, UPS also developed a set of "early warning signals" for each scenario to facilitate its executives and managers understanding of the evolving business environment. The objective had been to monitor changes that may indicate that the world was moving toward or away from any of the four scenarios. Having appreciated the ability of scenario planning to promote organizational learning about the long-term business environment and its effect on strategic decisions made by the scenario users, UPS continues to use scenario planning to help develop its long-range plans.

Notes

1. Dator, J. 2012. "On Looking into the Futures." In Deutsche Post AG, *Delivering Tomorrow: Logistics 2050—A Scenario Study*. Deutsche Post AG.
2. Scenario planning has an extensive body of scholarly literature of practical relevance. The interested reader is referred to the works of some of the field's leading scholars such as Ronald Bradfield, George Burt, George Cairns, Thomas Chermack, James Derbyshire, Liam Fahey, Paul Goodwin, Heiko von der Gracht, Robert Lempert, Rafael Ramirez, Rene Rohrbeck, Paul Schoemaker, and George Wright. Leading scholarly journals specializing in scenario planning include Futures, Foresight, Futures & Foresight Science, Technological Forecasting and Social Change. Neither list is exhaustive.
3. Spaniol, M., Rowland, N. 2019. "Defining Scenario." *Futures & Foresight Science*, 1(1), e3. doi:10.1002/ffo2.3.

4. Schwartz, P. 1991. *The Art of the Long View: Planning for the Future in an Uncertain World*. New York: Doubleday; van der Heijden, K. 2005. *Scenarios: The Art of the Strategic Conversation*. West Sussex: Wiley.

5. Bradfield, R., et al. 2005. "The Origins and Evolution of Scenario Techniques in Long-range Business Planning." *Futures*, 37(8), 795–812.

6. Ringland, G. 1998. *Scenario Planning: Managing for the Future*. New York: John Wiley.

7. Bradfield, et al., op. cit.

8. Ringland, op. cit.

9. Bradfield, et al., op. cit.

10. Bradfield, et al., op. cit.

11. van der Heijden, op.cit., p. 5.

12. Schoemaker, P., van der Heijden, K. 1992. "Integrating Scenarios into Strategic Planning at Royal Dutch/Shell." *Planning Review*, 20(3), 41–46.

13. Linneman, R., Klein, H. 1983. "The Use of Multiple Scenarios by US Industrial Companies: A Comparison Study, 1977–1981." *Long Range Planning*, 16(6), 94–101.

14. Schwartz, op. cit.

15. Wack, P. 1985. "Scenarios: Unchartered Waters Ahead." *Harvard Business Review*, 63(5), 73–89.

16. Bradfield et al., op. cit., p. 800.

17. Bradfield et al., op. cit., p. 801.

18. Phadnis, S. 2021. "Agent-Based Modeling Complements Intuitive Logics: A Commentary on Lustick and Tetlock 2021." *Futures & Foresight Science*, 3(2), e78. doi:10.1002/ffo2.78

19. Godet, M. 1986. "Introduction to La Prospective." *Futures*, 134–157.

20. Varum, C., Melo, C. 2010. "Directions in Scenario Planning Literature: A Review of the Past Decades." *Futures*, 42(4), 355–369.

21. Wack, op. cit. p. 84.

22. Schwartz, op. cit. p. 4.

23. Garvin, D., Levesque, L. 2006. "Strategic Planning at United Parcel Service." *HBS No. 9-306-002*. Boston: Harvard Business School Publishing, p. 6.

24. Porter, M. 1985. *Competitive Advantage: Creating and Sustaining Superior Performance*. New York: Free Press. p. 478.

25. Eisenhardt, K. 1999. "Strategy as Strategic Decision Making." *Sloan Management Review*, 40(3), 65–72.

26. Schoemaker, P. 1993. "Multiple Scenario Development: Its Conceptual and Behavioral Foundation." *Strategic Management Journal*, 14(3),

193–213; Kuhn, K. Sniezek, J. 1996. "Confidence and Uncertainty in Judgmental Forecasting: Differential Effects of Scenario Presentation." *Journal of Behavioral Decision Making*, 9(4), 231–247.

27. Meissner, P., Wulf, T. 2013. "Cognitive Benefits of Scenario Planning: Its Impact on Biases and Decision Quality." *Technological Forecasting & Social Change*, 80(4), 801–814.
28. Caplice, C. Phadnis, S. 2013. *Strategic Issues Facing Transportation: Scenario Planning for Freight Transportation Infrastructure Investment.* Washington, DC: Transportation Research Board; Phadnis, S., Caplice, C., Sheffi, Y. Singh, M. 2015. "Effect of Scenario Planning on Field Experts' Judgement of Long-range Investment Decisions." *Strategic Management Journal*, 36(9), 1401–1411.
29. The UPS case is briefly discussed in Phadnis, S., Schoemaker, P. 2022. "Visibility Isn't Enough—Supply Chains also Need Vigilance." *Management and Business Review*.
30. Garvin, D., Levesque, L. 2006. "Strategic Planning at United Parcel Service." *HBS No. 9-306-002.* Boston: Harvard Business School Publishing.
31. UPS Press Room, https://pressroom.ups.com/pressroom/ContentDetailsViewer.page?ConceptType=FactSheets&id=1426321596330-338.
32. Haddad, C. Ewing, J. 2001 (May 21). "Ground Wars: UPS' Rapid Ascent Leaves FedEx scrambling." *Business Week*.
33. Garvin & Levesque, op. cit., pp. 3–4.
34. The description of UPS scenario planning project is primarily based on Garvin & Levesque, op. cit.
35. Garvin & Levesque, op. cit., p. 5.
36. Ibid.
37. Wall Street Journal. 2001 (March 21). "UPS Strikes Cash Deal to Acquire Shipping Franchise Mail Boxes Etc."
38. Brooks, R. 2001 (December 31). "FedEx to Buy Kinko's for $2.2 Billion." *Wall Street Journal*. The heading is not completely accurate: FedEx paid $2.2 billion in cash but also assumed $200 million of Kinko's debt in addition.
39. Krause, K. 2002 (March 4). "One UPS Face." *Traffic World*, 26(9).
40. Salter, C. 2004. "Surprise Package." *Fast Company*, (79), 62–66; Foust, D., 2004 (July 19). "Big Brown's New Bag." *Business Week*, (3892), 54–56.

4

Designing Scenarios to Aid Strategic Planning in Supply Chains

Scenarios are created to influence managers' thinking, which influences their long-term planning and decision-making. To be considered credible and get used by the intended adopters, scenarios need to be designed purposefully and specifically for their decision context, requiring a systematic process of scenario creation. The scenario creation process that the MIT CTL research team employed is based on the Intuitive Logics School (ILS), with the addition of more concrete recommendations for executing different process steps.[1] These extensions are based on theories regarding operations executives' knowledge of different aspects of organizations and their environments.

Scenario Creation: A Primer

Scenario planning adopts an "open systems" perspective. This means that the exercise of scenario planning recognizes that an external environment affects an organization's strategic choices, yet the organization has some ability to influence this environment. The external environment includes not only actions of the suppliers, logistics service providers, and customers, but also, more broadly, geopolitical events, demands from a broad collection of stakeholders, media coverage, tax rates, and natural phenomena—all outside the organization's span of control. This external environment is the source of

© The Author(s), under exclusive license to Springer Nature
Switzerland AG 2022
S. S. Phadnis et al., *Strategic Planning for Dynamic Supply Chains*,
Palgrave Executive Essentials,
https://doi.org/10.1007/978-3-030-91810-1_4

opportunities for the organization and, at the same time, constrains its operations. In most cases, being able to anticipate a future environment allows the organization to prepare for and take advantage of it. Predicting the future environment is, of course, very difficult, especially as the planning horizon grows. For example, consumers' willingness to pay for environment-friendly products may be predictable for the next few months. However, it is difficult to predict its value for several years from now with high confidence. Furthermore, although outside its control, an organization can influence some aspects of the external environment. For example, a company planning to build a factory that would employ a large number of people could negotiate a favorable tax regime from a local government.

Analyzing a company's business environment to create scenarios requires answering two questions: (1) which aspects of its business environment can the company influence? and (2) which aspects are predictable? Certainly, the questions are not completely independent of each other; the ability to influence certain aspects of the environment may also provide at least some level of predictability. The first question helps managers distinguish between what they should be *prepared to respond to* (i.e., the aspects they cannot influence) and what they should *aim to influence*. The second question helps managers distinguish between the predictable aspects of the business environment, which they can prepare for with confidence, and the unpredictable aspects, for which they can only contemplate *contingencies*. A central part of scenario creation is the gathering of pertinent information about the organization's environment. The goal of analyzing these data is to develop a comprehensive understanding of different elements of the environment.

To describe the framework underlying the scenario creation process used by the MIT CTL team, a few key terms should be defined. These terms are used to describe the business environment relevant for scenario creation. Their use in scenario creation is illustrated using the case of Chemica (pseudonym), a South American multinational chemical business.

Scenario Creation: Some Terminology[2]

A set of scenarios depicts possible macro environments that an organization may encounter in the future. Developing those scenarios requires consideration of the strategic issues or decisions facing the organization and different aspects of the business environment relevant to those issues or decisions. The MIT CTL approach to scenario creation relies on classifying the different "variables" encountered in the strategic decision into three groups: *focal decisions*, *local factors*, and *driving forces*. These are depicted schematically

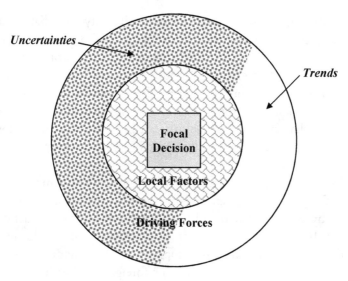

Fig. 4.1 Variables of organizational decision and environment for scenario creation

in Fig. 4.1. They primarily differ by the level of control or influence the organization has over the decision or environment.

- **Focal decision**: A decision about organizational action or structure (within the organization's control).
- **Local factor**: An element of the organization's external environment that the organization can influence but not control.
- **Driving force**: An element of the organization's external environment that the organization can neither influence nor control.

The set of driving forces are further partitioned based on the predictability of their value over the planning horizon of the focal decision:

- **Trend**: A driving force whose value over the planning horizon can be predicted with reasonable accuracy.
- **Uncertainty**: A driving force whose value over the planning horizon cannot be predicted.

To illustrate, a *focal decision* involving a firm's manufacturing strategy for a specific product line may consist of a make-or-buy decision; the production technology to use for the "make" products; locations and capacities of production facilities; choice of subcontractors and vendors, and so on. The considerations for these decisions are influenced by *local factors* such as product demand, raw material costs, availability of reliable suppliers, and licensing costs of production technology. Although the organization cannot control these factors, it can influence them through negotiations or other initiatives. For example, product demand can be influenced by advertising, pricing, promotions, and product bundling; parts and material costs can be influenced through supplier exclusivity, long-term contracts, or volume purchases; supply reliability can be influenced using long-term contracts, co-owning factories with suppliers, or using suppliers located in stable geopolitical regions.

These local factors are shaped by *driving forces*, which remain outside the organization's sphere of influence. For example, demographics (i.e., population sizes by age, gender, or ethnicity) are outside the influence of the organization but can strongly affect product demand. Trade agreements between the host country and the supplier's country modulate the costs of products and raw materials sourced from a foreign supplier. The rate of technological development or any regulations affecting access to the technology shape technology licensing costs.

Some of these driving forces may be predictable over the planning horizon of the strategic decision, in which case they would be called *trends*. For example, population demographics in most countries would be accurately predictable over five years; technological advances may be predictable over two- to five-year periods for several supply chain management technologies such as warehouse robotics. On the other hand, driving forces, such as the availability of quantum computing, may be unpredictable over a 10-year planning horizon; regulations governing trade between different nations or permitted uses of technology (e.g., regulations about drone operations) over the next five years may be unpredictable. Such driving forces are considered *uncertainties*.

Generic Scenario Creation Process

By definition, an organization cannot influence the driving forces of its environment. Consequently, it needs to be prepared to respond to contingencies that emerge from the confluence of those forces. As a result, driving forces are the fundamental ingredients of scenarios used to guide the focal decision. Driving forces are subdivided into trends and uncertainties, according to the predictability of the forces' future states over the planning horizon. When developing scenarios, each *uncertainty* is specified to take one of its extreme but plausible values in at least one scenario, such that all of its key extreme plausible values are captured across the set of scenarios. On the other hand, each *trend* takes its predicted value in every scenario. Thus, a *set* of scenarios that an organization may have to navigate will feature highly contrasting business environments *across* the scenario set, as defined by the underlying uncertainties.

Note that local factors and driving forces, including both trends and uncertainties, need to be identified and articulated by analyzing the business environment. The organization's ability to influence a given local factor is at least partly determined by the capabilities of its managers and senior executives. Likewise, the ability to predict the future values of local factors may depend on the quality of data and understanding of the factor's evolution. Thus, scenario creation involves extensive data collection (via desk research and interviews) from diverse sources and key stakeholders, inside and outside the organization. Information is then synthesized into a set of scenarios deemed plausible.

A seven-step scenario development process was used in the scenario planning projects by the MIT CTL team. This process is based on a set of axioms[3] about knowledge of local factors and driving forces among individuals within and outside the organization, as well as other data sources that may be leveraged for developing scenarios. The process is depicted in Fig. 4.2, while the key process steps are summarized at the end of the detailed description in Table 4.3.

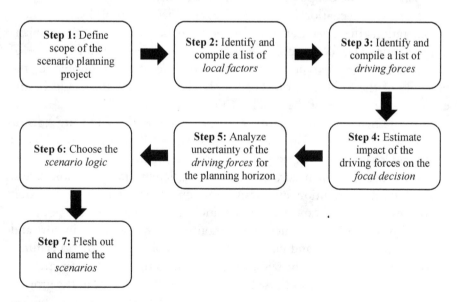

Fig. 4.2 Generic scenario creation process

The description of each step includes a brief example from the scenarios created for the South American business of Chemica in 2011, when the MIT CTL researchers were invited to conduct a scenario creation exercise with a group of 24 supply chain planners and three consultants. The planners were working on developing Chemica's regional distribution strategy for South America. The company wanted to use the scenario planning exercise to help the planners "think beyond cost and service" of day-to-day operations and consider broader issues, such as unpredictable import/export restrictions or quality of logistics infrastructure. The desired outcome of this workshop was to broaden the planners' thinking for formulating the company's regional distribution strategy. Thus, the company intended to use the process of developing the scenarios to build the planners' awareness of different macro-level forces that may be potentially relevant to the distribution strategy.

A three-day workshop was created for this exercise. Most of the supply chain planners participating in the workshop had operational and engineering backgrounds. The first day of the workshop was allotted to introducing the project and making the participants aware of the *qualitative*—as opposed to statistical—uncertainty, of the macro-level business environment. The first day also included an introduction to scenario planning as a method to manage such uncertainty and an introduction of the terminology to be used in the scenario exercise over the subsequent two days.

Step 1: Define the Scope of the Scenario Planning Project

The scope of a scenario planning project specifies the focal decision under consideration, the organizational functions to be involved, and the planning horizon. The focal decision may have multiple elements. The scope of the scenario project is typically defined by the executive responsible for the outcome of the focal decision. For supply chain strategy, this could be the executive responsible for the supply chain.

In the Chemica example, the *focal decision* was the company's distribution strategy for its South American business.[4] This decision included specifying locations and capacities of warehouses, transportation modes used for conveying the chemicals, capacities of different transportation assets, ownership of distribution and transportation assets, and an IT solution for processing import/export documentation. Accordingly, the scope of this project involved functions such as warehousing, transportation, import and export documentation, and customer service. Choices made by other functions, such as production or sales, were relevant to the distribution strategy; therefore, representatives of those functions were also involved in the project. The study used a planning horizon of 10 years because the distribution strategy included decisions to build, purchase, or lease long-lived assets such as warehouses, production facilities, and trucks.

Thus, determining the scope not only defines the boundaries of the scenario planning project but also helps in selecting the project team. The team needs representation from the organizational functions involved in the scope. It may also include representatives of the functions closely related to the functions in the scope, as either full-time or part-time team members. An ideal team member is knowledgeable about the function they represent, able to communicate outcomes of the scenario study back to their functional organization, and able to influence the implementation, in their function, of any initiatives resulting from the project.

Step 2: Identify and Compile a List of Local Factors

After defining the scope, the first data collection step for a scenario project looks at the organization's environment. It involves compiling a list of local factors that may affect the focal decision. Information about local factors is best obtained through exploratory, open-ended data collection methods such as semi-structured interviews. The exploratory nature of this data collection step means that the interviewer should not hold any preconceived ideas about what information may be relevant but simply record all information provided by the respondent. Semi-structured interviews encourage respondents to give deliberative, narrative answers characterizing different aspects of the business environment (as opposed to yes/no or agree/disagree answers). For this information to be relevant, the questions should be centered on the focal decision. Hence, the ideal questions probe respondents to depict the business environment to the fullest extent possible. For instance, "What aspects of the business environment that are outside of the organization's control can affect the focal decision?" These are then followed up with additional questions to explore the answers in further detail.

The raw data collected from different sources in this manner needs to be "normalized" because it generally consists of duplicate information and inconsistent terminology. Duplication refers to the description of the same aspect of the environment by different sources in similar terms and is generally easy to detect. Inconsistency refers to the descriptions of some aspect of the environment in different terms; it is a little harder to detect. The data analysis requires sifting and sorting through the raw data to identify the distinct and relevant elements of the business environment. Qualitative data analysis methods[5] aid this task. Such methods consist of grouping similar terms together and describing their essence in a single statement. It is useful to develop a terminology dictionary of all such statements. This qualitative analysis aims to produce a list of environmental features that covers all unique elements featured in the collected data.

For example, in the case of Chemica, different sources may mention, as different aspects of the business environment, availability of rail connections between different countries in South America, availability of single-versus-double track, condition of railcars and locomotives, and so on. Although worded differently, these aspects all may be grouped under an overarching factor titled "Cross-national Rail Infrastructure." The terminology dictionary for the scenario project would describe this phrase as referring to the capacity and quality of rail-transport infrastructure among various countries in South America.

The desired outcome of this analysis is a list of local factors relevant to the scenario study. Analysis of this data may also identify driving forces, which are discussed in detail in the next step.

In the case of Chemica, on the second day of the workshop, participants were divided into smaller groups for a brainstorming session to identify industry-level factors that would influence the performance of the company's distribution network. Collectively, the groups identified 30 factors, including availability of warehousing locations, customer delivery locations, availability of drivers, willingness of supply chain partners to collaborate, packaging requirements, and the price of diesel. They also included elements such as logistics services provided by third parties, adoption of barcoding and RFID among the service providers, availability and wages of logistics workers, and distribution channels used in the industry.

Step 3: Identify and Compile a List of Driving Forces

Driving forces are macro-level aspects of the business environment. They generally affect the organization through multiple local factors. For example, "road transportation time between a factory and a customer location" (a local factor) could be influenced by macro-level forces such as the quality of road transport infrastructure in the region, geographic characteristics, and weather conditions. Executives and managers with operational responsibilities may be aware of such relevant forces. Interviews with them (such as those conducted in the previous step) may identify several such relevant driving forces, describe their relationship with some of the local factors, and even provide some information about their recent evolution.

However, executives and managers are unlikely to be definitive sources of knowledge about developments shaping the nature and evolution of such forces. Understanding driving forces requires tapping sources of expertise relevant to the domain of each driving force. Such sources include, for example, regional economists knowledgeable about the history and contemporary plans for investments in transportation infrastructure; geologists knowledge-able about the features of the region's geography; environmental scientists knowledgeable about changing climate patterns in the region; construction engineers knowledgeable about the advances in construction materials and methods; political scientists knowledgeable about the discussions regarding multinational cooperation for infrastructure development, and so on. Infor-mation about driving forces comes from semi-structured interviews as well as from open literature (including scholarly publications, expert reports, weblogs, etc.), market research reports, and industry trade publications.

As in the previous step, the data collected by interviewing multiple sources may include duplicate and inconsistent records and thus requires normaliza-tion to identify all the unique driving forces mentioned in the data. Each driving force, along with its description, should be added to the terminology dictionary mentioned in the previous step.

In the case of Chemica, eight driving forces were considered for scenario creation: urbanization, availability of industry and supply chain talent, mobile computing, logistics infrastructure, the dominance of trading blocs, social fabric, environmental sustainability, and economic volatility. These forces were selected by the MIT CTL researchers in consultation with Chemica's South American supply chain leadership team. All eight were both highly relevant to the company's distribution strategy and highly unpre-dictable regarding their future evolution. On the second day of the Chemica workshop, after the aforementioned brainstorming session, the participants were given a series of short presentations by the MIT CTL team, describing the eight macro-level forces that shape the industry.

Once armed with a compilation of relevant local factors and driving forces, the next two steps involve analyzing the driving forces to develop scenarios. The first assesses their impact on the focal decision (Step 4), and the second estimates the uncertainty of their future states (Step 5). Both these steps involve soliciting input from different respondents internal and external to the organization. The respondents need to have a shared understanding of the local factors and driving forces. To this end, providing them with descriptions of the variables in the form of a terminology dictionary is helpful.

Step 4: Estimate Impact of Driving Forces on the Focal Decision
The first part of the analysis of driving forces estimates their impact on the focal decision. The objective is to identify the most impactful ones for designing scenarios. Because driving forces are typically macro-level elements of the business environment, their scope is much broader than that of a focal decision or a local factor. As a result, it can be difficult to assess the impact

of a driving force on a focal decision. However, it is generally easier to assess the impact of local factors on the focal decision due to their narrower scope.

Therefore, the scenario creation process estimates the impact of driving forces on the ultimate focal decision in three sub-steps. First, the project team assesses the impact of different local factors on the focal decision, by asking questions such as, "How strongly does [a local factor] affect the focal decision?" The answers could be recorded on a scale as simple as low/moderate/high or more elaborate seven- or nine-point Likert scales. Aggregating responses to such questions from a sufficiently large number of people knowledgeable about the organization and its local environment (as an average, the most common choices, etc.) can provide reasonably accurate estimates of relative impacts of different local factors on the focal decision.

Second, the project team estimates how strongly each driving force influences each local factor. This information can be gathered by asking "Does [a driving force] affect [a local factor]?", which would have a yes/no answer, or "How strongly does [a driving force] affect [a local factor]?", with answers collected on a Likert scale. The respondents answering this question need to have sufficient knowledge of the local factors and the driving force. The ideal respondents for this are industry experts who know the industry's local factors well and have a fairly broad view of the business environment to understand the effects of macro-level driving forces on the local factors. Assessing the relationship between every local factor and driving forces can be tedious; therefore, the exercise may be limited to the local factors that have the most impact on the focal decision, along with those related to any peculiar aspects of the business environment.

Third, the degree of association between local factors and driving forces—a measure that describes the extent to which a driving force is likely to influence a local factor—is used to assess the impacts of the driving forces from the impacts of local factors. The rationale behind this approach is that a driving force with a stronger influence on local factor should be more relevant for the local factor's impact on the focal decision, compared to a driving force with a weaker influence. A driving force with strong influence on several local factors having a strong impact on the focal decision would be more important for developing scenarios.

It is important to remember that these three assessments of the effects of driving forces and local forces on each other and on the focal decision are qualitative, even if they are diligently recorded in a spreadsheet as numbers from a Likert scale. An effect scored as "6" is not twice as powerful as one with a score of "3." Therefore, when using any quantitative analysis, one needs to avoid the intuitive tendency to seek numerical precision or to treat the exact values of the numbers as meaningful. Instead, the number should be seen as providing a *rough* and *relative* estimate of the relative importance of different driving forces or local factors and is used only to prioritize their consideration in subsequent deliberations.

In the example of the Chemica workshop, the participants had identified 30 local factors at the end of the workshop's second day. They were then asked to assess the impact of each on the focal decision using a five-point Likert scale. Table 4.1 summarizes the votes of the workshop participants assessing the impacts of local factors on this scale, ranging between 0 (no effect) and 4 (very strong effect).

The impact of each driving force was estimated by assessing its ability to influence the 10 most impactful factors[6] by itself. Working in three subgroups, each participant was asked to answer, for example, the following question: "How strong does a *driving force*, such as mobile computing, affect a *local factor*, such as customer locations where the company has to deliver goods?" The participants answered by selecting one of the three options: no effect (rated as 0), weak effect (1), or strong effect (2). The votes of the three groups were averaged to estimate how strongly different driving forces affected the chosen local factors. The impact of a driving force was estimated by adding the products of its association with each local factor to the impact of that local factor. Table 4.2 presents the summary results of this analysis.

As mentioned above, numerical precision is less important than the qualitative discussion the exercises force. Important insights emerge when participants are forced to put an objective value on a factor's impact or its relationship with a driving force and asked to explain the choice within the working group. The numeric result is a by-product of this exercise. The by-product is indeed useful as it provides a measure of the relative importance of different local factors and driving forces emerging from the deliberation, and facilitates subsequent steps for scenario creation.

Step 5: Analyze Uncertainty of Driving Forces
The second part of the analysis of driving forces includes an assessment of uncertainty regarding their future states. Kees Van der Heijden—the former chief of scenario planning at Shell—cautions that "deciding the boundary line between the predictable and the uncertain is not a trivial matter."[7] Uncertainty about a driving force over the planning horizon is based on the degree to which different experts disagree about the state of that driving force over the project's planning horizon. Therefore, uncertainty assessment involves a two-step process: information gathering and analysis.

First, wide-ranging research is conducted for each driving force, through independent expert interviews, industry reports, and relevant publications of

Table 4.1 Summary of Chemica's assessment of impact of local factors

| Local factors | Number of votes by impact score (0=no impact; 4=very strong effect) | | | | | Average impact |
	0	1	2	3	4	
Infrastructure availability of various transportation modes	0	0	3	10	9	3.27
Type of customers (big firms vs. small shops vs. individual consumers)	0	1	3	8	10	3.23
Customer delivery locations	0	0	3	11	8	3.23
Customer service requirements/levels demanded	0	2	4	7	9	3.05
Regulations specific to Chemica's industry	0	1	4	13	4	2.91
Availability of warehousing infrastructure	1	0	4	13	4	2.86
Import/export regulations	0	1	7	10	4	2.77
Availability of qualified logistics service providers	0	1	9	7	5	2.73
Technological solutions available for communication, visibility, and control	1	1	7	7	6	2.73
Demand ordering patterns	0	1	8	9	2	2.60
Level of talent available in industry	1	2	5	10	3	2.57
Prices of logistics services	0	3	8	7	4	2.55
EHS regulations for transportation and warehousing	2	1	6	9	4	2.55
Profit margin in Chemica's industry	0	3	7	10	2	2.50
Traffic restrictions in big cities	0	2	10	8	2	2.45
Strikes/lack of drivers	1	5	4	8	4	2.41
Logistics services offered by service providers	0	3	9	9	1	2.36
Adoption of barcoding, RFID	1	4	6	8	3	2.36
Availability of containers	0	4	9	7	2	2.32
Willingness of supply chain partners to collaborate	0	4	9	7	2	2.32
Supplier (raw material) network	2	4	5	6	4	2.29
Product prices and variations	1	6	6	4	5	2.27

(continued)

Table 4.1 (continued)

Local factors	Number of votes by impact score (0=no impact; 4=very strong effect)					Average impact
	0	1	2	3	4	
Price of diesel and variation in price	0	7	6	4	4	2.24
Customer preference for products	0	4	11	6	1	2.18
Availability and wages of logistics workers	0	7	7	5	3	2.18
Distribution channels primarily used in industry	0	2	13	5	0	2.15
Price of logistics land	2	3	9	6	2	2.14
Type of raw material suppliers (big firms vs. small firms)	2	3	9	6	2	2.14
Packaging standard for customers	1	5	12	4	0	1.86
Incoterms for inbound and outbound	2	8	6	5	1	1.77

top domain experts, to gather their predictions of future values of the driving force over the scenario study's planning horizon. Data gathering aims to collect a diverse set of opinions from reputable sources, not to seek consensus. One needs to steer clear of the groupthink trap here. To this end, the experts should be drawn from a wide range of organizations and be allowed to express their honest opinions without regard to other experts' opinions. The stewardship of scenario creation plays an important role here in avoiding groupthink.

Second, the predictions of the different experts are compared to assess the degree to which they agree. If the experts agree about the future state of the driving force over the study's planning horizon, then the driving force is considered predictable, is classified as a *trend*, and is assumed to take the state predicted by the experts for all the scenarios. Otherwise, the driving force is classified as an uncertainty and considered to potentially take an extreme range of values across different scenarios.

For a driving force categorized as an uncertainty, its plausible extreme values are identified from the aforementioned research, and the degree of uncertainty is estimated, qualitatively, based on the degree of disagreement among the experts. Expert interviews and published documents often include the rationale for a particular prediction. This information is also helpful for assessing the level of uncertainty. MIT CTL researchers found it adequate to label the uncertainty qualitatively for creating scenarios, as high or medium

Table 4.2 Summary of Chemica's assessment of relationship between local factors and driving forces

Local factors and their impact (from Table 4.1)		Urbanization	Availability of talent	Mobile telephony	Infrastructure	Trading blocs	Social fabric	Sustainability	Economic volatility
		Strength of association between local factors (first column) and driving forces (top row)							
Infrastructure availability of various transportation modes	3.27	2	0.33	0	2	1.67	0.67	1.33	1
Type of customers (big firms vs. small shops vs. individual consumers)	3.23	0.67	0	0.33	0.67	1	1	0.33	1.33
Customer delivery locations	3.23	1.67	0.33	0.33	1.67	1	1.33	1	1
Customer service requirements/levels demanded	3.05	0.67	0.33	1.33	1.33	1	1	1.33	1.33
Regulations specific to Chemica's industry	2.91	1.33	0	0	0.33	1.33	0.33	2	0.33
Availability of warehousing infrastructure	2.86	1	0	0	1.67	1.33	0	1	1.33

Local factors and their impact (from Table 4.1)	Urbanization	Availability of talent	Mobile telephony	Infrastructure	Trading blocs	Social fabric	Sustainability	Economic volatility
Strength of association between local factors (first column) and driving forces (top row)								
Import/export regulations	2.77	0	0	0	0.33	2	0.33	1	1.67
Availability of qualified logistics service providers	2.73	0.33	2	0.33	1	0.67	1	1	1.67
Technological solutions available for communication, visibility, and control	2.73	0	1.67	2	0.67	1	0.33	1	0.67
Level of talent available in industry	2.57	1.33	2	0.33	0.67	0.67	2	0.33	1
Estimated impact of driving forces	**27.2**	**18.3**	**13.4**	**31.1**	**34.5**	**23.4**	**30.5**	**33.2**

(with *trend* being the equivalent of low uncertainty); quantitative analysis was not necessary for this exercise in any of the MIT CTL scenario planning projects.

In summary, for all *trends*, the driving force is described as taking the value concurred by the experts about the future. For all *uncertainties*, generally, two extreme values ("low" and "high") are specified for the driving force. The uncertain driving forces are specified to take the low value in some scenarios and the high one in others.

In the Chemica exercise, the results of the second-day analyses (presented in Table 4.2) revealed that the four most relevant driving forces for Chemica's distribution strategy for South America were the dominance of trading blocs, economic volatility, logistic infrastructure, and sustainability. A facilitated discussion with the workshop participants led to the conclusion that economic volatility in South America was likely to remain high in the 10-year planning horizon for the project, but the evolution of the remaining three was unpredictable. Therefore, the three remaining forces were used to develop scenarios by considering their binary extreme values.

Step 6: Choose Scenario Logic

At this stage, the scenario creation process shifts to the design of scenarios as a decision-making aid for the organization's focal decision. The starting point for this step is the assessed impact and uncertainty of each driving force. Selection of a scenario logic involves defining the driving forces as the axes along which the different scenarios will differ. Peter Schwartz calls this one of the "most important steps in the entire scenario-generating process."[8] The driving forces chosen as the scenario axes are the ones with both high uncertainty and high impact on the focal decision.

The choice of scenario axes depends on the number of uncertain driving forces that dominate the focal decision space (Fig. 4.3). If only one driving force dominates—in terms of its high uncertainty and strong impact on the focal decision—then a single-axis logic with two scenarios is defined by the extreme low and high values of the dominating driving force (scenarios S1, S2 in Fig. 4.3a). This could be the case for the supply chain of a commodity with a global market (such as crude oil), where the price of the commodity is the dominating driving force. If two independent driving forces dominate the rest, then four scenarios can be formed as combinations of the low and high extreme values of the two driving forces (scenarios S1-S4 in Fig. 4.3b). If three driving forces dominate the rest, then rather than formulating eight scenarios (2 x 2 x 2), which would be too many, three scenarios can be formed. This is specified as combinations of the high (or low) values of two driving forces and the low (or high) values of the third. For example, scenario S1 in Fig. 4.3c can be defined as taking the high values of driving forces 2 and 3, and the low value of driving force 1.

Once the key driving forces are chosen as scenario axes, the potential scenarios are denoted as combinations of their extreme values. The remaining driving forces are specified in each scenario as taking the values compatible with those of the driving forces chosen as scenario axes. The result of this process is the specification of value taken by all driving forces in every scenario. These are "scenario seeds." They have all defining elements of the scenarios (in terms of driving forces) and are to be developed into full-fledged scenarios by elaborating the basic elements.

The following three-step approach helps define the scenario logic:

- Identify the key driving forces, i.e., those with high uncertainty and impact. It is also useful to choose, as scenario axes, the driving forces that do not seem correlated with each other. This ensures that all combinations of high and low values of the key driving forces are plausible. Accordingly, choose an appropriate scenario axes template and combinations of the key driving forces as scenario seeds. Before settling on a particular combination of key driving forces, explore the resulting scenario seeds with the project team members (who would be among the foremost users of the scenarios) to ensure that the candidates will lead to different yet plausible scenarios.
- After the key driving forces are chosen and scenario seeds defined, specify the remaining uncertainties in each scenario such that (a) all extreme plausible values of each uncertain driving force are mentioned in at least one of the scenarios, and (b) the value of each driving force included in each scenario seems plausible in the presence of the values taken by other driving forces specified in that scenario.

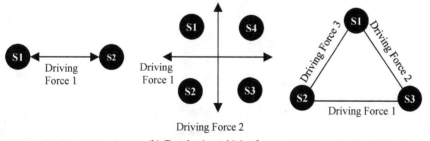

(a) One dominant driving force   (b) Two dominant driving forces   (c) Three dominant driving forces

Fig. 4.3 Commonly used scenario axes templates

- Describe all trends to take their respective forecast values (the consensus of experts) in all scenarios.

In the scenarios developed for Chemica, three driving forces stood out as being key: the dominance of trading blocs, logistics infrastructure, and environmental sustainability. They were used as scenario axes to develop three scenarios using the template shown in Fig. 4.3c. Three scenario seeds emerged from this scenario logic, as shown in Fig. 4.4.

Step 7: Flesh out and name the scenarios
The final step involves writing narratives for each scenario based on the driving force(s) specified in the scenario logic in the previous step. Narratives should include three important elements: a holistic scenario description, a pathway from today to the scenario's future, and a suitable, memorable scenario name.

First, the narrative should present a holistic description of the future business environment characterized by the scenario. In prior steps of the scenario development process, each driving force has been considered largely in isolation from others. Writing the narrative requires considering the driving forces together. Specifically, the narrative of each scenario should describe the future business environment *emerging* from the values taken by all the driving forces specified in that scenario. The interactions among different driving forces often produce interesting features of the environment that are not evident when the driving forces are considered in isolation. Therefore, narrative development is a process of integrating different driving forces to describe the emergent behavior of suppliers, competitors, consumers, and governments

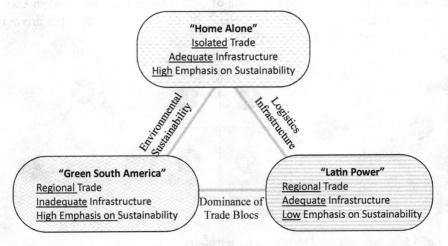

Fig. 4.4 Scenario seeds for Chemica's distribution strategy in South America

that make up the business environment. Because of the insights produced at this stage, the scenario project team should be involved in writing the scenario descriptions.

Second, the holistic picture of the future business environment described in a scenario should be believable. One effective way to achieve this is by showing the path that leads from the present business environment to this scenario future. This requires conjuring up plausible events—such as new regulations, technological breakthroughs, societal changes, ecological events—that push the trajectory of the business environment's evolution toward that specific scenario. For the events to be deemed plausible by the scenario users, they may be expressed in terms of the present-day developments. Key changes may be described as caused by "tipping points" in related domains. This step generally requires additional research to learn about different contemporary developments in various domains of the business environment. Thus, the narrative of each scenario includes a logical path from the present to the future described in that scenario.

Third, each scenario needs to be given a representative name. The scenario name often becomes a shorthand for the complex future described in the longer narrative. As mentioned in the UPS example in Chapter 3, scenario names provided a common vocabulary for talking about aspects of the future and the business that might fit a certain scenario. An ideal scenario name evokes the scenario's essence and is memorable by being short and even humorous. Thus, naming each scenario requires some thought.

Project team members play an important role in naming the scenarios because of their familiarity with the material after being involved in creating holistic scenario descriptions. They may also decide to rename a scenario after using it a few times and understanding its essence at a deeper level, to a catchier, more relevant name. One key naming tip is to avoid names that signal a preference (e.g., Preferred, Tolerated, Worst) or that forecast opinions (e.g., most likely, least likely). The name should only refer to the scenario itself, not its relation to other scenarios.

In addition to developing a verbal narrative, the scenario may include other collateral, such as physical artifacts, images, or videos representing objects and events in the fictionalized future world of that scenario. The goal is to develop materials that can allow scenario users to get an immersive experience of each scenario. The synthesized collateral can come in different forms, but would be fictional: statistics and charts, newspapers' front pages and magazine covers, audio and video news broadcasts, media and advertisements, blogs, and so on. These fictional media complement the textual narratives of the holistic scenario descriptions. Such collateral helps the participants to experience the scenario viscerally, creating a more powerful experience than simply reading the scenario narrative.

In the Chemica workshop, the first three steps were followed, but the rich media creation step was not, because the objective of the workshop was to demonstrate the scenario creation process and not to create scenarios for actual decision-making. After defining the scenario logic, the workshop participants split into three groups. Each group chose one scenario seed and developed it further (as described in the first two steps) in a 90-minute session, and finally named their scenario. The scenario names (Fig. 4.4), created by the teams on their own, suggest that the exercise had helped the workshop participants understand the essence of the scenario. For example, the scenario "Latin Power" describes a world where trade within the South American trading bloc is vibrant, enabled by adequate infrastructure, helping the bloc become an economic powerhouse. However, this has come at the expense of environmental sustainability. On the other hand, the scenario "Green South America" emphasizes environmental sustainability and regional trade within South America, both of which feature in the scenario name. The weak logistics infrastructure that was part of that scenario has prevented the bloc from becoming an economic powerhouse.

Table 4.3 summarizes the steps, personnel, and methods of the scenario creation process.

Table 4.3 Essential steps and elements of the scenario creation process

Process step	Personnel/resources involved	Data collection and analysis method
1. Define the scope of the scenario planning project	• Head of supply chain • Representatives of relevant functions	• Consider functions involved in and affected by strategic decision
2. Identify and compile a list of local factors	• Experienced organization members • Project team	• Exploratory, open-ended data collection • Qualitative data analysis
3. Identify and compile a list of driving forces	• Experienced organization members • External domain experts • Industry trade publications, market research reports • Expert reports and weblogs	• Exploratory, open-ended data collection • Focused data collection (by driving force) • Qualitative data analysis

(continued)

Table 4.3 (continued)

Process step	Personnel/resources involved	Data collection and analysis method
4. Estimate impact of driving forces on focal decision	• Experienced organization members • External domain experts, industry experts	• Assess the impact of local factors • Estimate association between driving forces and local factors • Analysis to map impact from local factors to driving forces
5. Analyze uncertainty of driving forces	• External domain experts • Industry trade publications, market research reports • Expert reports and weblogs	• Gather projections from wide-ranging reputable sources (by driving force) • Comparison of different predictions
6. Choose scenario logic	• Project team	• Key driving forces based on impact and uncertainty evaluations • Scenario axes templates
7. Flesh out and name scenarios	• Project team • Professional writers • Video creators, artists, etc. (optional)	• Narrative: Scenario description • Narrative: Pathways to each scenario • Scenario name • Develop rich media collateral (optional)

Notes

1. Phadnis, S., Caplice, C., Singh, M., Sheffi, Y. 2014. "Axiomatic Foundation and a Structured Process for Developing Firm-Specific Intuitive Logics Scenarios." *Technological Forecasting & Social Change*, 88, 122–139.
2. This material is based on Phadnis, et al., op. cit.
3. The axioms and the scenario creation process are described in Phadnis, et al., op. cit.
4. Although scenarios were not used per se for formulating the distribution strategy, their intent was to educate the team of distribution network designers and make them aware of the relevant uncertainties and trends affecting the strategy.
5. Qualitative data analysis is used for grounded theory research in social sciences. The following two references were particularly useful for the MIT CTL projects: Miles, M., Huberman, A. 1994. *Qualitative Data Analysis:*

An Expanded Sourcebook. 2nd ed. Thousand Oaks, CA: Sage; Strauss, A., Corbin, J. 1990. *Basics of Qualitative Research: Grounded Theory Procedures and Techniques.* Newbury Park, CA: Sage.

6. The choice of ten was not arbitrary. The numeric values of impact showed a step change between the top nine and the rest; "level of talent available in the industry" was chosen as a tenth local factor despite not featuring in top ten because none of the selected local factors related to "talent" (plus, this was eleventh most impactful). One additional reason for using such a simplistic approach was that the scenario exercise was used for educational purposes and not for creating scenarios for decision making.

7. van der Heijden, K. 2005. *Scenarios: The Art of Strategic Conversation.* 2nd ed. New York: Wiley.

8. Schwartz, P. 1991. *The Art of the Long View: Planning for the Future in an Uncertain World.* New York: Doubleday, p. 229.

5

Scenario Creation in Supply Chain Contexts

The MIT CTL team applied its scenario creation method in several industry projects. It was applied in organizations playing the three roles in supply chains introduced earlier: Hoppy Brew (functional role), Medford (business model role), and Future Freight Flows (infrastructural role).

Functional Role: Scenarios for Hoppy Brew

Recall the supply chain design challenge faced by Hoppy Brew's supply chain executives. The executives were wondering if the company had the "right supply chain" for a changing world characterized by environmental concerns, demanding consumers, changing regulations, and growing adoption of smartphones. The company decided to use scenario planning to guide its strategic initiatives in different parts of its supply chain.

Scope of Hoppy Brew's Scenario Planning Project (Step 1)

The project was launched by Hoppy Brew's Global Vice President of Operations and Logistics. Operations and Logistics at Hoppy Brew included five functional areas: procurement, brewing, packaging, distribution, and planning. The planning horizon for the scenario project was set to 10 years.

© The Author(s), under exclusive license to Springer Nature
Switzerland AG 2022
S. S. Phadnis et al., *Strategic Planning for Dynamic Supply Chains*,
Palgrave Executive Essentials,
https://doi.org/10.1007/978-3-030-91810-1_5

At the launch meeting, the Global VP of Operations set the goals for the project: identify the major drivers shaping the industry, articulate potential scenarios, and provide an approach for Hoppy Brew to prepare for and adapt to each scenario for the five functional areas. After subsequent discussions between the MIT CTL project team and Hoppy Brew's Operations leadership team, the scope of the project evolved in two significant ways. First, Hoppy Brew realized that the five chosen areas would be strongly influenced by the company's new product development initiatives. Therefore, the company's Global Vice President of Innovation & Development also joined the team. He expanded the project scope to include the company's research & development initiatives. Second, Hoppy Brew added one more deliverable to the project: a "playbook" that would enable the tracking of the evolving business environment and guide the executives' future decisions regarding its changing supply chain strategy.

Hoppy Brew kept the size of the project team deliberately small. The VP assigned one associate from the Operations team (a driven MBA graduate) to coordinate the day-to-day project activities with the MIT team. The VP of Operations was actively involved, along with the company's Global Director of Planning & Logistics. The Hoppy Brew team also arranged access to 18 senior executives for interviews and participation in the scenario development workshops.

Hoppy Brew Local Factors and Driving Forces (Steps 2, 3)

The first data collection step focused on gathering extensive information about Hoppy Brew's business environment. This information was collected from two sources: company executives and independent industry research reports. The company executives included five Global Vice Presidents, three Vice Presidents, six Global Directors, and three Directors. They headed functions such as Operations and Logistics, Distribution, Transportation, Packaging, Planning, Raw Materials Sourcing and Supply, Trade Marketing, Innovation and Technical Development, Revenue Management and Strategic Insights. Using exploratory interviews with open-ended questions, they were asked to characterize Hoppy Brew's business environment.

The second source of information was external to the company. This included extensive reviews of 16 different industries that interact with Hoppy Brew's business, such as Hoppy Brew's customers (supermarkets & grocery stores; wine & spirit wholesaling, beer, wine & liquor stores; convenience stores; and both chain and single-location full-service restaurants); competitors and substitute producers (distilleries, wineries); and suppliers (wheat, barley & sorghum farmers). The MIT CTL team also gathered additional information from various reports by domain experts, published by trade associations, consulting firms, non-profit organizations, and think-tanks, regarding input factors such as water and farm crops, regulations for the industry, and different channels through which Hoppy Brew's products are sold.

Analysis of this data uncovered 82 different aspects of the business environment. They included availability and cost of inputs and resources such as barley, specialty hops, water, and aluminum (for cans); competition for the inputs from other industries such as animal food; or shifts in arable land due to climate change. The data also included regulatory aspects such as government subsidies to farmers; excise and other taxes on alcoholic beverages; regulations affecting production, distribution, sale, and consumption of alcohol (including penalties for drunk driving). Industry dynamics such as competition from craft beers and wines, the purchasing power of wholesalers and retailers, and competition among retailers were also present in the list. It contained demographic trends such as consumers' health consciousness, ethnic composition of consumers, and their preferred tastes. Several technology-specific dimensions were mentioned as well, including advances in information technology, use of social media for sharing experiences, changes in brewing technology, and demand and technologies for customized beverages.

The multitude of aspects of Hoppy Brew's business environment captured through such a data collection exercise were examined to identify common themes. From this analysis, the MIT CTL team identified nine different driving forces shaping the business environment of Hoppy Brew. These driving forces and their classification in terms of trends versus uncertainties are presented in Table 5.1.

Impact and Uncertainty of Hoppy Brew's Driving Forces (Steps 4, 5)

After defining the driving forces, the MIT CTL team had to assess their impact on the focal decision and estimate their range of values over the 10-year planning horizon. This exercise was far from trivial. For example, consider the driving force: "Consumer preferences for consumption of beer and other alcoholic beverages." This driving force had over a dozen different dimensions, covering issues such as perceived health implications of different alcoholic beverages; demand for different types of alcoholic drinks (beer, ciders, mixed drinks, wines, spirits); type of product consumed (mass-market

Table 5.1 Driving forces of Hoppy Brew's business environment

Driving force	Description	Extreme values (under uncertainty)
Driving forces with HIGH uncertainty		
Consumer preferences for alcoholic beverages	Acceptance of GMOs; desire for customized drinks; preference for premium products; willingness to substitute among alcoholic beverages; the importance of production location; consumption location (e.g., restaurants, sports venues vs. homes, private parties)	*Extreme 1 (Customization)* *Extreme 2 (Brand)* The extremes are described as mentioned in the paragraph above
Resource availability	Access to specialty hops/ingredients; availability and cost of water used in beer production; climate change-related shifts in arable land; farmer incentives to grow barley vs. other crops	*Extreme 1 (Scarce):* Scarce access to and high cost of ingredients and water; strong farmer incentives to grow crops besides barley *Extreme 2 (Adequate):* Adequate access to ingredients and water; more arable land due to climate change; no particular farmer incentives to switch away from barley

Driving force	Description	Extreme values (under uncertainty)
Scope and intensity of regulations	Cost of obtaining and maintaining liquor licenses; excise and other taxes on alcoholic beverages; extent to which regulations dictate the structure of supply chain of alcoholic beverages	*Extreme 1 (Low)*: Cheaper liquor licenses, low taxes on alcoholic beverages; minimal regulations leaving markets to guide operations of liquor supply chains; minimal restrictions on alcohol consumption *Extreme 2 (High)*: High cost of obtaining liquor licenses; high taxes on alcoholic beverages; pervasive regulations about different aspects of liquor supply chains; more restrictions on where liquor can be consumed
Driving forces with MEDIUM uncertainty		
Competitive dynamics in the alcoholic beverages sector	Consolidation among wholesalers, retailers; retail industry structure; competition among retail formats and intensity of competition; alternatives to alcohol	*Extreme 1 (Strong)*: High consolidation in the wholesale and retail sector; strong competition; no major alternatives to alcohol *Extreme 2 (Weak)*: Fragmented retail and wholesale sectors with the presence of small stores; competition on par with the present; several alternatives to alcoholic products

(continued)

Table 5.1 (continued)

Driving force	Description	Extreme values (under uncertainty)
Consumer confidence and overall consumer spending	Consumer confidence; amount of money spent at liquor stores, restaurants, resorts; leisure travel within and outside the US; per capita disposable income	*Extreme 1 (High):* High consumer confidence and spending *Extreme 2 (Low):* Low confidence and spending
Other macroeconomic variables	Price of energy (average level and variability); strength of local currencies	*Extreme 1:* High and volatile energy prices, strong foreign currencies *Extreme 2:* Low and stable energy prices, strong US dollar
Driving forces with LOW uncertainty		
Advances in information, brewing technologies	The ability for consumers to create recipes to personalize alcoholic drinks; sharing of positive and negative experiences on social media; use of IT solutions to purchase liquor; visibility of how firms conduct their business	*Consensus:* All variables described were expected to be higher than the present (circa 2013)
Environmental concerns	Consumers' use of reusable containers; emphasis on recycling; regulations about emissions from trucks	*Consensus:* Slow increase in environmental consciousness and green policies among consumers, businesses, and regulations
General demographic characteristics of the society	Multi-cultural and multi-ethnic markets; consumer health consciousness; population by age and ethnic background; growth of cities; traffic and congestion and restrictions on goods transport in cities	*Consensus:* Continuation of trends observed at present circa 2013; growth in the percentage of the population living in the cities; increased traffic and congestion in cities causing more restrictions on goods traffic on city roads

vs. niche); acceptance of genetically modified organism (GMO) raw materials used to produce the drinks; brand loyalty; and importance of beverage consumption locations. Treating each of these dimensions in isolation would significantly increase the number of variables considered for scenario creation and complicate scenario development. However, collapsing them into one dimension such as "consumer preferences" also ran the risk of losing the nuances of these different aspects. Therefore, the team was left with the challenge of synthesizing this information while creating scenarios, without losing the richness contained in the multiple aspects of consumer preferences.

To this end, the MIT CTL team first assessed the importance of each aspect of Hoppy Brew's supply chain—a total of 82—by discussing them with the project team members. From this analysis, the team identified 25 aspects as unique and of significance for the supply chain. For each of these aspects, the team revisited the predictions about the component drivers gathered in its research and conducted additional industry research to evaluate their predictability over the next 10 years. If publications from different sources predicted similar values and predictions of different components of a driving force moved in a similar direction, then the uncertainty regarding that driving force was determined to be low, and the driving force was considered to be a *trend*. Conversely, if different sources gave conflicting predictions, or if predictions of different drivers moved in significantly different directions, then the driving force was considered to an *uncertainty*.

For example, consider consumer acceptance of GMO raw materials used for making alcoholic beverages. The team found articles from reputed sources such as Pew Research Center[1] and Packaged Facts[2] (a leading publisher of market research in the food and beverage sector) that showed consumers in Europe and Japan strongly objecting to GMO in food items; US consumers also opposed the use of GMO ingredients but to a lesser degree. Conversely, an opinion poll by another organization, Sustainable America,[3] found a more even split among US consumers supporting and opposing GMOs in food production (36 vs. 45%). Thus, the acceptance of GMOs in alcoholic beverages was deemed to be moderately uncertain among US consumers.

Another example was regulations on the distribution of alcoholic beverages. The United States has an idiosyncratic national mandate forcing a three-tiered supply chain—consisting of producers or importers, distributors, and retailers—for the distribution of alcoholic beverages in the country. This is a legacy of the repeal of Prohibition in 1933 through the Twenty-First Amendment to the United States Constitution. The first section of the Twenty-First Amendment repealed the Eighteenth Amendment, while the second section gave regulatory powers over alcohol trade to individual states.

Many states feared that the repeal of the Eighteenth Amendment would lead to a resurgence of the saloons, known for drunkenness, gambling, prostitution, and violence on their premises. Many saloons were also captive to producers of alcoholic beverages. Such vertical integration meant that a single organization could potentially control production, distribution, and retailing. Historically, many such organizations had connections to organized crime. The three-tiered system was introduced to prevent a single organization from controlling all three tiers.[4]

The legacy of the 1933 Amendment was still in place when the MIT team engaged with Hoppy Brew. Liquor producers and importers could not sell directly to consumers or even to retailers. They had to sell the products to distributors, who could only sell it to retailers (including restaurants), who were then allowed to sell the liquor to consumers. However, some states had been slowly chipping away at this requirement. Leveraging the power bestowed to them by the Twenty-First Amendment, these states had enacted laws that favored (not surprisingly) local alcoholic beverage producers. For example, New York and Michigan allowed in-state wineries to ship wine directly to consumers but maintained the three-tier requirement for out-of-state wineries. Calling this discriminatory, many small wineries banded together to fight these regulations. An eight-year battle by the small wineries finally culminated in a landmark US Supreme Court decision in 2005—known as the Granholm v. Heald case—that, by a 5–4 vote, ruled the discriminatory practice of the two states unconstitutional. Since this ruling, more states had allowed direct shipping of wine from any winery to consumers.

Another regulation, the Community Alcohol Regulatory Effectiveness (CARE) Act introduced in the US Congress in 2011, called for giving US states more power to promulgate rules regarding alcohol trade in the state. This would further diminish the three-tier system. The act was backed by the Wine & Spirits Wholesalers of America. However, several other organizations in the alcoholic beverage industry vehemently opposed it. The Brewers Association, WineAmerica, Distilled Spirits Council of the United States, Wine Institute, Beer Institute, and the National Association of Beverage Importers all called it unnecessary and harmful to consumers. They feared that states would enact protectionist measures.[5]

In 2013, when Hoppy Brew was developing the scenarios, it was not clear whether, how quickly, and to what extent the three-tier supply chain regulations would be relaxed for beer distribution in different US states. Yet, these potential regulatory changes could have a significant impact on Hoppy Brew. Such changes would determine whether the company could distribute its beer directly to retailers or sell directly to consumers through its own retail outlets. Moreover, there were also implications for future packaging modes, such as beer "cartridges" for in-home beer dispensing machines, which Hoppy Brew was considering. Thus, regulations related to the three-tiered system had both high impact and high uncertainty, making regulation a critical driving force for scenario creation.

The MIT CTL team conducted similar analyses for all shortlisted aspects of the business environment. The predictability of each driving force was assessed by considering the predictability of its component aspects. For example, for the driving force of "consumer preferences," six aspects, deemed significant for the supply chain, were examined in detail:

- Willingness to substitute among beers, wines, or liquors;
- Preference for the type of product (premium, mass-market, etc.);
- Demand for customizing drinks to taste;
- Importance of the production location in the consumer's perception of brand authenticity (e.g., whether a "German" brand beer is produced in Germany or the US);
- Acceptance of GMOs in alcoholic drinks; and
- The proportion of alcoholic beverages consumed at home vs. at eating establishments.

Opinion gleaned from public sources was diverse, just as it was among Hoppy Brew's executives about the future evolution of these dimensions of consumer preferences. As a result, the driving force "consumer preferences" was deemed to be *highly uncertain.*

Each driving force deemed uncertain was specified with two extreme yet plausible values. Defining the two extremes may not be straightforward. Consider, for example, "consumer preferences" and its six dimensions mentioned above. Which two values could express the uncertainty on those six dimensions? Based on the publications and interviews conducted earlier with Hoppy Brew executives, the "consumer preferences" driving force was defined as either "customized products" or standard "branded products." These two extreme values were defined as follows.

- *Customized products*: A strong consumer desire to customize drinks to taste; low desire to substitute among types of liquor; preference for taste and quality but not a brand; high importance put on production location; strong opposition to GMOs in alcoholic beverages; and consumption primarily at home.

- *Branded products*: Low consumer tendency to customize drinks to taste; a strong preference for premium brands; willingness to substitute among types of liquor; low importance for the production location; and consumption primarily at eating establishments.

The same exercise was performed for each driving force. Table 5.1 summarizes the analysis, showing the description, level of uncertainty, and plausible values for each driving force.

Hoppy Brew's Scenario Logic and Scenarios (Steps 6, 7)

The analysis of driving forces shaping Hoppy Brew's business environment, presented in Table 5.1, formed the basis for outlining Hoppy Brew's scenarios. The focus had been primarily on the driving forces with high uncertainty and with potential for high impact on Hoppy Brew's supply chain choices. The analysis and discussions of the analysis with Operations executives led to the realization that three driving forces were fundamental to creating the scenarios for the company. The three also seemed to have little correlation among them:

- Consumer preferences for alcoholic beverages,
- Regulatory environment (scope and intensity of regulations), and
- Resource availability.

Using the scenario axes template shown in Fig. 4.3, the driving forces were tied together in a scenario logic framework. Each scenario was defined by combining the "Extreme 1" values of two driving forces and the "Extreme 2" values of the remaining one. For example, one scenario (later named *Brew-nique!*) was formed by taking the "Extreme 1" values of Consumer Preferences (customization) and Resource Availability (scarce), and the "Extreme 2" value of Regulatory Environment (high). Figure 5.1 depicts the resulting scenario logic and three scenario seeds formed by combining the three driving forces (the names were decided upon only later in the process).

The three driving forces with medium uncertainty were added to each scenario such that each extreme value of the uncertainty appeared in at least one scenario and was consistent with the values taken by the three driving forces defining the scenario logic. Each driving force with low uncertainty (trend) was specified to take the same value in all three scenarios. The final step involved naming and writing narratives for each scenario. The writing of scenario descriptions helped the team generate scenario names: *Brand World*,

Fig. 5.1 Logic of Hoppy Brew scenarios

Brew-nique!, and *Group Drink*. Snippets of the scenarios are presented in Exhibits 9.1–9.3 in Chapter 9.

Business Model Role: Scenarios for Medford's Pharmaceuticals Distribution

A plethora of changes in various regulations, information and medical technologies, and market dynamics in healthcare industries had led Medford's executives to question if the company had the right business model in the evolving US pharmaceuticals supply chain. They wanted to determine their target customer segments, which products and services to offer, and which supply chain capabilities and resources to invest in. Before reaching these conclusions, however, Medford's executives needed to understand how the business environment might evolve in the coming years and affect the company's business. This was particularly challenging because the executives' attention was focused on tactical issues spanning no longer than a few weeks. Moreover, Medford's razor-thin profit margins left little room for error in any significant capital investment decisions. Medford decided to use scenario planning as a tool that could help its pharmaceutical distribution executives broaden their span of attention, step out of their tactical roles, and explore long-term issues.

Scope of Medford's Scenarios (Step 1)

The project was initiated by the Senior Vice President of Medford's Phar-maceuticals Distribution supply chain (who would soon become the busi-ness's president and CEO). Given the objective of broadening organiza-tional thinking, he involved his entire executive team in the project, which included another Senior Vice President, 12 vice presidents, 7 directors, and 4 managers, who oversaw distribution center operations, regulations, IT, strategy, human resources, environmental health & safety, and corpo-rate ethics. They were based in different regions of the US. This group met once a month at the company's headquarters to review the opera-tional performance of the pharmaceuticals supply chain, discuss tactical issues affecting the performance, and explore longer-term strategic issues. The Senior Vice President launched the scenario project when he realized that the monthly discussions were extensively focused on the short-term operational and tactical issues. Executives were struggling to cope with the slowly evolving longer-term developments affecting the healthcare industry.

The planning horizon for the scenario project was five years and included all areas pertinent to the pharmaceutical supply chain. The MIT CTL team was invited to one of the monthly meetings to present the idea of scenario planning (which was new to most of the executives involved in the project) and to launch the project. The team was granted access to all 24 members of Medford's executive team and had several engagements with them through interviews, workshops, questionnaire-based exercises, and presentations over one year.[6]

Medford's Local Factors and Driving Forces (Steps 2, 3)

The MIT CTL team started data collection by interviewing all the execu-tives involved in the project. The interviews were conducted by phone with each executive individually and recorded with their consent. The executives were asked to schedule the interview at a time when they would be able to think and deliberate, without any interruptions, about Medford's busi-ness environment over five years and what Medford would need to succeed in that environment. By listening to the recordings, a mental map was created for each executive. Each map showed different aspects of the business environment mentioned by the executive (color-coded by the domain refer-enced: industry dynamics, regulations, technology, etc.) and strategic actions advocated by the executive.

These maps were used in two ways. First, each map documented the executive's vision of Medford's business environment and strategies. They showed what each executive paid attention to, whether their attention focused predominantly on a narrow subset of the business environment, and what types of strategic actions they considered useful. In addition, comparing the maps of different executives also revealed where the group converged, where they diverged, and what was missing from their collective span of attention. Second, the elements of the business environment contained in all 24 maps were compiled to provide raw material to develop scenarios for Medford.

A notable feature of all Medford's executives' mental maps was that none of them included any variables related to the natural environment (e.g., carbon footprint, pollution, waste handling, natural resource consumption, deforestation). This could have been because the natural environment was either not relevant to pharmaceutical distribution or that it was a blind spot for the company. This was highlighted to the team, and environmental consciousness of the US society was included as one of the components in the scenarios developed in the project.

This data was complemented by information from external sources. The external data came from market research reports (provided by IBISWorld) for 15 industries relevant to the US healthcare sector, and reports specific to different industries from the relevant industry experts. These industries (followed by their NAICS[7] codes) included branded and generic pharmaceutical manufacturing (32,541), drug wholesaling (42,221), pharmacies and drug stores (44,611), life and health insurance (52,411), health & welfare funds (52,512), primary care and specialist doctors (62,111), home care providers (62,161), general hospitals (62,211), specialty hospitals (62,231), nursing care facilities (62,311), retirement communities (62,331), and biotechnology (54,171).

Qualitative analysis of the data collected from the interviews and the industry reports unearthed several aspects of the business environment. For instance, the market research databases provide "key external drivers." A total of 47 unique drivers were compiled from the industry research reports. Analysis of interviews with Medford's executives resulted in 55 different aspects of the environment (many of which were also included in the market research data). These aspects encompassed local factors and components of driving forces related to various domains of the business environment, such as:

- *Customer*: Magnitude of and the relative demand for pharmaceuticals from acute and non-acute care facilities, profitability of independent pharmacies, size of the government as a customer of pharmaceutical distributors, etc.

- *Supplier*: Market share of generic drugs, volume of patient-specific treatments produced by manufacturers, intensity of cost-reduction efforts of pharmaceutical manufacturers, etc.
- *Current and potential competitors*: Intensity of competition among the Big Three distributors, viability of regional distributors, entry of third-party logistics (3PL) companies like UPS and FedEx into pharmaceutical distribution, etc.
- *Regulations*: Enforcement of pedigree laws, enforcement of drug diversion laws, regulations about the transparency of drug prices, etc.
- *Societal issues*: Locations where medical care is provided (e.g., home, long-term care facilities, hospital), frequency of drug thefts, availability of pharmacists and nurses, etc.
- *Technology*: Use of e-prescription and Electronic Medical / Health Record technologies, proportion of biotech drugs in the mix of drugs produced, etc.

The difficulty with such a diverse set of variables was in identifying those likely to have the most impact on product distribution and assessing how they might evolve. Beyond that, the challenge was to group them into a few scenarios to simplify their deliberation by the company's executives without compromising the richness of the context. Guided by feedback from industry experts, the MIT CTL team identified 16 different driving forces shaping Medford's business environment. Several of these driving forces had highly uncertain futures.

Impact and Uncertainty of Medford's Driving Forces (Steps 4, 5)

The cataloging of the relevant driving forces was followed by an assessment of their impact on Medford's business and the uncertainty about the values they may take over the five-year planning horizon. Due to the project's goal to facilitate organizational learning, Medford's team members were involved extensively in this exercise.

The impact of any given driving force can be difficult to estimate because it typically influences multiple local factors that subsequently have varied impacts on the organization. However, the implications of local factors are easier to estimate due to their narrower scope. Therefore, Medford's team members were asked to assess the impact of a subset of 32 key local factors, representing unique aspects of the business environment on the company's supply chain performance. The reason for using a subset of the factors was to focus the team's discussion on salient unique aspects of the business environment while minimizing demand for the executives' time. Out of these 32 local factors, Table 5.2 lists the five key local factors assessed by the executives as having the strongest positive impacts and the five with the strongest negative impacts on Medford's supply chain. For example, manufacturers' reliance on distributors for delivering their products was considered strongly positive as it implied continued business for companies like Medford. In contrast, attempts by pharmacy chains, hospitals, and healthcare group purchasing organizations (GPOs) to bypass the distributors and procure the products directly from the manufacturers would negatively impact distributors' revenues.

Overall, a few recurring themes were noted during the analysis of the most impactful key local factors. Those with the strongest impact on Medford (either positive or negative) pertain to the reliance of its customers and suppliers on Medford's distribution operations. As upstream or downstream supply chain partners (hospitals, pharmacy chains, manufacturers) grow larger, the risk of bypassing Medford increases. Such "disintermediation" is a common business risk faced by companies in the business model role in many supply chains. This is also why strong growth of non-acute care facilities—which are typically small organizations primarily focused on healthcare and without capabilities to distribute pharmaceuticals—was seen as a strong positive by Medford's executives. In addition, customers' focus on price, leading to price wars, was seen as strongly negative, whereas customer demand for superior service (in terms of fast response, timely deliveries, etc.) was seen as

Table 5.2 Five key local factors with strongest positive and negative impact on Medford

Factors with strongest POSITIVE effect	Factors with strongest NEGATIVE effect
• Manufacturers' reliance on distributors for distributing drugs and devices	• Bypassing of distributors by pharmacy chains to buy directly from manufacturers
• Motivation of Medford's carriers to ensure reliable service to the customers	• Bypassing of distributors by hospitals and GPOs to buy directly from manufacturers
• Improvement in accessibility and quality of treatment due to technological advances	• Medford's customers' choice of distributor based solely on price
• Greater generic alternatives to patented drugs	• Fierce competition among the Big Three pharmaceutical distributors
• Significant increase in demand for pharmaceuticals at non-acute healthcare facilities (e.g., clinics, long-term care, homes)	• Increase in frequency of drug thefts

strongly positive. Such observations apply to many businesses and are typical for firms that rely on creating value through effective management of supply chains.

Driving forces with uncertain evolutionary paths could cause these local factors to move in different directions. Thus, the second part of the analysis assessed the association between different uncertain driving forces and the key local factors. Only two driving forces—the average age of the US population and the environmental consciousness of the US society—were considered predictable. The remaining 14 were considered unpredictable over the five-year planning horizon. The MIT team assessed how these 14 forces would affect different local factors. To simplify the analysis, the team focused on the key local factors with the strongest (either positive or negative) impact on Medford, as assessed by Medford's executives.

There is no objective way to assess the relationship between driving forces and local factors. Consequently, the project used a subjective method designed to help the Medford executives deliberate and learn about the ways that large macro-level forces affect the local factors in their industry and eventually affect Medford. The executives completed the assessments by answering the following question with a binary yes/no answer: "Does<a driving force>affect<a key local factor>?" The fraction of executives answering "Yes" to the question was used as a proxy for the strength of association between the respective driving force and the key local factor. Some driving forces were seen to have a strong association with several local factors, whereas others seemed to affect only a small subset.

For example, the driving force "complexity of the US healthcare supply chain" was deemed to have a strong influence on several key factors in Medford's business environment. These included the basis for customers' choice of a distributor (cost vs. service), the presence of 3PL carriers in drug distribution, hospitals' methods of acquiring pharmaceuticals, and so forth.

Due to its perceived ability to influence a large number of local factors that could strongly affect Medford's pharmaceuticals supply chain, this driving force stood out as one of the most impactful ones, next only to "cost pressure in the US healthcare sector." Without pharmaceutical distributors, manufacturers would have to provide financial credit services and set up accounts receivable for more than 200,000 healthcare providers across the country. Pharmacies and providers would have to carry weeks of inventory of each of the tens of thousands of products they sell and place individual orders from thousands of manufacturers for needed products daily.

This complexity was partly blamed for skyrocketing healthcare costs in the US, even though US healthcare performance was far from world-beating. The annual per capita health expenditure in the US had climbed from US$365 (equivalent to 7.2% of the US GDP) in 1970 to US$6,697 (equivalent to 16% of the GDP) in 2005[8]—the highest in the world and about 30% higher than that of the next most expensive country (Luxembourg). Furthermore, while the rate of growth had moderated lately, healthcare costs still amounted to 17.8 of the US GDP by 2019.[9] This was increasing pressure on government and non-governmental organizations to focus on healthcare costs.

Table 5.3 lists the driving forces by the level of uncertainty in the descending order, followed by their estimated impact. Two extreme values were specified for all uncertain driving forces.

Medford's Scenario Logic and Scenarios (Steps 6, 7)

As mentioned above, Medford's executives were deeply involved in the scenario creation process. The MIT CTL team facilitated the deliberation among Medford's executives to choose the scenario logic, using two dominant forces as shown in Fig. 4.3, by considering driving forces with both high uncertainty and strong impact on Medford. The group considered various pairs of driving forces with high uncertainty, wrote brief descriptions of all four scenario seeds created through each of their combinations, and finally chose the following two scenario axes because they presented four diverse and interesting scenarios.

- Complexity of the US healthcare supply chains
- Health of the overall US economy

The combinations of their extreme values created four scenario seeds, as shown in Fig. 5.2. The scenario names were chosen by Medford's executives after scenarios were fully defined.

Next, the team specified the values of all remaining driving forces to flesh out the four scenarios by considering two additional criteria:

- *Internal consistency among the values of different driving forces within each scenario*: Assessed logically by MIT CTL researchers and subsequently validated by Medford's executives
- *Variation among highly similar driving forces across four scenarios*: Created by considering correlations among Medford's uncertain driving forces, based on the fraction of Medford's executives who believed the driving forces

Table 5.3 Driving forces of Medford's business environment

Driving forces	Extreme values
Uncertainty: HIGH	
Cost pressure in the healthcare sector: Profitability and growth of pharmaceutical companies; R&D spending by Big Pharma; the power of group purchasing organizations (GPOs); profit margin of pharmaceutical distributors; total health expenditure; political and regulatory pressure to reduce healthcare costs	*Extreme 1:* Low *Extreme 2:* High
Complexity of US healthcare supply chain: Manufacturers' and retailers' choices for distributing pharmaceuticals; retailers' actions to drive sales of pharmaceuticals; cost advantage of selling drugs via mail order; cost of developing a good distribution network	*Extreme 1:* Low *Extreme 2:* High
Participation of government in the healthcare sector: Socio-political preference for access to healthcare; federal funding for Medicare and Medicaid; desire for creating standard laws across different states; new government regulations challenged and struck down in courts; creation of medical homes in PPACA	*Extreme 1:* Low *Extreme 2:* High
Volume of drugs sold in the US: Number of people in the US healthcare system; the volume of drugs consumed in the US; demand from pharmacies and drug stores in the US	*Extreme 1:* Same as 2009 *Extreme 2:* Much higher than 2009
Number of locations where the majority of healthcare is provided: Locations where healthcare is provided also relates to recovery time in long-term vs. short-term acute care, focus on preventive care	*Extreme 1:* Same as in 2009 *Extreme 2:* Much more than 2009
Climate sensitivity of drugs and treatments: Volume of biologic and specialty pharmaceuticals; development of biosimilar products; innovations related to the climate sensitivity of drugs and treatments	*Extreme 1:* Mostly temperature-insensitive *Extreme 2:* High volume of temperature-sensitive drugs
Health of the overall US economy: US unemployment rate, US GDP growth, per capita disposable income, investor uncertainty, world price of crude oil, stock market performance, housing price index	*Extreme 1:* Weak. Same as 2009 *Extreme 2:* Strong

(continued)

Table 5.3 (continued)

Driving forces	Extreme values
Uncertainty: MEDIUM	
Consolidation within the healthcare sector: Horizontal and vertical consolidation; number of pharmaceutical distributors, pharmacies, non-profit hospitals, specialty hospitals in the industry; pharmacy chains integrating upstream in the supply chains; number of group purchasing organizations (GPOs)	*Extreme 1:* Low *Extreme 2:* High
Proportion of generic drugs among the drugs consumed: Patents for branded products in patent pipeline; average price of drugs and treatments; prescription drug expenditure; use of generic drugs; reputation of quality of generic drugs; number of generic drug manufacturers; types of drugs manufactured	*Extreme 1:* Same as 2009 *Extreme 2:* Much higher than 2009
Nature of reimbursement policies: Reimbursement rates; insurance payments for outcomes; preferential treatment to mail-order and internet pharmacies	*Extreme 1:* Treatment-based *Extreme 2:* Outcome-based
Uncertainty: LOW	
Availability of IT solutions for healthcare management: Use of electronic medical records (EMR); advances in diagnostics, cure, and health management; the role and importance of IT in supply chains	*Extreme 1:* About same as in 2009 *Extreme 2:* Abundant
Availability of healthcare workers: Availability of nurses and pharmacists, cost of hiring healthcare workers, proportion of workers in service jobs, union memberships	*Extreme 1:* Scarce *Extreme 2:* Abundant
Health consciousness of the average citizen: Consumers' willingness to pay for service in drug delivery; consumer attitude about health and safety number of physician visits; importance of the relationship between patient and pharmacist; number of people with private insurance; consumer- vs. business-driven healthcare market	*Extreme 1:* Low *Extreme 2:* High
Predictable driving forces (TRENDS)	
Average age of US population: Average and median age; demand for Medicare; population of adults over 65 years of age; number of births; overall US population	*Consensus:* Higher than 2009
Environmental consciousness of the US society: Use of recycling; environmentalism; prevalence of "green" products	*Consensus:* Higher than 2009
Overall focus on drug security and safety: Focus on drug safety and security by the government and in media; health and safety awareness of consumers	*Consensus:* Higher than 2009

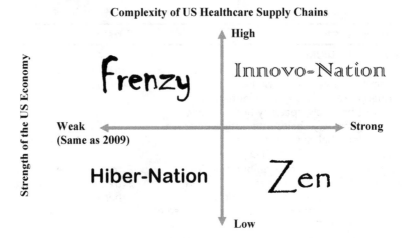

Fig. 5.2 Logic of Medford's scenarios

affected each of the key local factors considered in the analysis (shown in Exhibit 5.1)

Exhibit 5.1: Correlations among Medford's uncertain driving forces

	DF1	DF2	DF3	DF4	DF5	DF6	DF7	DF8	DF9	DF10	DF11	DF12	DF13	DF14
DF1: Availability of healthcare workers	1													
DF2: Availability of IT solutions for healthcare management	-0.37	1												
DF3: Climate sensitivity of drugs and treatments	-0.03	-0.12	1											
DF4: Complexity of US healthcare supply chain	0.14	0.16	0.32	1										
DF5: Consolidation within healthcare sector	0.57	0.10	0.29	0.37	1									
DF6: Cost pressure in the healthcare sector	0.61	0.02	0.39	0.51	0.92	1								
DF7: Health of the overall US economy	0.08	0.41	-0.06	0.04	0.70	0.51	1							
DF8: Health consciousness of average citizen	-0.04	-0.52	0.22	-0.13	-0.34	-0.25	-0.56	1						
DF9: Location where majority of healthcare is provided	0.19	-0.38	0.67	0.10	0.30	0.25	-0.10	0.63	1					
DF10: Nature of reimbursement policies	0.22	-0.01	0.53	0.43	0.41	0.43	0.12	0.05	0.39	1				
DF11: Overall focus on drug security and safety	-0.76	0.26	0.30	-0.27	-0.57	-0.60	-0.31	-0.04	-0.05	-0.15	1			
DF12: Participation of government in the healthcare sector	-0.19	0.08	0.44	0.69	0.22	0.29	-0.04	0.18	0.32	0.68	-0.01	1		
DF13: Proportion of generic drugs in all drugs consumed	-0.24	0.31	0.32	0.52	0.27	0.27	0.40	-0.05	0.14	0.54	-0.12	0.52	1	
DF14: Volume of drugs sold in the US	-0.45	0.21	0.71	0.28	0.28	0.19	0.33	0.03	0.51	0.51	0.40	0.58	0.60	1

Such use of correlations in scenario analysis is not common, so it is worth understanding its purpose. A high positive correlation between two driving forces indicates that the executives believe the two have the same effect on each key local factor; they either do or do not influence it. An attempt was made to specify all four combinations of the highly correlated pairs of driving forces across the four scenarios to increase cross-scenario variation among the paired driving forces.

For example, DF6 ("cost pressure in the US healthcare sector") and DF5 ("consolidation within the healthcare sector") had the highest positive correlation, because both were deemed, almost unanimously, to affect key local factors such as "competition among the Big Three," "presence of regional distributors," or "availability of talent," and to have little influence on factors such as "frequency of drug thefts" or "variations in pedigree laws." Therefore, each combination of the low and high extremes of DF5 and DF6 was described in one of the four scenarios. This was intended to facilitate exploration of a diverse set of implications for the local factors affected by the two driving forces jointly.

Once the driving force values for all four scenarios were specified, the scenario structure was presented to Medford's executives to ensure that each scenario was internally consistent and plausible. The executives were then split into four subgroups (one subgroup per scenario). Executives were assigned to the scenario group which they claimed to understand best. Each group evaluated its scenario's structure and suggested if any changes had to be made to the scenario to enhance its plausibility. In this process, Medford's executives came to realize that the driving force "overall focus on drug security and safety" would always take the same value ("high") in all four scenarios. Table 5.4 presents the final structure of Medford's scenarios.

After adjusting the structure, the MIT CTL team wrote the scenario narratives. This required additional industry research that was far more targeted than the broad scope of industry research conducted at the beginning of scenario creation. Research for the narrative sought specific examples to justify the different values taken by the driving forces in different scenarios to provide their realistic descriptions. Finally, the executives assigned to each scenario read and validated each scenario's content. Finally, they brainstormed to find a fitting name for their respective scenario. Preliminary narratives of the four scenarios are presented in Exhibits 9.4–9.7 in Chapter 9.

Table 5.4 Structure of Medford scenarios

Driving forces	Frenzy	Innovo-Nation	Hiber-Nation	Zen
Scenario axes				
Complexity of US healthcare supply chain	High	High	Low	Low
Health of the overall US economy	Weak	Strong	Weak	Strong
Remaining uncertain driving forces				
Availability of healthcare workers	Abundant	Scarce	Abundant	Scarce
Availability of IT solutions for managing healthcare	Same as 2009	Same as 2009	Abundant	Abundant
Climate sensitivity of drugs and treatments	Temperature-insensitive	Temperature-sensitive	Temperature-sensitive	Temperature-insensitive
Consolidation within the healthcare sector	High	Low	High	Low
Cost pressure in the healthcare sector	High	High	Low	Low
Health consciousness of an average citizen	High	High	Low	Low
Number of locations where the majority of healthcare is provided	Much more than 2009	Much more than 2009	Same as 2009	Much more than 2009
Nature of reimbursement policies	Outcome-based	Outcome-based	Treatment-based	Treatment-based
Participation of government in the healthcare sector	High	High	High	Low

Driving forces	Frenzy	Innovo-Nation	Hiber-Nation	Zen
Proportion of generic drugs in the volume of drugs consumed	Much higher than 2009	Much higher than 2009	Much higher than 2009	Same as 2009
Volume of drugs sold in the US	Same as 2009	Much higher than 2009	Much higher than 2009	Same as 2009
Predictable driving forces				
Average age of the US population	Higher than 2009			
Environmental consciousness in the US	Higher than 2009			
Overall focus on drug security, safety	High			

Infrastructural Role: Scenarios for Future Freight Flows (FFF) in the US

The MIT CTL launched the Future Freight Flows (FFF) project in spring 2010 to address the challenge posed in the NCHRP Project 20–83(01), described in Chapter 2. Two key tasks for this project were:

- To identify, categorize, and rank the driving forces and critical uncertainties likely to influence freight transportation flows within the US over the next 30 years, and
- To develop scenarios of the environment in 30–40 years, to aid any US transportation agency in planning transportation infrastructure investments.

The process used for developing and applying the scenarios, the analyses of local factors and driving forces, and the results of six workshops in which the scenarios were applied are described in detail in an online document[10] and a report[11] published by the US Transportation Research Board.

Scope of FFF Scenarios (Step 1)

The planning horizon for the FFF scenarios was 30 years, which befits the planning for long-lived infrastructure elements such as roads and ports. Some peculiar aspects of the ambitious NCHRP Project 20–83(01) defined the scope of the scenario project in ways that required adaptations of the well-established practices used for developing scenarios for Hoppy Brew and Medford. The FFF scenarios had four special requirements.

First, unlike the traditional scenario planning efforts in which the participants who develop the scenarios also apply them, the FFF scenarios had to be designed for use "out of the box" by decision makers other than those who helped develop them. Thus, the users of FFF scenarios would not have the benefit of scenario development deliberations that provide familiarity with the driving forces and key local factors in the scenarios. This meant the MIT CTL team had to create a set of collateral material that could expedite the scenario users' journey along the learning curve of the scenarios.

Second, the scenarios had to be general enough to be used by planning agencies in different parts of the US. This meant that the driving forces used to build scenarios had to be broad enough to be relevant nationally, and the scenarios had to avoid elements specific to any particular state or locale. One benefit of this approach was that it would provide a common set of scenarios to harmonize the long-term visions of planning agencies in different parts of the US, while entrusting the authority to make specific infrastructure investment decisions with the local and regional planning agencies.

Third, the scenarios had to be sufficiently flexible for planners in different levels of federal, state, local government to use without significant customization. This required the scenarios to be described at the national level. Moreover, it also meant that application of the scenarios required careful facilitation to allow planners at local, regional, or federal levels to draw implications of the scenarios for their desired level. As a result, the FFF scenarios were accompanied by a planner's guide and a facilitator's guide.[12]

Finally, the strategic questions or focal issues covered by different applications of the FFF scenarios would be diverse. Consequently, in contrast to traditional scenario planning where the scenarios are designed around a core issue, the FFF scenarios were created to enable any local transportation planning agency in the US to answer a general question: "Where should investments in freight transportation infrastructure be made [in location XXX] today to prepare for freight transportation needs in the year 2040?".

Local Factors of FFF (Step 2)

Identifying FFF local factors was challenging due to the broad geographic and jurisdictional scope of the project. The driving forces could have an unlimited number of impacts on different organizations in different parts of the country. Cataloging all such potential events is not only cost- and time-prohibitive but also futile, as the impacts felt on one transportation mode at one location may be meaningless for another mode or location (e.g., hurricanes seldom hit California; Wyoming has no seaports). Therefore, the MIT team decided to identify a few generic local factors that would be relevant for freight flows almost universally. Five such local factors were identified:

- *Sourcing patterns*: They capture changes in the locations where freight movements originate. This covers the procurement of raw materials, manufacturing, and distribution. The sources could shift globally (such as China, East Asia, Africa), within the country (different states, industrial areas, ports), or within a particular region itself (say, imported from outside the region vs. procured from local farms and fabrication centers).
- *Flow destinations*: They capture shifts in the locations of final demand. The destinations may shift among states, among different regions within a state (say, metropolitan areas vs. small towns), or within different parts of an urban area (say, downtown areas, suburban malls, individual homes).

- *Routing*: This includes any changes that affect the path the products take as they move from origin to destination, such as shifts in the modes of transportation (air, rail, river barges, trucks, and intermodal transport).
- *Flow volume*: Changes to a region's flow volume include any increase or decrease in the total tonnage or volume of goods moving from origin to destination along specific routes.
- *Value density*: This represents the monetary value per ton (or cubic feet) of freight and represents the characteristics of the goods being shipped. Value density is one of the primary criteria for the choice of transportation mode and for supply chain network design. Products with higher value densities (such as the latest models of consumer electronics or medical devices) tend to be shipped faster by more expensive modes (such as air) than lower value density products (such as gravel or grain shipped by rail).

To illustrate how the impacts on flow are used as local factors, consider the effect that containerization has had on supply chains. Containerization transformed sourcing patterns because it drastically reduced the costs of loading and unloading maritime cargo and transferring cargo between modes (vessel-to-rail-to-truck). This enabled the offshoring of production to regions across the globe, notably to China and East Asia. As a result, sourcing patterns within the US changed from domestic manufacturing locations scattered across the country to a handful of ports, mainly on the West Coast, that receive imported goods manufactured overseas. The impact on destinations was minimal because containerization did not change the location of the final demand (i.e., US population centers). However, it had a strong impact on routing, as the funneling of international sourcing sent more freight through fewer collection points (ports), resulting in greater use of rail-centric intermodal transportation to move the product inland. It has also affected the flow volume significantly as the number of containers moving through the US drastically increased. Yet, containerization has not significantly impacted the value density of the freight.

Driving Forces of FFF (Step 3)

The first major initiative for identifying driving forces was the FFF Symposium, held at MIT on March 11–12, 2010. Sixty handpicked non-MIT professionals participated as "expert practitioners." They came from 45 different organizations (shippers, carriers, 3PL providers, ports, transportation management software developers, academia, and the armed forces) and seven state transportation boards and the US Department of Transportation.

On the first day of the symposium, seven thought leaders presented different visions of the future in social, technological, economic, environmental, and political (STEEP) themes. The thought leaders presented the following broad themes:

- Aging, Changing Lifestyles & the Future of Freight (Dr. Joseph Coughlin, Director, MIT Agelab)
- Big Data and the New Age of Sensing (Prof. Sanjay Sarma, MIT Mechanical Engineering)
- Digital Fabrication: Transporting Bits and Atoms (Professor Neil Gershenfeld, MIT Center for Bits and Atoms)
- Wired for Innovation: How IT Is Reshaping the Economy (Prof. Erik Brynjolfsson, MIT Sloan School of Management)
- New Challenges for the Global Economy in 2010–2030 (Sara Johnson, IHS Global Insight)
- Measuring and Managing Sustainability (Dr. Jonathan Johnson, The Sustainability Consortium)
- Public Policy and Freight (David Luberoff, Harvard Kennedy School of Government)

The expert practitioners were asked to brainstorm transportation-relevant drivers in their industries as they listened to the thought leaders' presentations. After each presentation, the attendees noted the three most critical drivers from that presentation—drivers they thought might impact the future freight flows in the US. At the end of the day, each participant also provided a list of potential drivers that were missed during the presentations. Overall, the 60 expert participants provided more than 1,200 individual drivers that became raw material for identifying the driving forces of the FFF in the US.

The MIT CTL team analyzed this data to find common themes and synthesized it into 12 snapshot scenario snippets. The snippets included aging of the US population, increasing global trade, rising power of emerging markets, international climate regulations, rising protectionism, personal fabrication technology, "sense-able" network technology, sustainability regulations, consumer demand for sustainable products, increasing global security concerns, rising commodity prices, and additional points of entry of goods into the US.

The snapshot scenarios were presented back to the participants on the second day of the symposium for further analysis. The participants were divided into six groups, each including individuals representing all of the symposium's stakeholder groups, and were assigned two scenario snippets to evaluate in an interactive workshop. During this interactive exercise, each participant indicated their estimate of the driving force's evolution over five consecutive periods (0–2 years, 2–5 years, 5–10 years, 10–20 years, and 20–40 years) by choosing from five options: unlikely to happen (0–20% adoption), present at fringes only (20–40%), generally present (40–60%), widely present (60–80%), and omnipresent (80–100%). The participants also assessed the impacts of the snapshot scenarios on the five local factors, and how they might constrain the existing transportation infrastructure in the US. This analysis, its discussion, and subsequent feedback of the expert participants yielded 20 drivers of FFF.

Impact and Uncertainty of FFF Driving Forces (Steps 4, 5)

Next, a survey in April 2010 assessed the impact and uncertainty of the 20 drivers cataloged in the previous step. The survey yielded a total of 264 complete and usable responses from professionals across a variety of industries. The participants were asked to rate the magnitude of the impact of each driver on the existing US transportation infrastructure and the likelihood of its evolution in the specified direction (both on a five-point scale). The average value of impact was used as the estimate of impact; the variability in the likelihood values was used as an estimate of uncertainty. Drivers with similar themes and impact and uncertainty values were further synthesized. This produced a list of 10 driving forces. Table 5.5 presents these driving forces and summarizes their impact and uncertainty in qualitative terms.

FFF Scenario Logic and Scenarios (Steps 6, 7)

Two driving forces with the most impact and highest uncertainty—global trade and resource availability—became the two scenario axes along which the four scenarios varied. Figure 5.3 presents the logic of the FFF scenarios.

Aging population was found to be a *trend* and described similarly in all scenarios. Population dispersion was deemed fairly predictable as well due to increasing urbanization and was allowed to vary between mega-cities (New York City, Chicago, etc.) and second-tier cities (Madison, Burlington, Boise). Four scenarios were created for the project. Table 5.6 presents the scenarios and the scenario structure.

The narratives of the four scenarios—tweaked from their original publication for expositional clarity—are presented in Chapter 9 in Exhibits 9.8–9.11. Briefly, *Global Marketplace*, characterized by high global trade and

Table 5.5 Driving forces of Future Freight Flows, their impact and uncertainty

Driving forces	Impact	Uncertainty
Global trade: Re-shoring of manufacturing; increase or decrease in global trade, the rise of BRIC (Brazil, Russia, India, and China) and other emerging markets, new agriculture powerhouses, East Coast ports, strong non-US trading blocs	High	High
Resource availability: Water scarcity, commodity price volatility, green regulations, recycling regulations	High	High
Level of immigration: Global/regional/intra-country immigration; no immigration, disparity between manual labor and knowledge workers, changing cultural face of America	Low	High
Level of environmental awareness: Recycling regulations; customer demand for green products	High	Medium
Energy cost (level): Average cost of energy	High	Medium
Energy cost (variability): Variation in costs of energy	High	Medium
Population dispersion: Increasing urbanization, growth of mega-cities, growth of urban areas, growth of mid-sized cities	Medium	Medium
Energy sources: US dependence on foreign oil, natural gas, nuclear energy, battery-powered vehicles	Medium	Medium
Currency fluctuations: Dollar valuation, credit availability	Low	Medium
Aging population	Medium	Low

Fig. 5.3 Logic of FFF scenarios (Reference for scenario icons: MIT Center for Transportation and Logistics, "Scenario Planning Toolkit". Available at https://ctl.mit.edu/scenario-planning-toolkit)

Table 5.6 Structure of FFF scenarios

Driving forces	Global marketplace	One world order	Naftástique!	Millions of markets
Scenario axes				
Global trade	High	High	Low	Low
Resource availability	High	Low	Low	High
Remaining driving forces				
Energy cost (Level)	Low	High	High	Low
Energy cost (Variability)	High	High	Low	Low
Level of environmental awareness	Low	High	Same as today	High
Population dispersion	Growth in biggest cities	Growth in biggest cities	Growth in South West US	Growth in second-tier cities
Energy sources (majority)	Foreign	Domestic, foreign	North America	Domestic
Level of immigration	High global	High, global	High within the bloc, low across	Low
Currency fluctuations	Moderate	High	Low in bloc	Low
Average age of the US population	Older			

high resource availability, portrays a staunchly competitive world. Open trade promotes market-based approaches, immigration, and dramatic increases in global food production. This scenario represented what many believed, in 2010, as the most likely future.

One World Order, marked by high global trade but low or restricted resource availability, portrays a highly regulated world. Facing global scarcity of key resources, nations establish international rules to ensure their fair and sustainable use. Global trade thrives, albeit with a heavy orchestration through government regulations.

Naftástique!, characterized by low global trade and low resource availability, depicts a world where trade has moved away from a single global market toward several emerging regional trading blocs. China forms a bloc with Africa, while Europe and South America form their own clusters. The US leads an effort to make North America a self-sufficient economic zone.

Finally, *Millions of Markets*, characterized by low global trade and high resource availability, is a world where advanced technological breakthroughs have enabled the US (and other countries) to become highly self-reliant in terms of energy, agriculture, manufacturing, and other needs. It is defined by the trifecta of energy independence, intelligent manufacturing, and virtualization, enabled by digital technologies. Interestingly, this scenario was originally called *Technology Savior* but was changed when participants started associating any technological innovations with this scenario alone.

Supplemental Material for "Out of the Box" FFF Scenarios

As mentioned earlier, it was imperative to create supplementary material to provide rich descriptions of the worlds presented in the scenarios, and how the worlds might reach those states, for users not involved in the project. Two types of supplementary material were created for each scenario: a booklet detailing that scenario and a video of a newscast in that scenario.

In addition, the MIT CTL team developed a planner's guide and a facilitator's guide. The planner's guide detailed a 12-week timeline of events leading up to a scenario planning workshop. The facilitator's guide detailed how to conduct a one-day scenario planning workshop to use the scenarios effectively. The scenario booklets, videos, and the two guides were included in the Future Freight Flows Scenario Planning Toolkit.[13]

Scenario Booklets

To provide detailed descriptions of the scenarios, a booklet was created for each scenario to elaborate on the world it characterized. The booklet opened with a two-page narration of the scenario. This was followed by a timeline stretching from circa 1980 to 2040, showing the progression of different time series relevant to the scenario and different events that caused abrupt changes in the trajectory of events to take the world to that scenario's future state. These charts showed actual data and events until 2010 and fictional ones between 2010 and 2040. The time-series chart in each scenario booklet explains how the world evolved in that scenario. This was followed by more time series and other charts presenting relevant statistics to describe the scenario graphically. The fictional values of the time series were computed using the logic described in the scenario. Actual pre-2010 statistics and events were used to highlight the plausibility of each scenario.

To illustrate, Exhibit 5.2 shows the time series in the booklet for scenario *Naftástique!*. The timeline shows several actual historical events, such as the US–Canada trade dispute circa 1985, the formation of the World Trade Organization in 1995, the creation of the euro in 1999, and the Financial Crisis of 2008. It shows some pivotal fictional events such as the Energy Crisis of 2017—occurring seven years into the future at the time of the study—which leads to the formation of the China–Africa bloc, which sets off a chain of events that lead to the world described in the scenario.

Exhibit 5.2: Time series in the booklet of FFF scenario *Naftástique!*

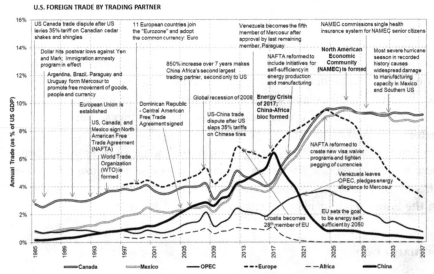

Figure 1. The level of trade as percent of U SGDP that the Unites States has with countries outside of NAMEC dropped dramatically in the 2020's with formation of regional trading blocks. The level of "intra-block" trade has increased accordingly with the re-domestication of many manufacturing industries back to North America.

Reference MIT Center for Transportation & Logistics, *Scenario brochure for Naftástique!*. Available at https://ctl.mit.edu/sites/ctl.mit.edu/files/attach ments/FWS_red_Naftastique_2.0.pdf

Exhibit 5.3 shows another illustrative example of a graphic in the booklet of *Naftástique!*. *Reference* It shows the source of energy in the US between 1960 and 2040. The chart plots real data for 1960 through 2010 and presents hypothesized levels from 2010 through 2040, reflecting the development described in the scenario.

Exhibit 5.3: Source of Energy in the US in FFF scenario *Naftástique!*

SOURCES OF ENERGY IN THE UNITED STATES

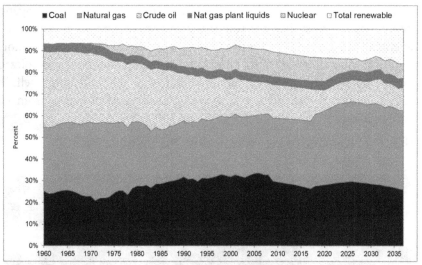

Figure 5. The mix of source of energy in the US changed significantly after the 2017 Energy Crisis, which spurred development in energy production from natural gas, solar and wind energy, and from clean coal technology. In 2037, only about 10% of the energy produced in the US comes from crude oil, produced primarily in the Gulf of Mexico and less than 7% from the nuclear power plants.

Reference MIT Center for Transportation & Logistics, *Scenario brochure for Naftástique!*. Available at https://ctl.mit.edu/sites/ctl.mit.edu/files/attach ments/FWS_red_Naftastique_2.0.pdf

Scenario Videos

Each scenario was accompanied by a video of a newscast in 2037. The newscasts described the events relevant to the scenario. For example, the newscast in *Naftástique!* showed a female TV anchor reporting that day's meeting in Toronto to mark the 10th anniversary of the North American Economic Community, featuring former US president Mr. Michael Castillo, the first US president of Hispanic descent, as the guest of honor. The newscast (called Netview) in *Millions of Markets*, a world defined by extensive technological advances, delivered a selection of news curated to the taste of the viewer and delivered by an avatar. It displayed a mix of video, audio, and text on the screen and progressed dynamically according to the viewer's interaction with the presented material.

Planning Guide

The planning guide was written to help a transportation planning agency to design, plan, schedule, and run the FFF scenario planning workshop. It described a timeline of activities and checkpoints in the process before, during, and after the workshop; noted the required resources and roles of different players; and provided guidelines to design the workshop itself. To illustrate, Exhibit 5.4 shows a snapshot of the timeline of events from the planning guide.

Exhibit 5.4: Timeline of events from FFF Planning Guide

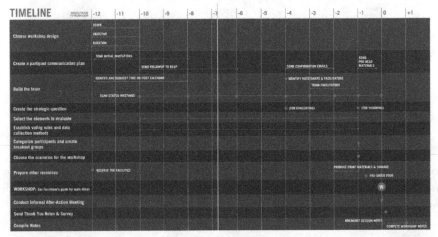

Reference MIT Center for Transportation & Logistics, *Scenario Planning Toolkit – Planning Guide*. Available at https://ctl.mit.edu/sites/ctl.mit.edu/files/PlannersGuide_Final.pdf

Facilitator's Guide

The facilitator's guide was a four-page document that could be printed on a single, double-sided 11 × 17 sheet and carried by the workshop facilitator with them on the day of the workshop. It provided a detailed timeline of different phases of the workshop, which involved, among other things, an introduction to scenario planning and the scenarios, exploration of implications, and cross-scenario analysis. It outlined the activities the facilitator needed to perform in different phases, the mindset to adopt in different phases, the questions to ask the participants, and the types of answers expected. It also listed about 10 salient features of each scenario to ensure that the participants identify them in their discussion of the scenario. To illustrate, Exhibit 5.5 shows a snapshot of one side of the facilitator's guide.

Exhibit 5.5: Part of FFF facilitator's guide

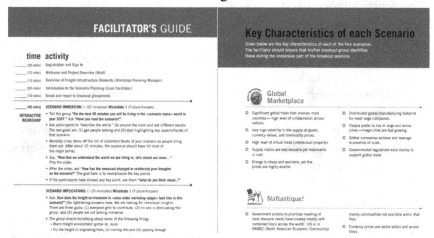

Reference MIT Center for Transportation & Logistics, *Scenario Planning Toolkit – Facilitators Guide.* Available at http://ctl.mit.edu/sites/ctl.mit.edu/files/FacilitatorsGuide_Final.pdf

Scenario creation has been described as a combination of science and art. As a science, the scenario creation approach presented in this chapter provides a structure for the scenario creation process. This structure focuses on human knowledge by recognizing the scope of knowledge of operations and supply chain executives and external experts, and by leveraging such knowledge appropriately in different steps of the scenario creation. As an art, the approach involves making choices about the scenario structure based on the subjective preferences of the scenario users when no objective criteria exist. The process presented in this chapter is adaptable to different project contexts, as evident in the diversity of applications in the cases of Hoppy Brew, Medford, and Future Freight Flows.

Notes

1. See https://www.pewresearch.org/global/2003/06/20/broad-opposition-to-genetically-modified-foods/.
2. See https://www.packagedfacts.com/Food-Formulation-Trends-8024542/.
3. See https://sustainableamerica.org/downloads/presentations/SustainableAmericaFinalDeck.pdf.
4. https://www.craftbeer.com/craft-beer-muses/three-tier-system-impacts-craft-beer.
5. https://www.prnewswire.com/news-releases/beer-wine-and-spirits-producers-urge-congress-to-reject-the-community-alcohol-regulatory-effectiveness-act-of-2011-118204069.html.
6. The data collected from Medford's executives are used in our study examining how supply chain executives think of business environment and strategies for long-term. Information in this section is referenced from: Phadnis, et al. 2017. "Strategic Cognition of Operations Executives." *Production and Operations Management*, 26(12), 2323–2337.
7. North American Industry Classification System (NAICS) is the standard used by US federal statistical agencies to classify different business establishments based on their economic activities.
8. Kaiser Family Foundation. 2007. *Health Care Costs: A Primer. Key Information on Health Care Costs and Their Impact* (Report# 7670). Washington, DC.
9. https://www.statista.com/statistics/184968/us-health-expenditure-as-percent-of-gdp-since-1960/.
10. Caplice, C., Phadnis, S. 2010. *Driving Forces Influencing Future Freight Flows* (No. NCHRP Project 20–83 (1)). http://www.trb.org/Publications/Blurbs/168695.aspx.
11. Caplice, C., Phadnis, S. 2013. *Strategic Issues Facing Transportation: Scenario Planning for Freight Transportation Infrastructure Investment*. Washington, DC: Transportation Research Board.
12. These documents are available at https://ctl.mit.edu/scenario-planning-toolkit.
13. Ibid.

6

Scenario Application: General Steps

Scenarios are a means to strengthen an organization's ability to adapt to changing environments. They provide a rationale for investments in robust and flexible assets, as well as timely actions to change organizational and functional strategies. Scenarios may be used to broaden the thinking of organizational decision makers and to facilitate a specific decision.

Using scenarios for making important organizational decisions or to anticipate the changes in the business environment requires a thorough understanding of the scenarios' environments. Concrete methods for detecting shifts in the environment toward or away from any given scenario(s) are also useful. Since different scenarios depict divergent views of the world, it is beneficial to first consider them individually until the scenario users become familiar with them, and only then contrast them with each other.

The MIT CTL researchers employed a six-step scenario application process in multiple scenario planning projects. The first five steps of the process are typically performed in a one- or two-day scenario planning workshop. Steps 1, 2, and 5 are essential in all applications of scenario planning; Steps 3 and 4 are primarily useful for decision-making projects, whereas Step 6 comprises an ongoing monitoring of the environment.[1]

© The Author(s), under exclusive license to Springer Nature
Switzerland AG 2022
S. S. Phadnis et al., *Strategic Planning for Dynamic Supply Chains,*
Palgrave Executive Essentials,
https://doi.org/10.1007/978-3-030-91810-1_6

Step 1: Immerse in the Scenarios (Individual Scenario)

Due to the short-term focus of their job, supply chain managers tend to be operationally focused. They are well equipped to make real-time decisions to address immediate concerns quickly and effectively. However, scenarios depict business environments several years or decades in the future, which are typically markedly different from the present business conditions. Therefore, scenario users need to immerse themselves, *mentally*, in the scenario. They need to understand the scenario thoroughly to ensure that their long-term decisions are based on the specific scenario and not on the present business environment nor their forecasts of the future made by extrapolating the present. In practice, this is often one of the most difficult aspects of scenario planning and requires extensive preparation.

Because the scenarios typically describe business environments that differ significantly from the present world, scenario users are asked to explore one scenario at a time until they become thoroughly familiar with each one. Before they come to the scenario planning workshop, each user is assigned to one scenario, asked to understand it well, and make notes about its salient features. At the workshop, each scenario is evaluated by a group of 8–15 individuals knowledgeable in a broad range of domains, with different groups assigned to different scenarios having similar compositions of domain expertise.

During the scenario planning workshop, a facilitator leads the users through a discussion of the key features of their assigned scenario. The facilitator needs to have a comprehensive understanding of the scenario and often carries a cheat sheet that lists the scenario's salient features. The facilitator should ensure that every member of that group has had a chance to express their understanding of the scenario. The facilitator may also present the collateral material such as a video or artifacts created to represent the scenario, to allow the participants to immerse themselves further in the depicted world. Finally, the facilitator may ask the participants to write down the salient features of the scenario to allow them to explicitly express their perception of the fictional world and cement the scenario's grip on their thinking.

Step 2: Identify Scenario Implications (Individual Scenario)

Immediately following scenario immersion, the facilitator asks the participants to identify the implications of the scenario for the organization and the project's focal decisions. Brainstorming is quite effective for this step. The group members are asked to identify and write the implications individually and may be asked to discuss them in smaller subgroups. These implications are then collected, typically, by asking the participants to write them on sticky notes and post them on a board. The collected ideas are then discussed by the entire group and refined.

Starting with individual idea generation before group brainstorming ensures that ideas from the quieter members of the groups are not overshadowed by the opinions of the more dominant participants. The facilitator also encourages participants to provide more specific descriptions of implications. For example, instead of simply writing that a certain scenario will "affect demand," the participants are asked to articulate the direction, magnitude, and specificity of the demand, such as: "likely to increase demand marginally for established high-value products in Latin American markets." More specificity leads to a deeper immersion in the scenario and better results.

The objectives and approaches for Step 1 (scenario immersion) differ from Step 2 (scenario implications). In the immersion step, the objective is to ensure all participants fully understand the scenario environment. The facilitator may need to be more assertive in this step to guide the group through the discussion to ensure that the participants understand the scenario correctly and comprehensively. In the implications step, the onus shifts to the participants because the objective is to identify any potential effects on the organization and its focal decision. The facilitator should encourage the participants to offer their opinions and avoid providing any of their own ideas. In other words, the facilitator's role shifts from instruction to elicitation between the two steps.

It is important to systematically record the output of Step 2, including salient points discussed during the group brainstorming, as it can be helpful in future discussions. Such notes can also provide the rationale for the strategic choices advocated for the scenario.

Step 3: Envision and Evaluate Strategic Initiatives (Individual Scenario)

Unraveling the implications of each scenario sets the stage for the participants to identify and assess strategic choices. In this step, the participants identify strategic choices that can help the organization prepare for the potential scenario implications. There are two ways to identify such strategic choices: visioning and evaluation. An organization may use either or both when scenarios are used for decision-making.

In the *visioning approach*, the facilitator guides the participants to envision initiatives that enable the organization to operate successfully in the scenario. In the MIT CTL-led scenario planning workshops, the team used brainstorming exercises for this approach. As with the immersion step, both individual and group brainstorming techniques were encouraged to generate ideas for potential strategic initiatives from all participants. Similar ideas are grouped and refined by leveraging the expertise of all participants in the group. In this approach, the participants work from a blank slate and synthesize ideas for new strategic initiatives.

In the *evaluation approach*, various strategic initiatives or specific projects have already been identified beforehand, and the scenarios are used to test their utility. The chosen initiatives or projects are typically those being considered for investment by the organization at the time of the scenario study. The number of initiatives evaluated in the scenario planning projects conducted by the MIT CTL team has ranged from 8 to 17. For the evaluation exercise, each initiative or project must be described in enough detail for participants to understand the initiative sufficiently and assess its value in different scenario worlds. The participants are then asked to evaluate the usefulness of investing in the initiative or the project in the context of the scenario being discussed. As before, the participants evaluate the initiatives and projects on their own first before engaging in group assessment.

The MIT CTL team used two general approaches for collecting the quantitative evaluations: (i) ask the participants to distribute a fixed number of points among the initiatives being evaluated such that those with higher utility for a particular scenario are assigned more points, or (ii) ask the participants to rate the utility of each initiative for the particular scenario on its own using a numeric scale. In both cases, it is useful to include a veto or a negative vote to indicate if investing in an initiative is detrimental to the organization under the scenario contemplated. Subsequently, the votes of all participants are summarized into the group's assessment of the initiatives under the scenario. They are then discussed to capture the rationale behind the assessment. It is particularly important to discuss the initiatives that receive votes favoring and opposing the initiative. This is where the utility of the initiative for the scenario is unclear, and the facilitator needs to elicit the rationale for the scenario users' assessment from the discussion. After this group discussion, the participants are given a chance to change their vote before the facilitator records the group's assessment of the initiatives for that particular scenario.

Step 4: Conduct Cross-Scenario Strategy Analysis

Until this point, each scenario has been analyzed in isolation by a subset of the users. Working separately, the groups assigned to different scenarios would have identified the implications of their scenario and created and/or evaluated strategic initiatives in the context of that world. In Step 4, the outcomes of Steps 2 and 3 for the different scenarios are compiled for cross-scenario analysis. This step aims to compare the strategic implications and initiatives across the scenarios.

Four terms are used to classify the utility of each initiative based on the cross-scenario comparison. Initiatives deemed useful in all scenarios are termed "No Brainers" (NB). On the other hand, initiatives found to be detrimental in all scenarios are termed "No Gainers" (NG). Since the utility of the NB and NG initiatives is not contingent on the future evolution of the business environment, decisions regarding them are easy: proceed with the NB and reject the NG initiatives. Initiatives deemed useful in some scenarios but not detrimental in any are termed "No Regret" (NR). These initiatives do not pose a downside in any scenario. However, because they have limited or no value in some scenarios, the organization may choose to delay their implementations. Finally, initiatives deemed useful in some scenarios and detrimental in others are termed "Contingent" (C). The decision to invest in them requires further assessment or a delayed decision. A common investment approach is to wait and see: monitor the evolution of the business environment and implement certain initiatives only when the future environment becomes less uncertain and a scenario in which a given initiative is helpful seems to be more likely.

The organization may also choose to implement an initiative in a flexible manner using "real options." The idea of real options was borrowed from finance and introduced in strategic management in the 1970s.[2] A real option is an "option" in that it is a right but not an obligation to take some specific action in the future at a specific cost; it is "real" as it pertains to tangible assets as opposed to financial securities. In the case of strategic supply chain planning, a real option implementation would involve making relatively small investments at present. However, such an investment can accelerate the future implementation of the initiative if a favorable scenario emerges. The investment can also be abandoned without significant sunk costs if the environment shifts toward an unfavorable scenario. Thus, an example of a real option for a transportation infrastructure planner is to acquire the land (or take a call option on the land) to build a multi-lane highway but delay the construction (or build only a two-lane highway initially) while projections of the traffic on that route remain uncertain.

In most scenario workshops, participants compare the initiatives qualitatively; any quantitative analyses for the contingent initiatives are conducted separately.

For the cross-scenario comparison in the workshop, all participants come together, including those who had hitherto evaluated only one scenario. The exercise begins with the presentation of all scenarios to the workshop participants. This is the first time the participants are likely to have seen the other scenarios. Representatives from each scenario are then asked to present the implications of their scenario and evaluations of the initiatives for that scenario. The presenters may also highlight the reasons—often, in terms of implications—for why they evaluated the initiatives in that particular way. Subsequently, the workshop's main facilitator presents the assessments of all initiatives in all scenarios juxtaposed with each other and classifies them into NB/NG/NR/C categories.

Step 5: Identify Scenario Indicators

Because scenarios describe potential business environments several years or decades into the future, the transition toward a particular scenario may not be evident in a slow-changing environment. This is particularly the case for supply chain managers who are focused on day-to-day operations and used to looking for faster-changing developments. Therefore, indicators of shifts in the business environment with reference to the future scenarios can be particularly helpful for operational managers to "see" such changes over time.[3] This step involves identifying such indicators for the set of scenarios developed. IT tools such as strategic radars can be useful to track the indicators and make sense of other developments in the business environment.[4]

Multiple sources can be used to identify the indicators. The scenario workshop itself is a useful event for identifying indicators. After deliberating scenarios and implications, and assessing the initiatives, the workshop participants have a good understanding of the scenarios. The participants may also have a rich knowledge of their industry and business environment. Therefore, they can provide valuable insights about indicators that may already be available and can be used for monitoring the environment. The participants may also be able to highlight other measurable developments or suggest new indicators. In addition, post-workshop desk research can be used to identify indicators that already exist in public and proprietary databases, such as government economic indicators and published industry surveys.

In addition to objective predefined indicators, the organization may also use contemporary events as ad hoc indicators to assess whether the business environment is evolving toward or away from any scenario. An organization may create an initiative to gather online news reports (using tools such as RSS feeds) and then ask its managers to determine whether the reported events indicate a move toward or away from each scenario. Alternatively, it may develop an AI application to determine this.

Step 6: Monitor Environment Using "Scenario Dashboard"

While the first four steps, and parts of the fifth, can be completed within a one- to two-day workshop, Step 6 is an ongoing activity for the organization. In this step, the organization creates a scenario dashboard managed with the aid of a formal organizational process and a supporting IT tool. The dashboard is used to monitor the business environment and assess the appropriateness of strategic choices in an evolving environment. Dashboard creation involves specifying the values of each indicator to correspond with the extreme values of its associated driving force and an appropriate logic to map multiple indicators to a particular driving force. Changes in the aggregate scores by updating the indicators over time can reflect shifts in the corresponding driving forces.

Key elements of the generic scenario application process presented above are summarized in Table 6.1.

Two more continuing efforts are recommended to operationalize the use of scenarios: organizing the supply chain function to make strategic decisions and dashboard reviews.

Table 6.1 Essential steps and elements of the scenario application process

Process step	Details
1. Perform scenario immersion (individual scenario)	• Users divide into subgroups with an assigned scenario
	• Each user reads the description of their assigned scenario (individually)
	• All users discuss key features of the assigned scenario (facilitated session)
	• The facilitator uses collateral to deepen the users' understanding of the scenario
	• Each user summarizes the key features of the scenario (individually)
2. Identify scenario implications (individual scenario)	• Each user identifies implications individually (individual brainstorm)
	• Users post individual ideas using sticky notes for group discussion
	• The facilitator summarizes similar ideas and leads discussion by the participants (group brainstorm)
	• The facilitator team records the output, including key points in the discussion
3. Envision and evaluate strategic initiatives (individual scenario)	• Visioning: Users generate ideas for strategic initiatives using individual brainstorming followed by group brainstorming
	• Evaluation (of chosen initiatives): Facilitator describes each initiative to the users, who then evaluate each initiative on their own and vote (individual brainstorming)
	• The facilitator summarizes individual votes and presents the group vote
	• Users discuss and explain their votes (group brainstorming)
	• Users submit vote changes, and the facilitator summarizes the final vote as the group's assessment

Process step	Details
4. Conduct cross-scenario strategy analysis	• All scenarios are presented to all users • Representatives from each scenario group present implications and evaluations of initiatives in their scenario • The facilitator presents NB/NG/NR/C assessment of all initiatives across all scenarios
5. Identify scenario indicators	• Users identify useful extant indicators and developments to be tracked by creating new indicators • The project team identifies existing indicators using desk research • The organization may create an initiative to gather and evaluate contemporary events as ad hoc indicators
6. Monitor environment using a scenario dashboard (recommended)	• The organization creates an IT solution to develop the scenario dashboard and creates a recurring process to monitor it • Scenario dashboard: define extreme values for each indicator to correspond with the extreme values of driving forces specified in each scenario  specify aggregation of indicator values to assess changes in the driving forces

Organizational Process for Making Strategic Decisions Using the Scenario Dashboard

Periodic reviews of the scenario dashboard are recommended to assess the most current levels of desirability of different supply chain capabilities. During the review, the executive team should discuss recent changes in the indicator values (e.g., sharp increase or decrease, high volatility, no change, etc.) to assess how the corresponding environmental factors may be changing. Next, the team should examine all capabilities undergoing a major change in their valuation since the last review. Accordingly, a key decision for the management team would be whether to implement a dormant capability or divest from an existing one.

The meeting should be attended by the leaders—or their representatives—of all functions whose capabilities are assessed using the scenario dashboard. Because one possible outcome of the meeting is the decision to change the capability portfolio, the representatives of each function should be knowledgeable about the functions' capabilities, be able to discuss their interdependence, and have the authority to decide to modify the organization's capability portfolio. Domain experts covering the company's business environment (e.g., agriculture, consumer trends, regulations) may also be invited to comment on critical developments in the business environment or implications of proposed capability changes. At the end of the review, the team would trigger the organizational processes to implement the group's strategic decisions.

Scenario Dashboard Meta-Review: Not to Be Overlooked

Finally, one important task relates to the meta-review of the scenario dashboard itself. This involves checking the relevance and completeness of the scenario dashboard's information and the validity of the scenario dashboard's assumptions. The meta-review would include the following tasks.

- Determine if any new capabilities need to be added to the scenario dashboard and then map the added capabilities to all environmental factors.
- Determine if any new environmental factors need to be added to the scenario dashboard and then map the new factors to each of the capabilities, define extremes of the new factors, and find appropriate indicators to track the new factors.

- Determine if the existing indicators are still appropriate for the environmental factors; add new indicators and their respective extreme values.
- Evaluate whether the existing capability/environmental factor mappings are still valid and update as needed.
- Determine if any capabilities or factors need to be removed from the scenario dashboard.

Finally, the meta-review should also examine if the scenarios being used are still relevant. If some uncertainties depicted in the scenarios have been resolved and/or new uncertainties have emerged, the firm may need to develop a new set of scenarios that reflect the contemporary uncertainties in the planning horizon.

Notes

1. Burt, G., van der Heijden, K. 2003. "First Steps: Towards Purposeful Activities in Scenario Thinking and Future Studies." *Futures*, 35(10), 1011–1026.
2. The term "real option" was coined in: Myers, S. 1977. "Determinants of Corporate Borrowing." *Journal of Financial Economics*, 5, 147–175. For an overview of real options theory, see Trigeorgis, L., Reuer, J. 2017. "Real Options Theory in Strategic Management." *Strategic Management Journal*, 38(1), 42–63.
3. Phadnis, S., Darkow, I. 2021. "Scenario Planning as a Strategy Process to Foster Supply Chain Adaptability: Theoretical Framework and Longitudinal Case." *Futures & Foresight Science*, 3(2), e62.
4. Schoemaker, P., Day, G., Snyder, S. 2013. "Integrating Organizational Networks, Weak Signals, Strategic Radars and Scenario Planning." *Technological Forecasting & Social Change*, 80(4), 815–824.

7

Scenario Application in Supply Chain Contexts

The MIT CTL team applied the scenarios developed to the companies representing the three different roles of supply chains.

Functional Role: Building an Adaptable Supply Chain for Hoppy Brew

In 2014, MIT CTL researchers facilitated the creation of three scenarios with the Hoppy Brew team: *Brand World*, *Brew-nique!*, and *Group Drink*, as described in Chapter 5. The scenarios were first used to evaluate various supply chain capabilities in a two-day workshop (Steps 1 through 5) in March 2014. Subsequently, the company developed a scenario dashboard (Step 6) for post-workshop use.

Exploration of Scenarios by Hoppy Brew Executives (Steps 1, 2)

On a daily basis, Hoppy Brew's supply chain executives dealt with operational issues such as the sourcing of barley and hops, packaging of beer in different types of containers (cans, bottles, kegs, barrels), and delivering the beer to distributors' warehouses. However, the company had to contend with

© The Author(s), under exclusive license to Springer Nature
Switzerland AG 2022
S. S. Phadnis et al., *Strategic Planning for Dynamic Supply Chains*,
Palgrave Executive Essentials,
https://doi.org/10.1007/978-3-030-91810-1_7

certain long-term issues, such as supplier availability, future delivery pack-aging formats, and the possibility of direct consumer sales should regulations change. The March 2014 scenario workshop was attended by Hoppy Brew executives battling such long-term issues. After highlighting the project's objectives, the MIT CTL researchers presented an anonymized summary of the views of the future business environment shared by the Hoppy Brew executives in pre-workshop interviews. In a way, this input reflected the company's "presumed future scenario" as envisioned by the executives. Subse-quently, the MIT researchers gave a brief presentation showing how major changes in several industries had caught leading firms and industry experts by surprise, thereby highlighting the challenges of predicting major industry shifts. These examples set the foundation for presenting scenario planning as an alternative way of preparing for major shifts in the business environment.

Setting the stage in this manner is indispensable. Using fictitious qual-itative narratives about the future to plan important strategic initiatives is not only novel to most supply chain executives, but it can also come across as downright absurd. Using qualitative stories for planning is antithetical to the concept of "rigor," presumably yielded by sophisticated quantitative forecasting techniques that supply chain executives are accustomed to. Such an attitude is common among engineers and quantitative analysts, notwith-standing the opacity of assumptions made in the forecast models or their validity in particular settings. Examples of forecasting failures at the start of a scenario planning workshop can help to pursuade supply chain execu-tives that using scenarios can be a useful means of considering fundamentally different, but plausible, future business environments for strategic planning.

Because the workshop launched the scenarios created for Hoppy Brew and was attended by only a dozen senior executives, all executives evaluated all three scenarios, instead of splitting the group into three small subgroups each exploring one scenario. Each scenario evaluation followed the same process and lasted approximately two hours. The sessions began with the executives reading the scenario description on their own followed by a facil-itated discussion of the salient features of that scenario. Once the facilitator felt that the relevant scenario features were identified and being discussed by the group, the executives were given the collateral material depicting typical consumers in the scenario. The facilitators used the material to push the executives to explore the scenario further. This process of *scenario immersion* continued until the facilitator determined that the executives had identified all the salient points of the scenario being discussed.

Each scenario immersion session then led to a discussion of the scenario's *implications*. The discussion began with open-ended questions regarding the effects of each scenario on Hoppy Brew in three broad areas: (i) Hoppy Brew's market environment (including consumers, competing products, and competing firms), (ii) availability of and access to natural resources (including water and farm products) and packaging materials, and (iii) other relevant industry factors (such as regulations of alcohol trade, technology, etc.). The process of identifying implications was similar to that of scenario immersion: each executive first noted the implications on their own and then discussed them with the group. The facilitator captured the salient points of this discussion on a flipchart.

Visioning of Supply Chain Initiatives for Hoppy Brew (Step 3)

The enumeration and discussion of the implications of each scenario led to the envisioning of supply chain capabilities necessary for that scenario in at least three ways. First, it primed the executives to *envision* ways to equip Hoppy Brew for the changing industry environment described in that scenario. Second, the list of implications captured on the flipchart allowed the facilitator to ask the executives targeted questions to envision the capabilities of different organization functions that could address specific implications. Third, the enumerated implications also provided a lens for evaluating the utility of the envisioned capabilities.

This process was followed for all three scenarios. During the post-workshop analysis, MIT CTL facilitators compiled a list of 65 unique capabilities envisioned across the three scenarios. Further refinement of this list with Hoppy Brew's project team eliminated duplicate and vaguely defined items. The result was a list of 48 specific capabilities falling predominantly in six general areas in the project team's scope: procurement, R&D, brewing, packaging, distribution, and planning.

Exhibit 7.1 presents a partial list of capabilities envisioned by Hoppy Brew's executives in the visioning session. The novelty of these capabilities in the context of Hoppy Brew's current operations, and the association between the capabilities and the scenarios, demonstrated the efficacy of scenario thinking. For example, the executives suggested several capabilities prompted by descriptions of resource scarcity in the *Brand World* and *Brew-nique!* scenarios. These included securing sufficient water resources, developing new breeds of cereal/grains, and approaching zero solid and liquid waste at the brewery.

Some supply chain capabilities needed to address the future described in certain scenarios could be traced back to the confluence of driving forces described in a particular scenario. For example, the capability to "produce same beer from alternative raw materials" suggested in the *Brand World* scenario (a world with resource scarcity and strong consumer preference for branded beer) was deemed necessary to maintain the brand's taste, even if disruptions in raw material supplies forced the company to brew with alternate materials. Similarly, the capabilities to "create and market a home craft brewing kit/recipe/formula" and to "efficiently deliver and service beer machines or dispensers" to homes were considered necessary in the world described in *Brew-nique!*, where consumers demand highly personalized products. In contrast, envisioning in the context of the *Group Drink* scenario (where product customization is driven by social experience instead of individual taste, regulations are limited, and resources are adequate) generated suggestions for capabilities such as the ability to "quickly create and launch new products or extensions" and to "postpone final customization of the product to near consumer location" to keep up with fickle and informed consumers. It also prompted the need to "highly customize packaging/labeling in very small lot sizes" to cater to small social events such as birthday and anniversary celebrations, weddings, and office parties. Overall, Hoppy Brew used the scenarios primarily as ideation devices to envision supply chain capabilities in various functions.

Exhibit 7.1: A partial list of novel capabilities envisioned by Hoppy Brew using scenarios

PROCUREMENT
- Identify and secure sufficient water sources
- Become more efficient in growing raw materials (e.g., barley)

R&D
- Quickly create and launch new products or extensions
- Understand and capture the sensory (taste, touch, feel, smell) essence of the company's brands

BREWING
- Approach zero solid and liquid waste at the brewery
- Create and market a home craft brewing kit/recipe/formula
- Produce same beer from alternative raw materials

PACKAGING
- Differentiate returnable bottles/packaging using design
- Highly customize packaging/labeling in very small lot sizes

DISTRIBUTION
- Efficiently deliver and service "beer" machines or dispensers
- Efficiently deliver in dense urban areas

PLANNING
- Accurately measure and track the end-to-end carbon footprint of all products
- Postpone final customization of the product to near consumer location

Scenario-Based Evaluation of Hoppy Brew's Capabilities (Steps 3, 4)

Each capability, such as those listed in Exhibit 7.1, arose from the needs envisioned when considering one of the three scenarios. An obvious question was whether a capability envisioned in one scenario would be beneficial under the other two scenarios as well. To perform this analysis, the Hoppy Brew project team decided to evaluate each capability in detail, delving into the specifics of each scenario. The team analyzed the benefit of investing in each capability by considering the extreme values of a detailed list of specific environmental factors that underpinned the entire scenario structure. From the data used for developing the scenarios, the team identified 25 environmental factors, components of different driving forces, representing different aspects of the relevant business environment. The executive team assessed the capabilities across six factors on the second day of the workshop and assessed the remaining 19 factors remotely using a structured questionnaire.

It is noteworthy that the request to perform such a detailed capability evaluation came from the Hoppy Brew executives themselves. While some executives evaluated capabilities only for the functions they considered themselves knowledgeable about, three team members evaluated all capabilities.

Capability Evaluations for Individual Environmental Factors

To perform the evaluation, each executive specified the desirability of each capability for Hoppy Brew under each of the two extreme values of each factor of the business environment. The executives, working independently, answered each question by selecting one of the four desirability options: "Must have/Essential," "Useful to have," "Nice to have/Minimal benefit," and "Bad to have/Detrimental." Exhibit 7.2 presents an example of the survey completed by a Hoppy Brew executive for 10 capabilities in the Brewing function under two extreme values of two environmental factors: the extent of regulations dictating structure of the beer supply chain (pervasive vs. minimal regulation) and climate-change-related shifts affecting the land capable of growing barley (more vs. less arable land).

Exhibit 7.2: Example of capability evaluation completed by one Hoppy Brew executive

Assessment of capability usefulness under extreme values of various environmental factors (Evaluator:)

Brewing Capabilities

Extent to which regulations dictate structure of supply chain (SC) for alcoholic beverages — Pervasive regulation | Minimal regulation

Capability to...	Pervasive regulation				Minimal regulation			
	Must have	Useful to have	Nice to have	Bad to have	Must have	Useful to have	Nice to have	Bad to have
Approach zero solid and liquid waste at the brewery								
Create and host platform for micro-brewers								
Create highly customized products of one								
Produce beverages in non-beer categories								
Produce same beer from various/local/alternative raw materials								
Create and market a home craft brewing kit/recipe/formula								
Create and market concentrated/powdered beer product								
Profitably brew in smaller batches								
Profitably brew beer faster								
Ensure quality of product from third party brewers using ████████								

Climate change related shifts in arable land capable of producing barley — More arable land | Less arable land

Capability to...	More arable land				Less arable land			
	Must have	Useful to have	Nice to have	Bad to have	Must have	Useful to have	Nice to have	Bad to have
Approach zero solid and liquid waste at the brewery								
Create and host platform for micro-brewers								
Create highly customized products of one								
Produce beverages in non-beer categories								
Produce same beer from various/local/alternative raw materials								
Create and market a home craft brewing kit/recipe/formula								
Create and market concentrated/powdered beer product								
Profitably brew in smaller batches								
Profitably brew beer faster								

Prepared by MIT Center for Transportation and Logistics   Page 2 of 35

All the completed questionnaires were compiled to obtain the group's assessment of the usefulness of the capabilities under different environmental conditions. One key issue was the small number of participating executives, which meant that the averaged results could be easily influenced by a single response. Therefore, the initial analysis was followed by an extensive discussion of the evaluation in another workshop conducted at MIT about six weeks after the initial scenario planning workshop.

For that discussion, the MIT CTL team first identified all capabilities that had received contradictory evaluations. For instance, the capability to "produce same beer from alternative raw materials" was assessed as being "Must have/Essential" and "Bad to have/Detrimental" by different respondents in six different environmental conditions: (i) pervasive regulation dictating the structure of supply chain of alcoholic beverages, (ii) scarce access to specialty hops/ingredients, (iii) high cost of obtaining and maintaining liquor licenses, (iv) strong farmer incentives to grow barley instead of other crops, (v) highly volatile energy prices, and (vi) unpredictable taxes on alcoholic beverages. The executives discussed all such divergent evaluations in the workshop. Surfacing the divergences during the voting led to further discussion and refinement of the executives' perceptions about how different environmental conditions would affect various capabilities. Typically, a second vote generated higher consensus on the rating of each capability under the environmental factors. The remaining capability evaluations under different environmental conditions that were unanimous were also reviewed and confirmed.

Cross-Scenario Analysis

Hoppy Brew used the scenarios again to determine capabilities that were robust to changes in the environment, so that Hoppy Brew could invest in them with relative certainty that they would be effective (i.e., they were "No Brainer"). For this, the evaluations of each capability under both extreme conditions of 25 different environmental factors were compiled, using a two-step approach (Exhibit 7.3). First, each scenario was expressed in terms of the value assigned to each of the 25 factors in that scenario condition, i.e., whether the scenario had a strong, weak, or no resemblance to either of the factor's extreme values. Second, the perceived utility of each capability for each factor corresponding to the extreme value described in the scenario was mapped.

Exhibit 7.3: Approach for assessing value of a capability in a scenario for Hoppy Brew

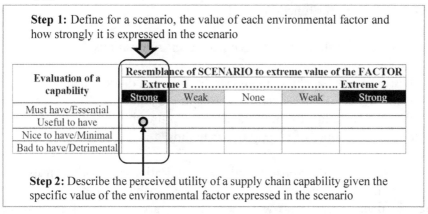

To illustrate this, Table 7.1 presents the descriptions of the three Hoppy Brew scenarios (columns) in terms of values of the 25 environmental factors (rows). Each cell in the three scenario columns depicts which extreme value of that row's environmental factor is likely to take in that column's scenario. The three right-most columns of the table illustrate the perceived utility of one capability—namely "quickly create and launch new products or extensions"—under the specific condition of the row's factor in the corresponding scenario. The four possible values of the perceived utility are indicated in table as follows: "Must have/Essential" (indicated with ++), "Useful to have" (+), "Nice to have/Minimal value" (0), and "Bad to have/Detrimental" (−).

Notice that the capability to "quickly create and launch new products or extensions" is essential under various conditions across the three scenarios. Specifically, consider the scenario *Group Drink*. In this scenario, the capability is deemed "Must have/Essential" in 15 different conditions (shown with ++ in 15 rows in the last column in Table 7.1 corresponding to the scenario) and "Useful to have" in six others. In three conditions, it has minimal value and is considered "Bad to have/Detrimental" corresponding to only one aspect of the scenario. Thus, the capability seems to be almost essential to have for the *Group Drink* scenario.

In the *Brand World* and *Brew-nique!* scenarios, the capability is seen as "Must have/Essential" in 11 and 12 different conditions, respectively, "Useful to have" in seven each, "Bad to have/Detrimental" in two each, and "Nice to have/Minimal" utility in five and four, respectively. As a result, the value of the capability in *Brand World* and *Brew-nique!* is rather limited. Therefore, across the three scenarios, the value of the capability is contingent and not robust.

Such a cross-scenario analysis revealed a handful of capabilities as robust across all three scenarios. The following are examples of four robust capabilities in four different functional areas:

- (Brewing) Capability to produce same beer from various, local, or alternative raw materials
- (Distribution) Capability to efficiently deliver in dense urban areas
- (Planning) Capability to sense and respond to point-of-sale demand signals
- (R&D) Capability to understand and capture the sensory (taste, touch, feel, smell) essence of Hoppy Brew's brands

A closer look at the scenarios and their implications revealed the reasons for considering these capabilities as robust. The capability to efficiently deliver beer in dense urban areas was deemed necessary in most of the environmental conditions. It was adjudged "Must have/Essential" regardless of the values taken by several factors such as the proportion of alcoholic beverages consumed at home vs. eating establishments, regulations (and their enforcement) about truck emissions, the footprint of the retail beer and wine stores, and types and predominance of leisure activities consumers engage in. In many other conditions, the capability was deemed to be "Useful to have" but not essential. Furthermore, no executive deemed the capability to be "Bad to have/Detrimental" under any environmental condition.

Table 7.1 Definitions of Hoppy Brew scenarios in terms of environmental factors and perceived utility of capability to "quickly create and launch new products or extensions"

Environment factor	Scenario description			Utility of chosen capability by scenario		
	Brand World (BW)	Brew-nique! (B!)	Group Drink (GD)	BW	B!	GD
Access to specialty hops/ingredients	Scarce	Scarce	Abundant	+	+	+
Availability (and cost) of water used in beer production	Scarce (High)	Scarce (High)	Abundant (Low)	−	−	0
Climate change-related shifts in arable land capable of producing barley	Less arable land	Less arable land	More arable land	0	0	−
Consolidation among beer, wine, and liquor wholesalers	Highly consolidated	Fragmented	Highly consolidated	++	++	++
Consumer acceptance of GMOs in the alcoholic drinks	−	Strong Opposition	General acceptance	0	+	++
Consumer confidence and overall consumer spending	High (Strong economy)	Low (Recession)	−	++	0	0
Consumer demand for the ability to customize drinks per their taste	Standard Products	Customized products	Customized products	0	++	++

(continued)

Table 7.1 (continued)

Environment factor	Scenario description			Utility of chosen capability by scenario		
	Brand World (BW)	Brew-nique! (B!)	Group Drink (GD)	BW	B!	GD
Type of products preferred by the consumers	Mass-market	Premium	Premium	+	++	++
Consumers' use of reusable containers for buying beer	Extensive	Extensive	None	++	++	+
Consumers' willingness to substitute among beer, wine, and liquor	Preference for type	Type-indifferent	Type-indifferent	+	+	+
Effort (and cost) required to obtain and maintain liquor licenses	Extensive (costly)	Extensive (costly)	Little (cheap)	0	0	++
Excise and other taxes on alcoholic beverages	Very high	Very high	Low/moderate	0	0	++
Extent to which regulations dictate the structure of the supply chain for alcoholic beverages	Pervasive regulation	Minimal regulation	Minimal regulation	+	++	++

(continued)

Table 7.1 (continued)

Environment factor	Scenario description			Utility of chosen capability by scenario		
	Brand World (BW)	Brew-nique! (B!)	Group Drink (GD)	BW	B!	GD
Farmer incentives to grow barley instead of other crops (corn, wheat)	Strong	Strong	None or weak	++	++	++
Footprint of the retail beer and wine stores	Same as in 2014	Nano-stores	Same as in 2014	+	++	+
Intensity of competition among retailers (grocery stores, hyper-marts)	Extensive	Minimal	Extensive	++	+	++
Predictability of taxes on alcoholic beverages	Unpredictable, changing	Predictable, stable	Predictable, stable	++	++	++
Predominant leisure activities	Sport	High-brow	Sport	++	++	++
Price of energy (VILC)	High	High	Low	+	+	+
Restrictions on the consumption of beer	Drink only where allowed	Drink only where allowed	Drink everywhere	++	++	++
Restrictions on public access to beer	Widely available	Widely available	Highly restricted	++	++	0
Restrictions on traffic in cities	Extensive	Extensive	Minimal	−	−	++
Sudden appearance of alternatives to alcohols	None	Several	Several	+	+	+
Type of leisure activity	Group	Individual	Group	++	++	++
Variability in the price of energy	Highly volatile	Stable	Highly volatile	++	+	++

Other capabilities deemed robust received similar patterns of assessments. However, the utility of most capabilities, including all capabilities envisioned in the Packaging function, was contingent on the state of the business environment. To use a "real options" investment in contingent capabilities, Hoppy Brew needed to be able to monitor the business environment. For this, the company needed to identify relevant indicators to watch.

Indicators to Monitor Hoppy Brew's Business Environment (Step 5)

The 25 factors of the business environment described in the scenarios served as the basis for identifying indicators. Several public databases, such as the World Bank Open Data initiative, publish time-series data that can be used as indicators. In addition, industry-specific guides, such as Industry Insights from the Beer Institute, make time-series data available by subscription. Hoppy Brew used both sources. The process for identifying indicators is identical for both sources: a targeted search process of the data sources (internet or databases) using the terms or synonyms related to the environmental factor yields a set of potentially relevant data series. The descriptions of the data series at the source can confirm if they are relevant to a factor of the business environment.

For example, consider the factor "availability (and cost) of water used in beer production." Although the factor cites beer production, water (and its price) plays a key role that extends far beyond the alcoholic beverages industry. Indicators are often publicly available for widely influential factors such as water prices. The OECD publishes data on the price of water in selected OECD countries.[1] The OECD lists prices for different representative localities in those countries. Exhibit 7.4[2] shows an example of monthly water charges in three US cities: New York, Dallas, and High Point (NC) as representative of a large city, an industrial area, and a rural area, respectively. The publication also lists the highest and lowest prices for industrial water in the country (in Exhibit 7.4, these were Virginia Beach, VA and Tampa, FL, respectively).

Exhibit 7.4: Price of industrial water in the US, as an illustrative example

UNITED STATES				
Monthly water charge (USD/Gallon)				
	Name	2-Inch Meter Light Industrial 50 000 CF	4-inch Meter Light Industrial 1 000 000 CF	8-inch Meter Light Industrial 1 500 000 CF
Large city	New York, NY	505.00	10 100.00	15 150.00
An industrial area	Dallas, TX	494.54	9 775.40	14 732.60
A rural area	High Point, NC	568.56	9 526.31	14 207.86
Minimum	Tampa, FL	450.00	900.00	1 350.00
Maximum	Virginia Beach, VA	1 381.70	27 350.00	41 105.00

Reference OECD. 1999. *Industrial Water Pricing in OECD Countries* (p. 55).

Another source for water prices was the Rickards Real Cost Water Index™, developed by Waterfund in collaboration with IBM Watson Research.[3] This index calculates the true cost of water production in different countries and cities. It is computed as a ratio of the total cost of water production (which includes capital and operating costs and subsidies) divided by the volume of freshwater delivered. Exhibit 7.5 shows an example of the index values in London, Manila, Sao Paulo, Singapore, and Uganda. The index is published quarterly and shows changes from the previous quarter.

Exhibit 7.5: Snapshot of the web page of Water Cost Index™

<table>
<tr><td colspan="2">water**fund**</td><td>Company</td><td>True Cost of Water</td><td>Insights</td></tr>
</table>

(powered by IBM Infosphere BigInsights)

Global Water Cost Indices

Location	Water Cost Index	% Change from	% Change from	Index % Change
	Q4 2015	Q3 2015	Q1 2008	Q1 2008
	in US Dollar (USD)	in US Dollar (USD)	in US Dollar (USD)	in Local Currency
Global	$1.80	▼ -4.0%	▲ 19.4%	▲ 32.9%
London	$2.78	▼ -4.0%	▲ 4.9%	▲ 33.7%
Manila, Philippines	$0.42	▲ 1.0%	▲ 23.8%	▲ 28.3%
Sao Paulo	$1.47	▼ -8.0%	▲ 15.3%	▲ 32.0%
Singapore	$3.65	▼ -4.0%	▲ 54.9%	▲ 33.0%
Uganda	$0.97	▼ -5.0%	▲ 1.1%	▲ 49.3%

Reference Waterfund. 2018. *Rickards Real Cost Water Index™ calculated by IBM*. Available at http://worldswaterfund.com/water-cost-index-overview. html.

The preceding two indicators closely match the environmental factor "availability (and cost) of water used in beer production." However, finding such good matches is not always possible. In such cases, one may choose a data series that is somewhat representative of the factor and use it to make judgments about any changes in the values of that factor.

For example, consider the factor "consumers' willingness to substitute among beer, wine, and liquor." This factor is specific to the alcoholic beverages industry, and thus, relevant indicators are likely to be found in industry-specific data sets. However, the factor also relates to consumers, and hence, some consumer surveys may contain the relevant data. The targeted search conducted as part of this project found no exact matches among publicly available sources but found indicators related to beverage preference that hinted at substitution patterns. For example, Gallup's annual Household Consumption Habits survey presents the percentage of respondents who report whether they drink beer, liquor, or wine most often. The survey also reports preferences by age groups, gender, and ethnicity, and the frequency of drinking for the preferred drink. This survey shows that although the percentage of Americans who report drinking alcohol (60%) has not changed since the 1990s, Americans' drinking preferences have shifted away from beer and toward wine. For instance, in 1992–1994, 71% of 18–29-year-old Americans reported beer as their preferred alcoholic drink; as of 2014, this number had dropped to 41% in this demographic. Over the same period, those reporting wine and liquor as the preferred drinks increased from 14 to 13%, respectively, to 24 and 28%. Exhibit 7.6 shows the aggregate trend since 1992. Another data source (a paid data set by Mintel[4]) provides statistics about mass-market beer, craft beer, and cider such as market sizes and forecasts, types of beer consumed, preferences by gender, on- vs. off-premise sales, beer purchase locations, brand loyalty, and so on.

Exhibit 7.6: Americans' alcohol preferences

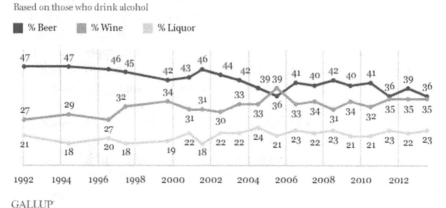

Do you most often drink liquor, wine, or beer?

Based on those who drink alcohol

GALLUP

Reference Gallup. 2013. *U.S. Drinkers Divide Between Beer and Wine as Favorite.* Available at https://news.gallup.com/poll/163787/drinkers-divide-beer-wine-favorite.aspx.

There are two important takeaways from the exercise of identifying quantitative indicators. First, a vast variety of data sources and statistics exist; one needs to look for the most relevant sources for measuring the environmental factors described in the scenarios. Second, the scenarios also make it easier to understand whether and how a particular statistic or time series is relevant for the company's strategic decisions. Thus, scenarios can be useful for sorting through the abundant supply of data and statistics. The selected indicators can help supply chain executives to understand how the business environment is changing, which of those changes are relevant for the company's supply chain, and how those changes may affect the functioning of the supply chain.

Scenario Dashboard for Hoppy Brew (Step 6)

The last step in the Hoppy Brew scenario project was to design an IT tool and an organizational process to monitor the company's business environment. The MIT CTL researchers designed a prototype database tool called

"Playbook" by Hoppy Brew. Similar tools have been developed and used for monitoring changes in the business environment under names such as dashboards and strategic radars. In addition, the MIT CTL team specified organizational processes that would use the information provided by the tool to reevaluate supply chain capabilities in the evolving business environment.

The Playbook uses the indicators identified in Step 5 to track the environment in terms of the driving forces vis-à-vis the scenarios using two processes. The first assigns responsibility to a manager to maintain the Playbook's data by updating the indicators regularly. The second specifies schedules for meetings to analyze and review the indicator values for any changes in the business environment and to make decisions about adapting the supply chain strategy. In a high-velocity environment, these meetings are likely to be held more often, as frequently as every quarter. In a slower-changing environment, the review may be performed as infrequently as once a year.

The Playbook stores the latest values of the indicators, translates them into the values of the environmental factors on a scale delimited between the two extreme ends, and computes the corresponding utilities of the supply chain capabilities. The latter two functions require additional computation. First, translating indicator values into the states of an environmental factor (between its two extremes) requires quantifying the factor's extremes values, which hitherto had been expressed only qualitatively. Second, an algorithmic expression was needed for estimating the utility of each capability as a function of the estimated values of the environmental factors. Once these two functions are built, the Playbook can be easily extended to conduct what-if analyses, enabling managers to understand how a change in the value of a specific environmental factor may impact the desirability of multiple capabilities.

The scenario dashboard should have an appealing and user-friendly graphical user interface to display the values of different driving forces in relation to their extreme values, the state of the present business environment in relation to the scenarios, and the changing desirability of different strategic initiatives.

Computing Extreme Values of Environmental Factors

During scenario development, participants envisioned two extreme qualitative states for each environmental factor (e.g., "high" or "low" material prices, and "strong" or "weak" consumer preferences), which were then associated with one or more quantitative indicators in the scenario dashboard. Relating the measured or what-if values of the indicators to the state of an environmental factor required specifying the numerical values of the indicators that would correspond to the extreme states of the environmental factor.

Estimating these extreme values can be challenging because the values need to be extreme but plausible. Such values may (or may not) be outside of historical ranges. Therefore, setting numerical extreme values requires a deep understanding of the driving forces and how the forces are measured by the indicator. The rationale of these settings also needs to be accepted by the executives involved in the scenario planning project. For example, the environmental factor "availability (and cost) of water used in beer production" has two qualitative extreme values: "Scarce (high cost)" and "Abundant (low cost)." As described above, two quantitative indicators measure this factor: the price of industrial water in the US and Rickards Real Cost Water Index™. Table 7.2 shows the extreme values chosen for the two indicators to correspond to the two qualitative extremes values of the environmental factor they measure and the rationale for the choice of those values. The value of the environmental factor was computed by averaging the normalized values of the two indicators.

Table 7.2 Quantitative indicator values to measure qualitative environmental factor

Indicator	Corresponding value		Rationale for the choice of extreme values
	High cost	Low cost	
Price of industrial water in the US	6.76	0.03	High cost: Based on the maximum price among countries and an increase of 5% per year for 15 years (1999–2014) Low cost: Based on the minimum price among all eight countries in the report
Rickards Real Cost Water Index™	3.37	0.42	High and Low costs: Based on the maximum and minimum values of the index in the data, compounded using the highest and the lowest growth rates observed in the five years of data

Assessing Value of Supply Chain Capabilities

The desirability of each supply chain capability depends on the value of the different environmental factors and the association between the factor and the capability. The four levels of association between Hoppy Brew's supply chain capabilities and environmental factors (Essential, Useful, Minimal, Detrimental) were given weights of (+3, +1, −1, −2). The research team also tested the use of weights of (5, 1, 0, −2) and (3, 1, 0, −1) to ensure that the capability evaluations were not sensitive to the weighting scheme used. The weights (+3, +1, −1, −2) were chosen because this scheme provides a penalty for investing in capabilities of minimal desirability. The desirability of each capability was computed using these weights, the assessed relationships between the capabilities and environmental factors, and the values of the environmental factors.

Because different indicators are likely to be measured using different units and scales that may differ by orders of magnitude, it is necessary to normalize the indicator values before aggregation. Normalization involves subtracting the average value of each indicator from each actual value and dividing the difference by the standard deviation. One also needs to specify the weight assigned to each indicator as they are aggregated, to produce a proxy value for the driving force. A simple approach is to assign equal weights to all indicators. Aggregation provides a single value for each driving force and is used to track its movement toward its extremities.

As indicators are updated, the values of corresponding environmental factors are computed again, consequently updating the desirability ratings of the supply chain capabilities. Figure 7.1 shows a schematic representation of Hoppy Brew's Playbook. The left side of the Playbook lists all environmental factors and their present values, shown using arrows between the two extremes. The right side of the Playbook lists all supply chain capabilities, shown with a vertical black line on a linear scale ranging from detrimental (the "Low" end) to essential (the "High" end). Updating the indicator values changes the values of the environmental factors on the left, which in turn changes the desirability ratings of the supply chain capabilities on the right.

Finally, the MIT CTL team made specific recommendations for setting the process of making decisions using the playbook and meta playbook reviews.

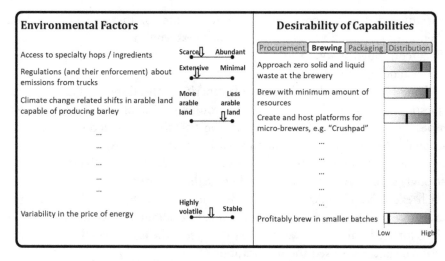

Fig. 7.1 Schematic representation of Hoppy Brew's Playbook

Business Model Role: Anticipation of Environmental Changes at Medford

In 2010, Medford's Pharmaceuticals Distribution business embarked on a year-long collaborative scenario planning research project with MIT CTL.

The goal of this scenario exercise was to enable ongoing organizational learning about the evolving healthcare environment in the US. No particular strategic investments were chosen to be guided by the scenarios. Therefore, the scenario application at Medford covered the first four steps mentioned in Table 6.1 and was limited to understanding scenario implications. Neither an indicator-identification nor a scenario-monitoring system was included in the scope of the Medford project.

Chapter 5 presented the process followed by the Medford executives resulting in the four scenarios. The executives then explored the implications of each scenario followed by a cross-scenario analysis.

Scenario Exploration by Medford's Executives (Steps 1–3)

After an extensive scenario development process, Medford's executives had developed an appreciation for the scenario practice and its intended objective of facilitating organizational learning. Furthermore, each executive had multiple opportunities to examine one scenario thoroughly. They had evaluated the scenarios for internal consistency, assessed and validated the scenario narrative, and had subsequently chosen a name for the scenario based on their intimate understanding of the business environment it represented. They continued working with their assigned scenarios to develop a deeper understanding of the world.

The first structured exploration of scenario implications used a web-based questionnaire consisting of the 32 environmental factors, describing various aspects of the driving forces used in the scenario construction. The questionnaire listed a particular state for each factor and asked the executives to note their level of agreement—on a scale of "−2: strongly disagree" to "+2: strongly agree"—that the factor could take the specified state in their scenario. Each executive completed the exercise individually. In most instances, the executives examining each scenario concurred about the scenario's implications for the local factors. Where they disagreed, the executives discussed their rationale and reassessed the implications.

Table 7.3 presents the average values of implications of the four scenarios for the 32 key local factors. A high positive (negative) score, say +1 or higher (−1 or lower), suggests that a particular implication is highly likely (unlikely) in the given scenario. Scores between −1 and +1 indicate less certainty about the implication being experienced in a scenario.

For example, consider the implication that manufacturers will consolidate across branded, generic, and biologic segments. This is considered to be highly likely in the scenario *Frenzy*, almost certain in *Hiber-Nation*, and fairly unlikely in *Zen*, whereas its occurrence is uncertain in *Innovo-Nation*. The diversity of implications across different scenarios, seen in Table 7.3, attests to the efficacy of scenarios as a tool that can facilitate strategic conversation about the unpredictable environment. It allows executives to discuss contradictory views about the future operating conditions in their industry and their implications for the company, neatly organized into different scenarios of the future.

Cross-Scenario Analysis of Scenario Implications (Step 4)

Medford's cross-scenario analysis was also based on the scenario implications. This analysis identified seven implications as robust across all scenarios and three as strongly contingent on specific scenarios.

Table 7.3 Implications of Medford's scenarios

Scenario implications	Frenzy	Innovo-Nation	Hiber-Nation	Zen
Interpretation of results: +2: strongly agree; 0: neither agree nor disagree; −2: strongly disagree				
3PL carriers will be significant competitors in the distribution business	0.50	0.67	1.60	0.75
The Big Three will still remain the three biggest distributors	2.00	1.00	0.00	1.25
The Big Three will compete fiercely on price	1.50	1.33	1.00	1.00
Carriers will be motivated to ensure that Medford's customers get good and reliable service	1.75	1.33	1.00	1.00
Climate control during storage and transportation will be regulated	1.00	2.00	1.20	0.00
Companies will experience a scarcity of talented and dedicated employees	0.00	1.00	−0.40	2.00
Customers will choose distributor based only on price	0.50	−0.33	−0.20	−0.50
Demand at acute care facilities will be a lot higher than today	0.25	−0.33	−0.20	0.00
Demand at non-acute care facilities—such as clinics, long-term care, home—will be a lot higher than today	1.25	2.00	1.40	1.00
Distributors will be held responsible for drug safety	2.00	1.67	0.20	0.50
Drug manufacturers will try to reduce cost	2.00	1.67	1.00	0.25
Drug prices will become more transparent due to regulation	1.50	1.33	1.80	−0.25
Environmental regulations will be much stronger and more pervasive than in 2009	1.75	1.67	1.40	1.00
Fee-for-service model will be the dominant model in industry	0.25	1.00	0.00	0.25
Frequency of drug thefts will increase	0.00	0.33	1.40	−0.25

(continued)

Table 7.3 (continued)

Scenario implications	Frenzy	Innovo-Nation	Hiber-Nation	Zen
Hospitals, GPOs will bypass distributors and buy directly from manufacturers	−0.50	−1.00	1.40	−1.50
Hospitals will become more specialized by disease needs	1.50	1.33	1.00	0.50
Independent pharmacies will struggle to be profitable	0.75	1.00	1.60	0.25
Manufacturers will consolidate across branded, generic, and biologic segments	1.25	0.33	1.80	−1.00
Manufacturers will focus less on branded drugs, more on niche and biotech drugs	0.75	1.00	1.40	1.25
Manufacturers will have to rely on distributors for distributing drugs, devices	0.50	0.33	−0.40	1.25
Most drugs will be distributed direct to patient	−0.25	−1.00	−0.20	−1.00
Payers will lower reimbursement rates	1.50	1.67	1.60	0.25
Payers will pay for outcome, not treatment	1.75	0.67	0.40	−1.75
Pharmacies will bypass distributors and buy directly from manufacturers	−0.75	−0.33	0.60	−0.75
Technological advances will improve accessibility and quality of treatment	0.00	0.67	1.20	2.00
The number of care delivery locations will increase	1.50	2.00	−0.20	1.75
There will be more generic alternatives to patented drugs	2.00	1.67	1.40	0.75
There will be one federal pedigree legislation that all states follow	−0.75	0.00	0.00	0.50
There will be only very few regional distributors	1.25	1.00	1.80	0.75
Volume of drugs sold to mail-order pharmacies will be much higher than in 2009	1.50	1.67	1.20	1.50
Volume of drugs sold to warehouse pharmacies will be much higher than in 2009	0.50	1.00	0.80	0.50

Robust Implications for Medford

The following represent the seven robust operating conditions Medford was likely to experience in its future business environment.

- Volume of drugs sold to mail-order pharmacies will be much higher in the future.
- Demand at non-acute care facilities (e.g., clinics, long-term care, home) will be a lot higher.
- Environmental regulations will be much stronger and more pervasive.
- Carriers will be motivated to ensure that Medford's customers get good and reliable service.
- The Big Three distributors will compete fiercely on price.
- There will be more generic alternatives to patented drugs.
- There will be very few regional distributors.

The first five were considered highly likely in every single scenario. In fact, at least 14 of 16 executives completing this exercise, regardless of the scenario, rated each of the implications to be either somewhat or highly likely in their scenario. The dissenting votes had only "somewhat disagreed" with the implication for their scenario. The last two implications were considered highly likely in three scenarios and somewhat likely in the remaining one.

Contingent Implications for Medford

Three implications stood out as contingent across the four scenarios.

- *Payers will pay for the outcome, not treatment*: This was the most contingent implication. It was considered highly likely in *Frenzy* and highly unlikely in *Zen!* All executives in each scenario concurred in their evaluation of the likelihood of this factor in their scenario. This implication was directly related to the driving force "nature of reimbursement policies" and in these two scenarios, the implications parallel the description of the driving force in the scenario. However, the likelihood was less certain in the remaining two scenarios.
- *Manufacturers will consolidate across branded, generic, and biologic segments*: This was the second most contingent implication. It was considered highly likely in *Frenzy* and *Hiber-Nation* and highly unlikely in *Zen*. This implication seems to derive from the confluence of two driving forces: "proportion of generic drugs in the volume of drugs consumed" and "consolidation

within the healthcare sector." The two scenarios in which this was deemed likely described a much higher proportion of generic drugs, which have lower profit margins for the manufacturer and high consolidation in the healthcare sector.

- *Hospitals and GPOs will bypass distributors and buy directly from manufacturers*: While this was considered to be highly likely in *Hiber-Nation*, the implication was deemed highly unlikely to occur in *Innovo-Nation* and *Zen*. This implication seemed to relate to the confluence of two driving forces: "availability of healthcare workers" and "locations where the majority of healthcare is provided." The two scenarios in which the implication was considered unlikely had been described as having a large number of locations of care delivery (hence the need for greater scale and competence in managing distribution) and likely to experience scarcity of healthcare workers (hence the inadequate staff to manage distribution).

Thus, the cross-scenario analysis provided a way for the executives to understand factors of Medford's business environment that were highly likely to be experienced vs. unpredictable factors that were contingent on how the environment evolved. Thus, the analysis helped resolve some uncertainty about the future of local supply chain factors (i.e., the robust implications) and provided more clarity about when some contingencies would resolve in a particular way.

Exploration of the implications of the four scenarios marked the end of the MIT CTL team's involvement with the Medford team. Although no specific decisions related to strategic supply chain planning were taken in this exercise, the participating executives acknowledged having a much richer understanding of the US healthcare sector and its future through the use of the scenarios.

Infrastructural Role: Transport Infrastructure Planning

The MIT CTL team presented the Future Freight Flows (FFF) scenarios and the process for applying them during six one-day workshops conducted between November 2010 and June 2011.[5] The workshops were held at three state departments of transportation (DOTs) (Minnesota DOT, Washington State DOT (WSDOT), and Georgia DOT), the US Federal DOT, a regional planning agency (Delaware Valley Regional Planning Commission), and the Port of Long Beach. The MIT CTL team's involvement was limited only to the participating organization's workshop. As a result, the application of the methodology was limited to the first four steps of the process.

The general process was followed in all FFF workshops. A few process steps are exemplified by their use at the workshop conducted at the WSDOT in Seattle in March 2011.

Pre-Workshop Activities

Planning for each FFF workshop began approximately three months in advance. The pre-workshop activities defined nine aspects of the workshop's design. These were defined by the host agency's leader (e.g., the WSDOT leader) overseeing the planning of its freight infrastructure. Typically, the leader was a senior manager or director-level person.

Scope

The time horizon for all workshops was 30 years and the geographic region typically covered, but was not always limited to, the jurisdiction of the planning agency hosting the workshop. For instance, the WSDOT workshop evaluated various segments of freight infrastructure within the state of Washington but also considered nearby connecting or competing infrastructure segments such as the East–West highways in Canada with access to the neighboring Washington State. Similarly, the workshop at the Georgia DOT evaluated ocean ports in its neighboring states in addition to several in-state infrastructure segments.

Objective

The workshop objective was to either envision new initiatives or evaluate predefined infrastructure investments, or a combination of both. The workshop at Minnesota DOT was primarily a visioning exercise and was conducted to complement an ongoing project. The workshops at the Delaware Valley Regional Planning Commission (DVRPC) and US DOT were used purely for the evaluation of predetermined infrastructure segments. The remaining three combined both objectives but were primarily focused on evaluation.

Table 7.4 Participants from different types of organizations in WSDOT workshop

Organization classification	Participants
Academics, consultants	4
Carrier	8
Community association—Tribe, labor	4
Government planner—Federal (incl. military)	5
Government planner—State	10
Government planner—Local	12
Port	8
Shipper	10
Total invitees	**61**

Workshop Duration

The very first workshop (DVRPC) was scheduled as a half-day exercise. However, this duration was found inadequate given that many workshop participants had no previous experience with scenario planning. As a result, all subsequent workshops were scheduled as one-day workshops.

Participants

Participation in all six workshops was by invitation only. The participants were selected for their first-hand knowledge of the region's freight infrastructure needs. They included transportation planners at the local, state, and federal levels; regional shippers (manufacturers, retailers, farmers, etc.); freight carriers from different transportation modes; and community and environmental groups. The number of participants was capped at approximately 60, to limit each scenario's group discussion to 15 participants to ensure that all participants had adequate opportunity to contribute their expertise to the workshop discussion.

The WSDOT workshops had the most participants (61). They represented various constituents, as depicted in Table 7.4.

Strategic Questions

All workshops addressed the same general question: what investments in freight infrastructure should the planning agency make considering the four scenarios looking 30 years into the future? Different workshops used variations of this broad question. For example, the WSDOT workshop was designed to address three specific questions:

- "Which freight investment segments (among the chosen 16) will be the most critical for the [next] three decades?"
- "What will be the primary and secondary freight corridors in the [next] three decades?"
- "What are some initiatives that WSDOT should take to improve the freight corridors?"

Evaluation Elements

Selection of the freight infrastructure segments to evaluate was the most discussed aspect of workshop design in the pre-workshop planning. The segments were finalized as late as two weeks before the workshop. Generally, each segment consisted of a continuous single-mode (i.e., a highway, a rail line, a waterway, etc.) freight artery in the region. The WSDOT workshop evaluated 16 different segments (listed below). Each segment was plotted on a map and presented to the workshop participants. Exhibit 23 in the appendix shows a grayscale version of a chart depicting the 16 segments used in the workshop.

- Highways (6): I-5 and North/South highways in Western Washington State, North/South highways in Eastern Washington State, I-90 (major East/West highway), etc.
- Rail lines (5): North/South rail lines parallel to I-5, Stevens Pass East/West rail line, etc.
- Waterways (2): Columbia and Snake Rivers, Strait of Juan de Fuca & Puget Sound
- Cargo airports (2) in Western and Eastern Washington
- Pipelines (1): the network of all major pipelines in the state of Washington

The US DOT workshop was an exception. Because its scope spanned all 48 contiguous states of the US, no specific infrastructure segments were evaluated. Instead, the workshop evaluated three categories of infrastructure segments. The *gateways* include points of entry and exit from the US; the *corridors* include major highways, rail lines, waterways, and pipelines; and the *connectors* include local roads and freight connectors, short-line rail, and intermodal facilities.

Evaluation Mechanism

All workshops used some form of voting to collect the participants' assessments of the usefulness of various infrastructure segments. All FFF workshops (except the Minnesota DOT workshop that used scenarios for visioning) used veto votes to indicate the segments that should *not* be invested in. Each workshop participant was forced to veto at least one and up to three segments in each workshop. This was done to enforce the idea that strategy "renders choices about what not to do as important as choices about what to do."[6] In each voting session, the workshop participants first decided their votes individually, then placed the votes publicly on a voting sheet, and then discussed the rationale for the vote.

Scenarios

Four of the six workshops used all four FFF scenarios. The workshops at Port of Long Beach and Georgia DOT each used three because of the smaller number of participants vs. the design intention of having between 10 and 15 participants deliberate each scenario. The scenario omitted for each workshop was the one considered least relevant to the host agency: *Millions of Markets* at Port of Long Beach and *Global Marketplace* at Georgia DOT.

Debrief

Each workshop ended with a debrief session with all participants. Some workshops (such as the WSDOT workshop) also included a debrief session only for the members of the planning organization. This allowed the planners to delve deeper into the results and to understand infrastructure segment evaluations in light of the workshop participants' comments. Such qualitative input is helpful for understanding the rationale for the vote and can be useful to planning agencies when they prepare project funding requests.

Exploration of FFF Scenarios at WSDOT (Steps 1, 2)

The exploration of FFF scenarios started before the day of the workshop itself.

Pre-workshop Scenario Exploration

Once the participants in a workshop were confirmed, each one received an emailed document describing the purpose of the workshop and the list of infrastructure segments to be evaluated (along with their descriptions). The participants were asked to evaluate, using a web-based questionnaire, whether each segment required investment, by considering their estimates of the demands placed on it over the next 30 years. At this initial evaluation, the participants had not yet seen the scenarios. Simultaneously, the MIT team and the planning agency assigned the participants to different groups, ensuring that each scenario had between 10 and 15 participants. Once a participant completed the pre-workshop evaluations of the infrastructure segments, they were emailed the booklet for their assigned scenario along with a one-page description of the scenario planning methodology. Each participant was asked to read and understand their scenario and come prepared to discuss it at the workshop.

Participants' evaluations of infrastructure segments before reading the scenario (i.e., the pre-scenario evaluations) were used as a baseline to compare with the post-scenario evaluations later to assess the effect of scenarios on their recommendations.

Scenario Exploration During the Workshop

The in-person workshop began with a briefing to all participants about its purpose and an overview of infrastructure segments to evaluate, followed by a presentation by the lead facilitator of the MIT CTL team. The facilitator introduced the scenario planning methodology, shared several examples of the difficulty of long-term predictions, and explained how scenarios would be used in the workshop. Subsequently, participants were grouped according to their assigned scenarios.

The WSDOT workshop featured four break-out groups each assigned to one of the four FFF scenarios. The facilitator of each break-out group asked the group's participants—seated in a U-shaped layout to face each other and the facilitator—to describe the scenario they had read. The facilitator went around the room, asking all participants to share their understanding of the scenario and making sure that the key attributes of the scenario were pointed out. After about 20 minutes, when most of the important features of the scenario were highlighted, the facilitator showed the five-minute video of the newscast in that scenario. After watching the video with the group, the facilitator asked if the group had missed any key points and continued the discussion to ensure that the participants thoroughly understood their assigned scenario.

Following this immersion exercise, the participants were asked to identify the implications of the scenario for the freight environment being considered in the workshop. This session aimed to get the participants to draw implications of their scenario for freight in terms of the five local factors: sourcing, destination, routing, volume, and value density. During the discussions of scenario features and implications, the facilitator emphasized that the participants should act as if the scenario had materialized and they were "living" in that world.

Envisioning and Evaluating Infrastructure Investments at WSDOT (Step 3)

Building on the understanding of the scenario's implications, the facilitator continued the previous session by having the participants *evaluate* the workshop's infrastructure segments for usefulness in their scenario. Thus, for each infrastructure segment, the participants argued if an investment in the segment should be made now to prepare for the future scenario discussed by the group.

Participants decided their vote individually and then revealed it by placing poker chips on appropriate squares of a voting sheet representing the infrastructure segments. The workshops asked for two types of votes: positive points to indicate preferences for investing in a segment (with more points indicating a greater need for investing), and vetoes to indicate that investing in a segment would be a waste of resources.

The facilitator tallied the vote, which then led to further discussions of the rationale behind the vote. The infrastructure segments prioritized for this discussion were those receiving a large sum of investment points and vetoes (strong divergent opinions), followed by those receiving a large sum of points (strong consensus of support), those heavily vetoed (strong consensus of rejection), and those receiving few investment points or vetoes (weak support or rejection potentially caused by uncertainty). The participants were allowed to change their vote after discussing the rationale behind different participants' votes. The facilitator tallied the final investment points and vetoes for each infrastructure segment to summarize the group's investment evaluations.

Figure 7.2 presents the evaluation of 16 infrastructure segments to prepare for *One World Order* in the WSDOT workshop. The darker vertical bars with positive values in the figure present the fraction of investment points received by the corresponding segment; the lighter bars with negative values represent

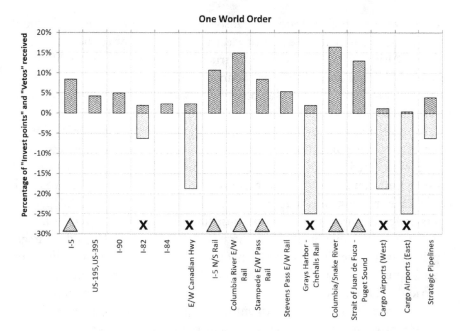

Fig. 7.2 Evaluation of infrastructure segments for *One World Order* in WSDOT workshop

the fraction of vetoes. Triangles and crosses next to the segment names at the bottom of the chart indicate if the segment was highly favored or disfavored, respectively, in the scenario. The absence of either symbol indicates an absence of a clear preference.

One World Order presents a highly regulated world marked by high global trade but low or restricted resource availability. The group allocated a total of 1,310 investment points and 16 vetoes. The vote shows that Columbia/Snake River Waterway, Columbia River East/West Rail, Juan de Fuca/Puget Sound Waterway, I-5 highway, I-5 North/South Rail, and Stampede Pass East/West Rail are clear favorites for investment in preparation for *One World Order*. On the other hand, Cargo Airports in the East and West of the state, Grays Harbor/Chehalis Rai, East/West Canadian Highways, and I-82 were clearly unfavorable for investment under this scenario.

The rationale for this is fairly straightforward. *One World Order* is severely resource-constrained, has high and volatile energy costs, and has a very high awareness of environmental sustainability. As a result, the participants favored investing in energy-efficient modes of transportation such as rail and water transport. However, the group also voted to invest in I-5 North/South Highway. This is a major artery in the state of Washington, and the participants believed that it needed expansion even though road transport is not the most energy-efficient mode of transportation. However, this mode could be energy-efficient with the use of electric trucks and other non-polluting vehicles. Although electric heavy-duty trucks were not available in 2010, the scenario approach helped the participants to unshackle themselves from the present-day reality and assess the long-term investment by remaining open to future possibilities.

The evaluations in each scenario were followed by a *visioning* session in which the participants were asked to identify a primary and a secondary corridor—formed by joining different segments of the infrastructure—of greatest importance for their scenario, and to envision initiatives WSDOT could take to improve freight flow along those corridors. The participants concluded that the corridor consisting of Columbia River East/West Rail Lines, Columbia/Snake River Strategic Waterways, I-84, and Strategic Pipelines would be the most vital in *One World Order*. They identified the most important initiatives for success in *One World Order*: improvement of railroad operations and infrastructure, creation and/or improvement of port-barge-rail connectors, and investment in dredging and building locks. Again, these initiatives focused on energy-efficient modes of transport.

Cross-Scenario Analysis of WSDOT Infrastructure Investments (Step 4)

After each group had fully discussed its scenario and its recommended investments, all workshop participants reconvened for cross-scenario analysis. The session began with a video of each scenario, followed by the group's presentation of their evaluation of infrastructure segments in that scenario. The presenters also described the rationale for their group's votes and discussed it with the other participants. The session repeated the video-presentation-discussion cycle for all scenarios used in the workshop. This is the first time all participants had a chance to learn about the other scenarios.

The workshop facilitator concluded this part by showing a slide juxtaposing the evaluations of segments in all four scenarios. Figure 7.3 presents the cross-scenario comparison for the WSDOT workshop. The darker vertical bars with positive values show the fraction of investment points received by each segment in different scenarios in the following order: *Global Marketplace*, *Millions of Markets*, *Naftástique!*, and *One World Order*. The lighter colored bars of negative depths show the fractions of vetoes received by the segments in the respective scenarios. The icons at the bottom show the net evaluation of segments as being highly useful (triangles), highly wasteful (crosses), or of uncertain utility (circles) in the four scenarios. This graphical

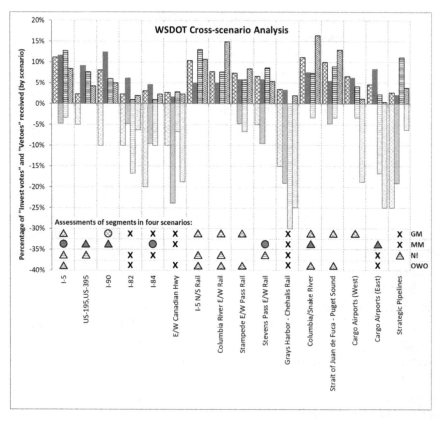

Fig. 7.3 Cross-scenario evaluation of infrastructure segments in the WSDOT workshop

presentation facilitates the discussion of robust and contingent investments. Using Fig. 7.3, the segments can be classified as follows:

- No brainer (robust; useful in all scenarios): I-5 (the utility in scenario *Millions of Markets* is somewhat uncertain but largely positive)
- No regret (robust; useful in some scenarios, wasteful in none): I-5 North/South Rail, Columbia River East/West Rail, Columbia/Snake River, Juan de Fuca/Puget Sound, US-195 & US-395, and Stampede Pass East/West Rail. Also, potentially I-90 and Stevens Pass East/West Rail
- No gainer (robust; useful in none): Grays Harbor/Chehalis Rail, I-82, East/West Canadian Highways, and potentially I-84
- Contingent (useful in some, wasteful in some): Cargo Airports (West), Cargo Airports (East), and Strategic Pipelines.

Incorporating Workshop Feedback into Traditional Planning Processes

Each transportation planning agency typically has well-established processes targeting different planning horizons. The output of a scenario planning workshop should be incorporated into these processes. For example, state DOTs in the US develop statewide transportation improvement programs (STIPs) based on the transportation improvement programs developed by the separate city and regional jurisdictions in the state. These typically span four years and designate funding for specific investments in the transportation infrastructure. State DOTs also create long-range statewide transportation plans (LRSTPs) that span 20 years and define future goals, strategies, and projects for the state's transportation infrastructure. The FFF workshops' recommendations would feed into the LRSTP plans created at the state and regional levels.

The three scenario applications in this chapter demonstrate how scenarios and scenario planning can be deployed as cognitive and strategic decision-making tools to help organizations make sense of and prepare for the changing business environment. Immersion in a scenario allows supply chain executives and managers to think about how their systems may need to adapt to potential long-term changes in the business environment. The use of scenarios for decision-making enables envisioning supply chain capabilities that may not seem useful in the existing business conditions but can be critical in a future scenario.

Notes

1. See OECD publication "Industrial Water Pricing in OECD Countries" published by OECD's Working Party on Economic and Environmental Policy Integration.
2. OECD. 1999. *Industrial Water Pricing in OECD Countries* (p. 55).
3. See webpage on Waterfund website: http://worldswaterfund.com/water-cost-index-overview.html
4. https://store.mintel.com/us-beer-market-report.
5. Detailed descriptions of all workshops and their results are available in the following document, which is also the basis for the material in this section: Caplice, C., Phadnis, S. 2013. *Strategic Issues Facing Transportation: Scenario Planning for Freight Transportation Infrastructure Investment.* Washington, DC: Transportation Research Board.
6. Porter, M. 1996. "What Is Strategy?" *Harvard Business Review,* 74(6), 61–78 (p. 77).

8

Learning from Scenario Applications

Just as fables of animals teach us important life lessons, scenario planning encapsulates exercises in foresight and organizational learning in stories about fictional futures. Unlike fables, though, scenario planning projects require extensive effort. Therefore, a natural question is about its consequence: *does it work?*

Answering whether a scenario planning initiative (or any strategic management intervention, for that matter) "worked" is not easy. At the very least, evaluation of its outcomes must wait several years or decades—the length of the planning horizon. Even after the outcome is known, assigning the cause is not possible—that a particular organization succeeded because it practiced scenario planning and not due to some other factors such as smart leaders, other strategy processes used by the organization, or just plain luck. Conducting systematic, double-blind scientific experiments, in which some organizations are assigned to the "treatment group" (i.e., scenario practitioners) and others to the "control group" is not feasible.

Despite more than half a century of its use in numerous long-range planning projects in business firms and government agencies, the evidence of the effectiveness of scenario planning has remained largely anecdotal. The three cases presented in this book could become additional feathers in scenario planning's heavily adorned cap of such accounts. In that sense, they aim to provide some objective evidence of the effects of scenario planning on organizational learning, managerial judgment, and strategic choices. The MIT CTL

S. S. Phadnis et al., *Strategic Planning for Dynamic Supply Chains*, Palgrave Executive Essentials, https://doi.org/10.1007/978-3-030-91810-1_8

team also has drawn some conclusions regarding how scenario interventions may be evaluated systematically.

Evaluation of a Scenario Planning Application

The opening chapter highlighted three challenges prevalent in strategic planning in supply chains: a difficult decision-making context, operational focus of organizations, and inadequacy of operational planning methods for making strategic decisions. Scenario planning was introduced as a method to facilitate long-range planning by simplifying the complexity of the supply chain decision context and distilling its major uncertainties across multiple scenarios. To assess whether this approach was effective, or to answer whether a scenario planning initiative worked, one needs to check whether the initiative achieved its objective. Given its use as an aid for organizational thinking and decision-making, the effectiveness of a scenario planning initiative can be assessed by answering the following two questions:

- Did the use of scenarios change the perspective of its users about the decision context covered in the scenarios?
- After using the scenarios, did the decision makers change their judgment of any strategic decisions or propose any new initiatives in the context covered in the scenarios?

The questions are rather straightforward; answering them, however, is not.

Difficulty in Evaluating Scenario Planning

Assessing whether an organizational initiative has changed its practitioners' thinking is fraught with challenges. First, companies seldom keep records of what their managers know or anticipate, or how they evaluate specific issues at any given time. Thus, there exists no documented basis for comparing participants' thinking from one period to another. Second, in place of such records, one may choose to ask the decision makers whether the scenario initiative influenced their thinking. Such evidence is sometimes found in publications describing scenario planning initiatives. However, the objectivity of such evidence is questionable because individuals' assessments are severely affected by cognitive biases.

For instance, hindsight bias causes people to mistakenly believe that what they know in the present was obvious to them in the past. It also leads individuals to underestimate the uncertainty they had experienced in the past.

Thus, decision makers may believe that what they know after participating in a scenario planning initiative was evident to them even before the exercise. In addition, those championing the scenario planning initiative may be deceived by confirmation bias and mistakenly believe that the initiative (they championed) did indeed help them learn something new and change their perspective.

Third, even if any change in the decision makers' perspective before and after the scenario planning exercise was correctly captured, it is difficult to attribute the change solely to the exercise, without ruling out the influence of other events experienced by the organization or other information received by the decision makers while the scenario exercise was underway.

Assessing whether the scenario planning exercise influenced any organizational decisions, or the decision makers' judgment of specific decisions, is hampered by similar challenges. The organization may not possess records of the decision makers' judgment about specific projects, unless it keeps immaculate logs of minutes of its meetings or preserves other forms of communication (e.g., emails, presentations) in which such projects or initiatives are discussed. Such records can help assess the scenario planning initiative. Furthermore, if the records also report the decision makers' rationale behind their judgment, it is easier to check whether any judgment changes were influenced by the particular scenarios used. Yet, keeping such records is infeasible, not least because it can influence what managers are willing to share in an exchange of information and opinions.

Approach for Evaluating Scenario Planning Initiatives

However, not all hope is lost. Scenario planning initiatives can be evaluated using a general three-pronged approach: record information before and after a scenario planning intervention, assess any changes in the information between before and after the intervention, and attribute any changes to scenario planning exercises through systematic design of the study.[1] The approach is summarized in Table 8.1.

In the case of one-time scenario applications, the relevant information should be recorded immediately before and then immediately after the scenario planning intervention. In the case of ongoing application, the relevant information may be collected and recorded multiple times, starting before the method's first use and then either after significant episodes of the scenario use or after important events in the organization or its environment. The kinds of information recorded would depend on the objective of the scenario initiative.

Table 8.1 Approach for evaluating scenario planning initiatives

	Organizational thinking	Organizational decision-making
Recording information	• Mental maps of decision context: Relevant issues, strategic initiatives, and relationships among them (open-ended questions) • Implications and predictions of the issues (structured questionnaire)	• Rating of or recommendation for pursuing predefined strategic initiatives (structured questionnaire) • New strategic initiatives (open-ended questions) • Rationale for the judgment
Assessing change after scenario intervention	• Issues and initiatives added to or dropped from mental maps • Network densities of mental maps • Assessments of impact and future outlook of issues	• Change in rating or recommendation for pursuing predefined strategic initiatives • Additional strategic initiatives proposed or dropped from recommendation
Attributing change to scenario planning initiative	• Compare changes of those participating in the scenario planning initiative to those not participating in the initiative • Collect information immediately before and after scenario intervention	

Evaluating the Effect on Organizational Thinking

When scenario planning is practiced to broaden organizational thinking, the challenge is ascertaining the degree to which the exercise actually influenced the participants' thinking. An effective way of recording "thinking" is through mental maps. To create a mental map of thinking about the decision context targeted in a scenario exercise, the decision maker is asked to describe the context using open-ended questions. The decision context pertains to the organization's business environment addressed in the scenario exercise and related strategic initiatives. Using open-ended questions is essential to ensure that the information collected in the interview comes entirely from the respondent and is not inadvertently supplied through the interviewer's questions or probes. The information thus collected may then be represented using mental maps that depict issues and strategic initiatives as well as relationships among them. The issues and strategic initiatives represent the respondent's *attention* relevant to the decision context. These are the factors the individual is likely to consider in making the decision. On the other hand, connections between them show the respondent's salient *cognitive associations* among the concepts, which describe the respondent's view of their interdependence and may influence the individual's interpretation of different events.

The mental maps may be complemented by asking respondents to assess the implications of different issues (i.e., whether they are opportunities or threats for the company, or how they affect different strategic initiatives of the company) or to predict their future states (i.e., likely to get stronger, weaker, or remain the same). Such information about implications and predictions is captured most effectively using structured questionnaires to represent each respondent's *interpretation* and *future outlook* about the decision context.

Comparing the mental maps created at various points in time would reveal any changes in the individual's thinking. Such changes may occur either in the person's attention or cognitive associations. The ideal way to attribute changes in the mental maps to a scenario planning exercise is to compare the changes observed among the participants of the exercise with non-participants. However, conducting assessments with two sets of employees twice in a short period may not be feasible. Alternatively, mental maps may be developed immediately before and after a scenario planning exercise, so that the scenario user is unlikely to be exposed to any information or issues, other than those discussed in the exercise.

Evaluating the Effect on Strategic Decisions

When scenario planning is used to facilitate decision-making, its effects can be assessed using specific initiatives proposed by the decision makers or their judgment of specific strategic initiatives. Using structured questionnaires, decision makers may be asked to evaluate a particular initiative on a seven-point scale ranging from -3 (strongly negative) to $+3$ (strongly positive). Alternatively, the decision maker could be asked to make a Yes/No recommendation for investing in the initiative and express their level of confidence in that recommendation. Such a quantitative approach is effective for evaluating a predefined set of initiatives. If scenarios are used as idea-generation tools, their evaluation could be based on the quantity, quality, or scope of the envisioned strategic initiatives.

In both cases, it is helpful to ask the decision makers to provide the rationale for their recommendations. This can provide insights into what caused the decision makers to change their assessment of any predefined initiatives or suggest new ones, and help attribute the changes to the scenario intervention or specific scenario used.

Outcomes of Featured Scenario Planning Projects

The outcomes of the three scenario planning projects discussed throughout this book add to the body of anecdotes regarding the impact of scenario planning.

Functional Role: Outcomes for Hoppy Brew

With the help of the scenario planning exercise, Hoppy Brew aimed to answer the question: "Do we have the right supply chain to support the business in this changing environment?" Among the 48 capabilities spanning six functional areas considered in the exercise, eight had been assessed as robust across the three scenarios. Hoppy Brew decided to prioritize its focus on those eight. Two of these capabilities were in the Distribution function: "Efficiently deliver in dense urban areas" and "Efficiently deliver in small lots." As a follow-up to the scenario study, Hoppy Brew launched a new project with the MIT CTL's Megacity Logistics Lab to examine the capabilities to deliver small lots efficiently in dense urban areas. This project was a direct outcome of the scenario planning study, which had highlighted this particular challenge, thereby enabling Hoppy Brew to focus on it, from a collection of a few dozen examined using the scenarios.

Business Model Role: Outcomes for Medford

Medford's objective for conducting scenario planning was to facilitate organizational learning among the senior executives of its pharmaceutical distribution business. The exercise involved 24 senior distribution executives in the team. Although the project team did not have an opportunity to assess any changes in the executives' thinking *after* the use of scenarios, the ongoing process of scenario creation provided several learning opportunities. Two notable examples of learning in the Medford project centered on individual reflections on the exercise and observed patterns of aggregate perception of the executive team.

Breaking from Operational Focus to Think About Long-Term Issues

Medford's executives noted that the interviews conducted to capture individual perceptions of the business environment and preferred strategic choices helped them break free from their operational focus and think about long-term issues. However, several participants admitted that this was not an easy exercise for them, and it had pushed them to think about issues they did not usually consider. The interviews to document the executives' perceptions of Medford's future business environment and strategies were followed by a short survey to find out if the interview itself facilitated learning (i.e., made you think differently, made you think about new things, etc.). A majority of the executives responded, and two out of three noted that just the one-hour, open-ended interview itself had been a good learning experience, and suggested continuing the discussion. Admittedly, these quotes should be taken with a grain of salt because of the potential influence of cognitive biases mentioned earlier. An element of "virtue signaling" or, in this case, reluctance to say that a management-directed activity was a waste of time, may also be present. With these caveats in mind, some of the quotes received from executives participating in this exercise were as follows:

"[It's] easy to get caught up in what impacts my operation daily and I don't spend enough time following market drivers and analyzing their potential impact in the future. The conversation prompted some strategic thinking on my part."

"It made me think about a long-term strategy for the company. We typically think about 12–18 months out—this made me focus on longer term."

"Yes, it did make me think about things… It's a good starting exercise, but I do think it would be worth further discussion."

Some of the comments also highlighted the difficulty created by the operational focus of their jobs when the executives thought about the long-term issues.

"There was sufficient time for our discussion, but not enough for me to have given proper 'soak' time to think through the questions posed."

"Due to my schedule, I didn't have a ton of time to put some extra thought prior to the call, which is my fault."

Such comments reveal how the grip of operational focus can restrict strategic thinking, and Medford's executives are by no means an exception. Most senior supply chain executives face competing demands and time pressures that challenge long-term strategizing, which requires them to not only take time away from the constant barrage of operational issues but also switch mental gears from short-term issues to long-term concerns.

Focus on Threats but Optimistic Outlook

After validating the mental maps, the MIT CTL researchers collected Medford's executives' assessments of the impact and future outlook of the 32 key local factors using a structured questionnaire.[2] The factors were described in statements such as "Drug prices will become more transparent due to regulation," "There will be only very few regional distributors," "There will be more generic alternatives to patented drugs," and so on. For each factor, the executives answered two multiple-choice questions individually:

- What effect would the factor have on Medford? (Answer choices: Hurt extremely, Hurt somewhat, Neutral, Benefit somewhat, and Benefit extremely)
- How strongly do you agree that the factor would materialize as described, in the next five years? (Answer choices: Strongly disagree, Disagree, Neutral, Agree, and Strongly Agree)

Each factor in this questionnaire had been obtained from one or more executives' validated interviews and, thus, could be traced back to the specific executive(s). Knowing the impact and likelihood of each local factor as perceived by each executive, and knowing which of the 32 factors were mentioned by an executive and which were not, helped understand the issues the executives focused on and how they perceived the future defined by those issues. Data from over 600 assessments of impact and likelihood showed three statistically significant patterns.

First, the likelihood of an executive rating a factor as having an "Extreme" impact on Medford (either positive or negative) was 0.40 (on a 0–1 scale, with 1 representing certainty) if the factor was mentioned in the executive's description of the future, and 0.31 if it was not. This suggested that, on average, the executives' future outlook was defined by disproportionately more factors that they considered to have an extreme impact on the company, and may overlook the factors they assumed to be less relevant.

Second, the likelihood that an executive would consider a factor as having a negative impact (either "extreme" or "somewhat") on Medford was 0.51 if the factor was included in the executive's description of the future, and only 0.40 if it was not. Thus, before using scenarios, the executives were likely to pay disproportionately more attention to factors they considered as threats to Medford. As a result, their preferred supply chain strategies, influenced by aspects of the business environment they paid attention to, were likely to be defensive or focused on threat mitigation more than what would be rationally justified.

Third, Medford's executives were optimistic despite such preoccupation with threats. Their average estimate of likelihood of negative factors to materialize in the next five years was 0.64 vs. 0.79 for the ones they considered positive. Similarly, the fractions of factors they considered unlikely to materialize over the same period were 0.24 for the negative factors and 0.12 for the positive ones.

These results were eye-opening for Medford's executives. It was the first time they had seen not only their individual strategic thinking mapped but also the systematic biases in their thinking about strategic issues affecting pharmaceutical supply chains.

Time constraints prevented a repeat of the mental-mapping exercise after Medford's executives used the scenarios. Such an exercise would have helped detect changes in the executives' strategic thinking as an indication of the scenarios' influence. The initial exercise was still helpful in documenting the nature of strategic thinking of operations executives.[3]

Of the three results, the first may be fairly common. Business executives, pressed for time, are likely to focus their attention on aspects they consider to be highly impactful for the firm. It is unclear if the second result is peculiar to Medford, a company in a cost-competitive business, or an industry riddled with high uncertainty about different aspects of the business environment and subject to regulatory attention. The opposite—i.e., disproportionately more focus on positive aspects of business environment—may characterize start-ups or firms in rapidly growing industries. Finally, the third result could be an attribute of executives in a company succeeding in a highly competitive industry, or of senior executives in general. Psychological research shows that optimism is associated with strategies that seek to reduce or eliminate challenges imposed on organizations by their environments. An optimistic disposition may have helped Medford's executives reach their current positions by successfully navigating companies they worked for through organizational challenges in their careers.

Infrastructural Role: Outcomes in Future Freight Flows (FFF)

The effects of scenario planning on managerial thinking and strategic decisions were also tested in the FFF project.[4] The FFF workshops were an exceptional context for such an assessment as all participants in each workshop were invited because of their expertise and knowledge regarding the region's freight infrastructure needs. They were asked to evaluate real invest-ments in infrastructure segments and knew that their input would influence those investment decisions. Such workshops were also somewhat familiar settings to participants; transportation planning agencies in the US often hold workshops to seek input from different stakeholders to inform the policy and investment decisions.

Before each FFF workshop, each participant completed a questionnaire individually to evaluate the infrastructure investments considered in that workshop. These assessments reflected their present perceptions about the region's freight environment. Each participant then completed the same ques-tionnaire twice again, individually, at two other points during the exercise. A comparison of these evaluation enables examination of the effect of scenarios on their judgment.

Expert Judgment Changes After Participating in a Scenario Planning Workshop

Changes in participants' evaluations of different infrastructure segments were tested in two workshops conducted at the Washington State Department of Transportation (WSDOT) and Port of Long Beach (POLB). Through a ques-tionnaire, each participant was asked to make a two-part evaluation for each infrastructure segment: whether the planning agency should invest in that segment (Yes/No) and their confidence level in their recommendation. The evaluations were completed less than one week before the workshop, during the workshop after the single-scenario evaluation (to test effects of single-scenario evaluation), and one week after the workshop (to test effects of the scenario planning workshop/multi-scenario evaluation).

The WSDOT workshop included 343 data samples in which a partic-ular infrastructure was evaluated by the same participant before and after the workshop (i.e., after seeing all scenarios). In 189 of them (55.1%), the participants changed their judgment, either by switching their yes/no investment recommendation or by changing their confidence in that recom-mendation. Similarly, the POLB workshop yielded 285 instances in which an infrastructure segment was evaluated by the same participant before and after the workshop. Here too, a large majority (198 or 69.5% of instances) of participants changed their judgments. The greater proportion of changes in POLB than WSDOT could be because confidence was measured on a finer seven-point scale in POLB, as opposed to a four-point scale in WSDOT. This evidence of the influence of scenarios on judgments of experts is noteworthy. However, this is only a minor part of the story.

Changes in Expert Judgment Were Systematic and Could Be Traced Back to the Scenarios Used

Even more remarkable is how the changes in experts' judgments related to the scenarios they used in the single-scenario evaluation. To study this, the participants' pre-workshop evaluations were compared with those completed immediately after single-scenario evaluation. Figure 8.1 summarizes the results from the WSDOT and POLB workshops.

The WSDOT workshop produced 433 instances in which a participant evaluated a segment in both pre-workshop and post-single-scenario evaluations. The latter was conducted during the workshop and had more responses than the aforementioned post-workshop analysis, which had 343 data samples with matching pre-workshop evaluations. In 248 of them (57.3%), the experts changed their judgments. Among them, if a particular segment was found useful for the assessed scenario (based on the votes received in scenario evaluation), the participants were more likely to become favorable to investment in it (54 out of 86; 62.8%). This was shown by either switching their recommendation to invest from "No" to "Yes," keeping their recommendation as "No" but lowering the confidence in their opposition to it, or maintaining their recommendation as "Yes" and increasing their confidence in this endorsement. Similarly, the participants were more likely to become less favorable (44 out of 64; 68.8%) to investing in segments deemed wasteful for the scenario used. There was also a tendency to become less favorable to investment in segments that could not be clearly identified as either useful or wasteful in the scenario used (59 out of 98; 59.2%).

The POLB workshop showed similar results for the 404 samples in which the same participant evaluated a segment in pre-workshop and after single-scenario evaluations. Judgments changed in 288 of them (71.3%). Among them, the participants were more likely to become favorable to investment

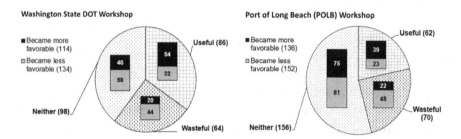

Fig. 8.1 Changes in expert judgment after single-scenario evaluation (Adapted from: Phadnis, et al. [2015] Effect of Scenario Planning on Field Experts' Judgment of Long-Range Investment Decisions. *Strategic Management Journal, 36*[9], 1401–1411)

in the segments found useful (39 out of 62; 62.9%) and less favorable to investment in the segments found wasteful (48 out of 70; 68.6%) for the scenario they used. There were no systematic tendencies to become more or less favorable to investments in segments that could not be clearly identified as useful or wasteful in the scenario (81 out of 156, or 51.9%, became less favorable but the difference was not statistically significant).

Experts Prefer More Flexible Options After Multi-Scenario Evaluation

Another question is whether scenario-induced changes were limited to judgments about long-term investments, or do they also affect the manner in which strategies get implemented? This question was tested in the FFF workshop in Washington, DC in June 2011. The participants were asked to recommend the best option for implementing investments in 13 types of infrastructure segments (such as border crossings with Canada and Mexico, road and rail corridors to population centers, intermodal connections) among the four generic options listed below. They range from the least to the most flexible:

- OPTION 1: Identify specific regions and projects where investments should be made, allocate funds, and start implementing the projects.
- OPTION 2: Identify specific regions and projects where investments should be made and allocate funds to the projects, BUT DO NOT START IMPLEMENTING them.
- OPTION 3: Identify specific regions where investments should be made and allocate funds to those regions, BUT DO NOT ALLOCATE FUNDS TO PROJECTS.
- OPTION 4: Allocate funds to this segment, but do not allocate funds to individual regions within the segment.

The 13 segments were evaluated by 27 expert participants in both pre-workshop and post-workshop assessments for a total of 351 samples of before-and-after data on the segment evaluations. Figure 8.2 presents the distribution of the vote among the four options before and after participation in the scenario planning workshop. Before the workshop, a majority of the participants (229 out of 351; 65.2%) recommended Option 1, which is the least flexible. One possible reason for such a strong expression of urgency could be the widely perceived deteriorating quality of the US transportation

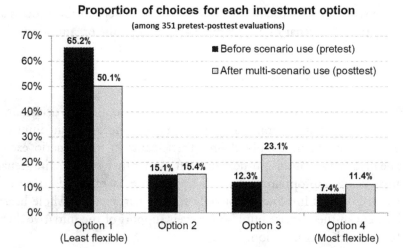

Fig. 8.2 Preferences for four options for implementing infrastructure investments (Adapted from: Phadnis, et al. [2015] Effect of Scenario Planning on Field Experts' Judgment of Long-Range Investment Decisions. *Strategic Management Journal, 36*[9], 1401–1411)

infrastructure.[5] After participating in the workshop, Option 1 was recommended in only half of the evaluations (176 out of 351; 50.1%), indicating a significant drop in the tendency to prefer the least flexible implementation of long-term infrastructure investments. Moreover, the preference for a more flexible option (Option 3) increased from 12.3% (43 out of 351) before the workshop to 23.1% (81 out of 351) after.

Ensuring Success of a Scenario Planning Initiative

A scenario planning initiative is unlike typical projects undertaken in supply chain management. In contrast to projects such as installation of new equipment, implementation of an IT system, signing of a contract with a supplier, building of a new logistics facility, or expansion of a highway, the critical outcome of a scenario project—scenarios created, strategies contemplated or implemented—cannot be tested easily using an objective quality standard. This could impede the acceptance of scenarios by supply chain executives, managers, and associates, who may expect to assess the quality of a product or process with concrete metrics. The "proof" of a scenario intervention's quality is in the practice of scenario creation and application. Besides using a theoretically sound process, such as the one presented in Chapters 4 and 5, the following six factors are useful for "selling" different steps in this process and to ensure that the scenarios are accepted and used by the organization.

Start with a Clear Definition of Purpose

Scenarios are used to provide *foresight* to make long-term decisions, as opposed to the *forecasts* commonly used for making short- and medium-term decisions for managing supply chains. Participants in the scenario exercise must be made aware of this purpose upfront so that they evaluate the scenario initiative using appropriate criteria (i.e., learning as opposed to accurate prediction). This is important not only for the participants' whole-hearted involvement in the exercise but also for their support of the initiative during its practice in the organization.

Involve Supply Chain Executives in Scenario Creation from the Beginning

The involvement of executives and senior managers from the supply chain and related functions from the inception of the scenario exercise is vital. This begins with the interviews that explore the business environment relevant for the scenario study. Their involvement ensures that the scenarios address the issues that are deemed relevant by the organizational leaders. The organizational leaders should also be involved in assessing the implications of various driving forces and local factors for scenario creation. Often, such organizational members are the only reliable sources for assessing the effect of different local factors on the organization. Their participation ensures that scenarios are constructed by considering the most relevant factors of the environment.

Failure to involve appropriate executives and managers in scenario creation could result in the scenarios being rejected as irrelevant because they either fail to include the issues considered pertinent by the organization or because the impact of various local factors on the organization is misunderstood.

Refer to Authoritative Sources During the Scenario Creation Process

Scenarios describe multiple future states, most of which are unlikely to resemble the contemporary business environment. The only way to justify such scenarios is through logical arguments about their plausibility, based on credible, existing information collected through expert opinions, reports of current operating conditions, or predictions from market research reports. This information forms the foundation on which the fictional futures (i.e., scenarios) stand. For the scenarios to be considered plausible, this foundational information needs to be considered reliable by the scenario users. If the sources are considered suspect, the scenarios are less likely to be believed or used by the intended users.

The second source of authority relates to the facilitators guiding scenario creation. Several choices and steps in the scenario creation process—such as the data sources used to inform scenario content, the assessment of uncertainty, or the selection of scenario logic—are influenced by the judgment and advice of the facilitators guiding the scenario creation. Despite the growing theoretical basis for scenario creation,[6] such steps do not typically have clear right and wrong options. If organizational members involved in scenario creation do not agree about the resolution of specific steps, mediation by experienced facilitators can prevent stalling of the scenario project, even if the ultimate choices shaping the scenario content are not enthusiastically endorsed by all organizational members.

Note that deference to authoritative sources is not the same as "appeal to authority," which is a logical fallacy in which the only proof offered for a claim is an expert's opinion. The structured process to guide scenario creation, as presented in this book, requires gathering information from a broad range of authoritative sources to avoid this logical fallacy. The process defers to experienced facilitators only when the scenario project risks stalling and no logical way to break the deadlock exists.

Involve the Scenario Project Team in Finalizing the Scenario Logic and Content

In addition to their involvement at the beginning of scenario creation, organizational leaders must be involved in choosing the scenario logic and defining the scenario structure. This is done to ensure that the executives and managers involved have an opportunity to deliberate different choices about scenario structure, understand their pros and cons, and appreciate the choices made that influence the scenario content. This helps gain their acceptance of the scenarios and subsequently promotes the use of scenarios among their subordinates.

Characterize Unofficial Future as One of the Scenarios

Most executives have a tacit view of the future environment of their organization. If the supply chain executives at an organization come from a fairly homogenous background, their individual visions of the long-term future may share several common elements. These commonly held beliefs about the future business environment constitute the group's "presumed future scenario." This vision can be identified from the interviews of the organizational leaders. It is helpful to include this vision as one of the scenarios. First and foremost, it is one of the plausible future environments and hence constitutes a legitimate scenario. Furthermore, it is also the most likely scenario in the minds of the supply chain executives. Therefore, not recognizing the unofficial future in any scenario can lead the executives to question the entire set of scenarios and reject them as works of fiction.

However, there is a downside to describing the unofficial future in one scenario. Such a scenario may become a magnet, leading the executives to disregard the remaining scenarios as less likely to occur. To counter this, the scenario facilitators need to emphasize that all scenarios should be considered equally likely when used for organizational learning or strategic decision-making. The focus is on "what if" thinking in scenario planning, not on "what will."

Measure Effects of Scenario Intervention

Measuring the effects of a scenario intervention is useful, although not essential, to ensure the success of a scenario planning initiative. An organization planning to embark on a scenario planning initiative may appreciate the difficulty in doing so for the reasons mentioned earlier in this chapter. However, systematically measuring and demonstrating any changes in judgment or decisions as a result of scenario intervention can provide concrete evidence about the practice's effectiveness. This can be especially helpful to get operationally focused managers and executives to gain confidence in ongoing scenario planning practices and resort to their regular use to think about the long-term business environment.

To conclude, it is important to recognize that scenario planning is a method to facilitate organizational learning and foresight, which can be used to navigate structural changes in the business environment. It is not a forecasting technique. The creation and application of scenarios is a resource-extensive exercise, as evident from the examples given in this book. The approach for evaluating a scenario planning initiative presented in this chapter describes how organizations can measure the effectiveness of such an extensive intervention. This can be particularly helpful if scenario planning is used for applications in strategic supply chain management, where the scenario users may be heavily involved in day-to-day operations and be accustomed to using quantitative performance metrics in their operational duties. Managers may be more willing to cogitate long-term issues facing the organization and to prepare for seemingly unpredictable shifts in its environment using scenario planning if they see measurable improvements in their strategic thinking by using this method.

Notes

1. An excellent reference for designing such quasi-experiments is Campbell, D., Stanley, J. 1963. *Experimental and Quasi-experimental Designs for Research*. Chicago: Rand McNally.
2. Phadnis, S., Sheffi, S., Caplice, C., Singh, M. 2017. "Strategic Cognition of Operations Executives." *Production and Operations Management*, 26(12), 2323–2337.
3. Theoretical lessons from the Medford study were tested in a survey and published in Phadnis, et al. op. cit.
4. Phadnis, S., Caplice, C., Sheffi, Y., Singh, M. 2015. "Effect of Scenario Planning on Field Experts' Judgment of Long-Range Investment Decisions." *Strategic Management Journal*, 36(9), 1401–1411.
5. Infrastructure Report Card by the American Society of Civil Engineers (ASCE): https://www.infrastructurereportcard.org/.
6. For example: Wright, et al. 2013. "Scenario Methodology: New Developments in Theory and Practice—Introduction to Special Issue." *Technological Forecasting & Social Change*, 80, 561–565; Phadnis, et al. 2014. "Axiomatic Foundation and a Structured Process for Developing Firm-Specific Intuitive Logics Scenarios." *Technological Forecasting & Social Change*, 88, 122–139.

9

Appendix

Exhibit 9.1: Hoppy Brew scenario "Brand World" (Circa 2014)

 This is a world marked by extensive resource scarcity. Governments have failed to provide any recourse; not because they do not desire to, but because they cannot agree on what regulations could be helpful. This world is also defined by consumers who appreciate the status recognition they get by associating themselves with major brands—by consuming products of the major brands, following the brands on social media, and wearing merchandise bearing the brand logos. Fortunately, consumers' acceptance of mass-produced items helps cope with the resource-scarce business environment.

The scarcity of earth's resources has become a painful reality. The shift in climate pattern has hurt the production of grains—rice, wheat, barley, corn, to name a few—all over the world. Unpredictable crop yields make it difficult to assure their supply for the production of food and beverages. Compounding this problem for food and beverage producers is that the grains previously used in food sources are now also used for fuel production. The food and beverage producers find themselves competing with large energy firms for their share of grain. This should not have been a complete surprise though: the continuing scarcity of crude oil experienced from the start of the twenty-first

S. S. Phadnis et al., *Strategic Planning for Dynamic Supply Chains*,
Palgrave Executive Essentials,
https://doi.org/10.1007/978-3-030-91810-1_9

century meant that it was only a matter of time before energy firms started looking at other natural sources all over the world to produce fuel. However, no other natural resource is as painfully constrained as the one most abundant on this planet—water! It's not that the amount of water has suddenly diminished, it is the extreme and unpredictable fluctuations in the availability of water—the unprecedented juxtaposition of the bouts of draughts and floods in different parts of the world—that makes usable water scarce. In the hindsight, this was inevitable as twenty-first century governments failed to invest in the infrastructure to harvest groundwater aquifers or in the construction of large dams.

If anyone thought that the governments had fallen to the most abject levels of ineptitude possible 10 years ago, things are worse. Bickering between governments of different countries as well as fights among political parties within countries have reached a point where almost nothing gets done by governments. Political parties are more interested in adhering adamantly to their ideologies (however baseless they may be in the global world) than compromising even a little to get things done. It is not uncommon for several states within a country to have very different regulations that match the political philosophies of the parties that rule the state. There are even more blatant acts of politicking where the change in power at a state leads to the annulment of some unpopular regulations. The bickering continues at the global level as well. There are no global agreements regarding the taxing of carbon emissions; governments routinely flout the World Trade Organization mandates to provide subsidies to their home industries to win a few political votes in the bitterly divided world. The revelations of intelligence agencies in some countries listening to the private phone and email conversations of leaders of other countries some 10 years ago have destroyed whatever trust was built among groups of countries after World War II.

While resources are scarce, failure of governmental action means resource scarcity is managed through market mechanisms. This engenders price volatility. Because of the dysfunctional governments, no wide-ranging laws guide the business activity. Instead, laws are made locally to please the local stakeholders without any regard to their global implications.

Consumers in this volatile world appreciate the consistency of taste and experience obtained when consuming or using a particular branded product. While it is the taste or quality that first attracts a consumer to a particular product, what keeps him/her hooked is the brand's code of conducting its business, especially its environmental stewardship, which has become a key brand differentiator in this resource-starved world. Brand-conscious consumers of this world flaunt their loyalty to mega-brands by following the latter on social media, supporting sports teams sponsored by the brands, wearing apparel bearing the brand's name and logo, and so on. The brands associated with global green initiatives are among the "coolest" to follow! Following a brand on social media is a way consumers indicate their appreciation for values the brand espouses—be its low carbon footprint, local production, ethical conduct, organic raw materials, or support of local charities. These intangible attributes make it even harder for competing firms to "steal" consumers away from other brands.

Consumers' preferences for the consistent taste delivered by branded products are often regional. They also prefer environmentally friendly and healthy products. Their choices are stable too. Consumers purchase their food and packaged goods items mainly from large grocery or retail stores. That is the environmentally responsible way to make purchases at an affordable price, which is also important in their purchase decisions.

Exhibit 9.2: Hoppy Brew Scenario "Brew-Nique!" (Circa 2014)

BREW-NiQUE! This is a world where consumers crave individuality in all things—from the food they eat, the beverages they drink, the clothes they wear, to furniture they buy for their homes. Most consumers aspire to be considered unique rather than part of a group, club, or team. While there is strong demand for environmentally sound and healthy products, the desire for extreme differentiation is the most dominant.

Several factors influence consumers' purchase decisions. With the ubiquity of information access enabled by almost universal Internet connectivity and mass adoption of wearable electronics, consumers are able to identify attributes of a product before making a purchase. The product information consumers consider important could be a product's nutritional value or health implications based on scientific studies, or information about the firm, such as its sustainability practices, ethical conduct, parity of employee compensations, and so on.

One factor that does not affect purchase decisions is the brand! No longer is it necessary to use the brand as a proxy for the information that was hard to come by just 10 years ago. Above all, consumers crave individuality: they pick and choose the product that meets their idiosyncratic needs. Mass customization has finally hit its full stride with consumers being able to modify most products they purchase at points of sale, easily and economically, in many cases. For example, each member of a family typically has customized versions of juices, snacks, toothpaste, and several other items. Customization and personalization options range from labeling to packaging to actual product formulations. The use of direct-to-home product delivery has increased dramatically due to this high level of customization.

Interestingly, of the many alcoholic beverages on offer consumption of wine has increased dramatically. This is mainly due to the perception that each vineyard produces a "unique" product. There has been an explosion of niche vineyards—many of which are nothing more than buyers of wine from other vineyards that then blend and re-label with a unique name.

This world is also marked by an extensive scarcity of natural resources such as various crops and water. Businesses are caught between highly demanding consumers and severely constrained resources. If advances in information technology have helped to create the "Me First!" consumer, it is by no means a world of "Me Only!". Consumers care a lot about the environment. What has magnified society's environmental concerns is the global resource scarcity. No other natural resource is as painfully constrained as the one most abundant on this planet—water! It's not that the amount of water has suddenly diminished. Extreme and unpredictable fluctuations in the availability of water (droughts and floods) across the globe have made usable water scarce. The shift in climate patterns has also hurt the production of grains—rice, wheat, barley, and corn, to name a few—all over the world. The unpredictability of yield from year to year makes it very difficult to assure their supply for the production of food and beverages. What does not help either is the adamant resistance of consumers to genetically modified organisms (GMOs) in their food—despite inconclusive scientific evidence of their harm—which could make the crops more drought-resistant and increase their yield.

Governments in most countries and various jurisdictions within countries have taken it upon themselves to "help" businesses navigate this treacherous world by creating a plethora of regulations that guide economic activity. These laws have a significant impact on businesses. Government quotas, rather than market mechanisms, are used to allocate resources to businesses. These allocations can change each year depending on how "efficiently" a particular firm is perceived to have used its resources in the previous year. Shipment of products between regions and countries has become an exceptionally complex process.

Governments also scrutinize new ventures much more closely for their ability to conduct business in a resource-efficient manner before allowing them licenses and permits to start the venture. Each new production facility, transshipment center, and vehicle fleet must pass strict inspection before being put into productive use. Existing assets are inspected frequently with the same rigorous eye.

These supply-side regulatory initiatives are complemented by demand-side mechanisms—excise duties, tariffs, and taxes—to control demand, especially for the products made from and/or delivered using constrained resources. One of the results of this system is the high cost of many items such as out-of-season produce and organic foods. Regulators also harness consumers' choosiness to make sure that firms make appropriate information available to help consumers make their purchase decisions. Routine audits, enabled by IT solutions, help regulators ensure fidelity of the information provided by businesses regarding their products and practices.

Exhibit 9.3: Hoppy Brew scenario "Group-Drink" (Circa 2014)

GROUP DRINK This is a world where experience is more important than the product for most consumers. Consumer purchase decisions are influenced by a variety of factors, but none matter as much as how the product contributes to the social experience in which the consumers intend to use it. Consumer tastes tend to mirror social aspirations. Consumers will go to great lengths to search out specific products that are used by favored movie stars or sports celebrities in order to emulate them. Buying behavior indicates that consumers want to be known for being members of particular groups. Unfortunately, consumers are fickle, and their allegiance to a particular good or brand tends to be short-lived.

Universal Internet connectivity allows consumers to obtain ideas for the product that will provide the experience they are seeking. Consumers will go out of their way to find a specific product or brand. Smart devices and wearables, which are widely adopted, are used to scan the product being considered to determine if other consumers are enjoying the product. Searching for a specific desired experience is common as is the downloading of formulations and recipes of products that can provide such an experience. Product recipes are freely shared in standard formats that can be sent to the custom food and drink producers to replicate the taste. Of course, a consumer can always resort to one of his/her recipes stored on a cloud server. Ultimately what matters to the consumer is the quality of experience they have—either with a bunch of friends at a restaurant or home, or in the solitude of wilderness—when the product was consumed. It is not so much about picking a product in the market that satisfies the individual, but rather creating a product that enriches the occasion.

Just like they have enabled consumers to move from a product-centric world into an experience-centric world, technological advances have also rendered the means to exploit the earth's limited resources much more efficiently. At times, technology has even reversed the resource scarcity. The use of genetically modified organisms (GMOs) in crops allows farmers to get a much higher yield from each hectare of their farm and grow crops that are much more resistant to a variety of diseases. The opposition to GMOs in certain parts of the world—specifically, Europe—has significantly dwindled as consumers realize that the use of GMOs leads to a more sustainable world by allowing humans to extend the productive value of the planet's finite resources. Significant advances in the profitable harvesting of solar and wind energy, complemented by large finds of natural gas in North America, allow for an adequate supply of energy for commercial and personal activities at a reasonable—and stable—price. The actions taken by businesses and individual households for improving the energy efficiency of their facilities, homes, and activities in the last couple of decades have helped as well. Overall, this is a world where technological advances have ensured that lack of resources never becomes a hurdle in meeting the needs of increasingly sophisticated consumers.

The management of water to ensure adequate supply of this vital resource has improved significantly thanks to the diligent efforts of businesses and social enterprises in collaboration with local community groups. Organizations such as the 2030 Water Resources Group have built platforms that allow social entrepreneurs to bring their innovations that improve the efficiency of water use or clean water to potable standards using cheap portable devices, to communities all over the world. Such innovations have become widely available: from more efficient irrigation plans developed from the analysis of local soil conditions and more accurate weather predictions, more efficient processes in water-intensive industries (such as textiles, mining, or meat production), inexpensive advanced leak detection systems in water distribution networks, solar-powered desalination units, to solutions such as Slingshot™ that convert dirty water to potable standard, and many more.

However, the most surprising change in the world over the past decade is not what technological developments have enabled—but it is the change in the regulatory environment across the world. Government agencies have learned to not interfere with the business sector and complicate matters in this technocratic world. They seek to simplify the regulatory environment to support innovation and entrepreneurial activity. They limit their role to ensuring that firms are providing accurate information to the consumers and ensuring that individual freedoms and intellectual property receive full protection. Governments see their job as creating a secure environment for individuals and enterprises to thrive and enabling transparency of individual and business conduct.

Marijuana has become more widely accepted—especially in the US where it is legalized in 40 of the 50 states. Interestingly, the substance has moved away from being a commodity; specialty marijuana brands are being marketed and endorsed by different celebrities. Younger consumers have dramatically increased their use of marijuana over alcohol.

Exhibit 9.4: Medford Scenario "Frenzy" (Circa 2010)

Frenzy

Seven years since the global economic crisis, the US economy has still not rebounded back to the health it enjoyed in 2006–07. The unemployment rate in the US hovers in the high single digits; the financial condition of those employed is not too rosy either. Over the last five years, per capita disposable income has grown by a meager 2% annually.

In addition to failing incomes, families also have to endure high cost of living, primarily led by high energy prices. The socio-political turmoil in the African and Middle East nations that started in 2010 has created an environment of uncertainty not seen since the 1973 oil crisis. This uncertainty drove oil prices higher globally; the US was no exception. The lukewarm US economy has reduced the tax revenue of the federal government. To respond to the rapidly burgeoning budget deficit under the shrinking tax revenues, Congress has resorted to aggressive spending cuts. Medicare and Medicaid budgets have been slashed. Wall Street does not see an optimistic future either; analysts are bearish on the growth of US companies.

In the stagnant US economy, smaller players find it difficult to compete and larger players struggle to grow. This has resulted in the consolidation of businesses in all industries in the healthcare sector. Firms have used horizontal as well as vertical consolidation as a means for growing their revenue. Very few small and regional distributors remain in the industry. They either have exited the business or have been acquired by the distributors. Pharmaceutical companies, struggling to maintain revenues after the patents of their blockbuster drugs expired, bought fledgling biotech companies. Large warehouse pharmacies, which benefit from high economies of scale and scope, have acquired many independent and regional pharmacies that were struggling under the higher costs of capital necessary to compete against the national chains. Large warehouse pharmacies have also increased their foothold in the distribution of drugs from manufacturers to retail stores. Manufacturers and pharmacies have found synergies in connecting directly and sharing demand and inventory information for high-volume drugs in the post-investment-buying, fee-for-service era.

In this stagnant economy, there is strong pressure to reduce the cost of healthcare. To cope with the lowered budget, Medicare and Medicaid have reduced their reimbursement rates. This forces other stakeholders in the healthcare sector to squeeze costs out of their balance sheets. Consolidated hospitals are much bigger and collaborate to exert pricing pressure on manufacturers and distributors. The price discounts received by hospitals regularly exceed 15%, which the GPOs were able to provide in 2010. The manufacturers of branded drugs are spending more money on R&D with the hope of developing new blockbuster drugs to improve their profitability in the long run. After a decline in R&D spending in 2009 due to economic slowdown, pharma R&D spending has steadily increased over the last five years, reaching $150 billion globally in 2014. However, they have not been able to replace the high revenue and high profits brought in by blockbuster drugs, such as Lipitor or Plavix, after their patents expired. This increased R&D spending, coupled with high pricing pressure from the market, has put a serious dent in the manufacturers' short-term profitability. With a significantly higher volume of generics, the distribution fees make up a higher proportion of the total cost of delivering pharmaceuticals. Under the high cost pressure, this has put pressure on the fee-for-service model in pharmaceutical distribution; no alternate model has emerged.

The US population continues to age; the median age today is 37.5 years. About 15% of the 325-plus million Americans are 65 years or older. On its own, the 47 million residents aged 65 years and older would make the US one of the 30 most populous countries in the world, as populous as Spain, or as Canada and Cuba combined! The average US resident is also more health-conscious today than five years ago. S/he is conscious of the food choices and portion sizes at grocery stores and restaurants, stays more physically active, uses nutritional supplements, and undergoes regular medical checkups. This shift has been enabled by multiple factors, such as nutrition programs of grocery stores (such as Safeway's SimpleNutrition program), consumer education programs of pharmacies for chronic disease patients, as well as government policies that encourage spending on preventive care and regulations (such as those requiring chain restaurants to display caloric content under the Affordable Care Act of 2010). The "Patient Education" programs promoted by the American Pharmacists Association are no longer limited to reactive focus on medicines and illnesses; they proactively educate patients about healthier life-styles choices. These have helped create a stronger bond between a patient and his/her pharmacist. This has boosted demand at the remaining, once-struggling independent pharmacies, which leverage their personal connections with patients better than the national chains. Health-conscious consumers value this interaction with their local pharmacists. This pharmacist is often at a mom-and-pop pharmacy or a grocery store where the consumer shops. Grocery chains and independent pharmacies sell a much higher volume of drugs today compared to five years ago. They have captured the market share of warehouse pharmacy chains as well as that of mail-order pharmacies.

US healthcare supply chains have become a lot more complex due to the convergence of many factors. The focus on preventive care through patient education has greatly increased the number of locations where healthcare is provided. Pharmacies and hospitals have set up clinics for routine health checkups and cures for common illnesses. Their omnipresent health-consultation centers provide advice on healthy eating and living choices. "Patient-centered medical homes" are now ubiquitous. Most major retailers and manufacturers have built or acquired internet-based mail-order platforms to ship medicines directly to their consumers. Mail-order has become an attractive channel for acquiring drugs. The weaker economy has also forced retailers to come up with creative solutions to increase sales of medicines. Retailers often have monthly or weekly promotions to drive the sale of generic medicines. Many retailers collaborate with long-term care facilities and deliver medicines to their residents on a regular schedule. While these programs increase demand for retailers, they also generate huge swings in demand for the medicines making supply chain planning more difficult. There is also heightened awareness and focus on the security and safety of medicines. Firms have to take greater care in ensuring that the pharmaceuticals released into the supply chain are safe for consumption. Different states have created a variety of regulations addressing this issue, adding to the complexity of the supply chain. Overall, this increase in the number of care-delivery locations, demand variability, and the number of government regulations have made US supply chains more complex than ever before.

Stemming from the increased awareness in the general population and the policies that encourage preventive care, payers—both public and private—have started to reimburse for health care delivery based on the outcomes, not the treatment. Payers have been developing more sophisticated metrics to measure physician quality. The models for measuring outcomes are not perfect but are viewed as having the potential to improve the effectiveness-to-cost ratio of the US healthcare system and are strongly supported by the government. Healthcare providers have begun to shift to providing care that is team-based, preventive, and comprehensive, rather than one-on-one, fee-for-service, or managed. Payers encourage consumers to use these facilities, as preventive care is more cost-effective in the long run.

Fortunately, there is an abundance of healthcare workers in the US to cater to this aging and health-conscious nation. Because of cuts to Medicare and Medicaid benefits, many aging workers have postponed their retirements and many retired workers are working part-time to get health benefits. Pharmacists are one such group. According to the Pharmacy Manpower Project, over 90% of all licensed pharmacists are actively practicing pharmacy; a significant increase from 86% in 2004. There is no longer a shortage of nurses either. The number of first-time US-educated nurses has continued to grow at a little over 7% annually for the last 15 years since 2000. Because of this steady supply of US-educated nurses, more than 3 million registered nurses work in the US healthcare sector today. This pool of nurses is adequate to meet the need of the aging US population.

The US government is much more active in the healthcare sector today than it was a decade ago. The provisions of the Affordable Care Act of 2010 are fully in place. These include guaranteed insurance coverage regardless of preexisting conditions, a cap on annual deductibles, increased visibility to various insurance policies via health insurance exchanges, Medicaid and subsidized coverage for low-income families, etc. Different states have enacted laws for tracking the pedigree of drugs from manufacturer to consumer to protect patients from contaminated or counterfeit drugs. Different states have adopted laws that suit their interests best, creating a variety of pedigree laws across states. This variation is seen in the method of tracking pedigree (electronic vs. paper), level of serialization (unit doses vs. boxes), the origin of pedigree tracking (manufacturer vs. distributor), etc. Following the lead of the US Drug Enforcement Administration, all 50 states and the District of Columbia now have established Prescription Drug Monitoring Programs (PMP) to prevent illegitimate use of prescription drugs. However, the programs are not uniform across states; different states monitor different schedules of substances, and different parties are eligible to access a patient's prescription drug utilization data.

Generic drugs dominate the market today. This is not a surprise given that pharmaceutical manufacturers did not have many patented drugs in the branded drug pipeline to replace the ones that lost patent in the last five years. Any fears about the quality or safety of generic drugs have been quelled by a deliberate effort by the Food and Drug Administration (FDA) to assure people that generic drugs are held to the same high standards as the branded drugs and that they have the same performance as their branded equivalents. One motivation for the FDA's effort was to encourage providers and patients to rely more on generic drugs as an attempt to reduce the cost of healthcare. The proportion of biologic drugs in the total volume of drugs consumed in the US has not changed much since 2010. The high cost pressure in the US economy has compelled payers to require providers to rely more on low-cost generic drugs and less on biopharmaceuticals, which are much more expensive to make and distribute. A majority of the drugs consumed today consist of the generic versions of traditional, small-molecule pharmaceuticals.

Even though access to and affordability of healthcare has greatly increased due to the Affordable Care Act of 2010, the volume of drugs sold has not increased dramatically. This is primarily due to the increased focus on preventive care and healthier lifestyle choices. The strict enforcement of prescription drug monitoring programs, which typically carry significant fines for violation, has forced physicians to be sparing and careful in writing prescriptions for their patients. This has had a noticeable impact on reducing prescription drug abuse. The 2014 National Survey on Drug Use and Health by the US Department of Health and Human Services reported that the number of US residents 12-years and older reporting the use of psychotherapeutic or pain reliever drugs for nonmedical purposes had fallen to 5.3 million (less than 2% of the population) from a high of 16 million (6.3%) in 2009.

In the last five years, although computational and biological sciences have continued to make theoretical advances, the conversion of scientific discoveries into practicable technologies has been somewhat stagnant. One of the reasons for this has been the weakness of the US economy. Firms have used their limited budgets for maintaining existing assets and capabilities instead of investing in new technologies whose returns are risky in the short run. The same has happened with electronic medical records (EMR). Even though EMR technologies have continued to make advances in the last five years, their adoption in that time has practically been stagnant. Hospitals, already struggling to remain profitable, have chosen to invest in human resources—nurses, physicians, etc.—instead of capital-intensive technologies.

American society is highly environmentally conscious. The social movement of environmental conservation and improvement that became popular at the turn of the millennium was not a short-lived fad. Americans are much more likely to reduce-reuse-and-recycle than before. Sensing this societal trend, companies also focus on making their operations "greener". This has led to an increase in the use of renewable sources of energy as well as higher fuel efficiency automobiles.

Exhibit 9.5: Medford Scenario "Innovo-Nation" (Circa 2010)

Innovo-Nation

The world is more democratic and safer than it was five years ago. The social movements of 2010–11 in African and Middle Eastern nations have led to political reform there. The threat of terrorism has diminished significantly owing in part to targeted crackdowns on terrorist networks facilitated by the treasure trove of information gathered from Osama bin Laden's compound. This has also lessened fears of a disruption in the oil supply and has resulted in lower oil prices.

The US economy has grown steadily since January 2012. This growth has primarily been fueled by innovations in the energy and biotech sectors; market analysts are bullish on the growth of these two sectors. The US unemployment rate continued to drop as the economy grew; it reached below 5% in fall 2013 and has remained there since.

The crowning glory of the second decade of this millennium has been the innovations in biotechnology. Combined with the advances in genetics and computational biology, biotechnology has produced a vast array of biopharmaceuticals that target the underlying causes—not mere symptoms—of many serious diseases. The fruits of mapping the human genome completed more than 10 years ago are also beginning to pay off in the form of gene therapy products. Consolidation in the healthcare sector experienced five years ago has significantly slowed down. Firms prefer to compete as small niche players in emerging industries (such as biotech manufacturing, specialty clinics and pharmacies) because it affords them the agility to rapidly develop and market the products of their emerging technologies. Pharmaceutical companies have staunched their desire to buy small biotech companies, as they realized that the productivity of a biopharmaceutical manufacturer suffers when brought under the bureaucratic control of a large, old-technology pharmaceutical company. The rumor of an impending bitter divorce between Sanofi-Aventis and Genzyme, barely four years since their merger, is one prominent example. Large hospital chains and warehouse pharmacies realized that they have a lot to learn before they can simply acquire the niche clinics and pharmacies specializing in gene therapies.

US healthcare supply chains have become a lot more complex due to the convergence of several factors. Focus on preventive care through patient education has greatly increased the number of locations where healthcare is provided. Pharmacies and hospitals have set up clinics for routine health checkups and cures for common illnesses, and health-consultation centers for getting advice on healthy eating and living choices. "Patient-centered medical homes" are now ubiquitous. Most major retailers and manufacturers have built or acquired internet-based mail-order platforms to ship medicines directly to their consumers. Mail-order has become an attractive channel for patients to acquire drugs. Advances in biotechnology have fostered a proliferation of specialty clinics and pharmacies all over the US. The clinics specialize in different types of biotech treatments, while the pharmacies specialize in handling the sensitive biologic products used in testing as well as treatment. Biotechnology has also enabled patients—especially those with chronic conditions—to treat themselves at home. Home-based healthcare is now ubiquitous. The net result of this is that healthcare is now provided in millions of settings, including traditional settings such as hospitals as well as specialty clinics, retirement homes, and patient's own homes.

However, biologic drugs, which represent a large portion of the drugs used in the US, contain living organisms and need to be maintained in a temperature-controlled climate from the time they are manufactured until they are introduced into a patient's body. In general, there is a heightened awareness and focus on the security and safety of medicines. Firms have to take greater care in ensuring that the pharmaceuticals released into the supply chain are safe for consumption. Different states have created a variety of regulations addressing this issue, adding to the complexity of the supply chain. Overall, this increase in the number of care-delivery locations, volume of temperature-sensitive drugs, and the number of government regulations have made US healthcare supply chains more complex than ever before. An upshot of this increased complexity and a stronger economy for the distributors is that the competition from 3PL providers has withered away. Parcel companies have found plenty of opportunities to grow revenues in their traditional domains, where they don't have to worry about managing the complexities of operating a cold chain and complying with a plethora of climate control regulations.

The sharp rise in the use of biologic drugs, which are generally expensive because of their specialty and sensitive nature, has increased healthcare costs in the US. Healthcare costs are again in the political spotlight, and the healthcare sector is facing high pressure to reduce costs. Firms in all industries of the US healthcare sector are trying to squeeze costs out of their balance sheets. Today, it is rare to find a US hospital that does not have membership in at least one Group Purchasing Organization (GPO). Today, hospitals expect even more cost savings from their GPOs than before. The GPOs, in turn, have started putting more pricing pressure on the manufacturers and distributors they purchase pharmaceuticals from. Manufacturers of branded drugs have been investing more in R&D with the hope of developing new blockbuster drugs to replace the ones whose patent protection expired in the last five years. After a decline in R&D spending in 2009 due to economic slowdown, pharma R&D spending has steadily increased over the last five years, nearing $150 billion globally in 2014. However, this increased R&D spending, coupled with high pricing pressure from the market, has put a serious dent in the manufacturers' short-term profitability.

Even though biopharmaceuticals have grown significantly in the last five years, the total volume of drugs in the market is dominated by generic drugs. This is not a surprise because pharmaceutical manufacturers did not have sufficient patent-protected drugs in the branded drug pipeline to replace the ones that lost patent in the last five years. Any fears of the quality or safety of the generic drugs were allayed by a deliberate effort by the Food and Drug Administration (FDA) to assure people that generic drugs are held to the same high standards and that they have the same performance as their branded equivalents.

As expected, the US population continues to age; the median age today is 37.5 years. About 15% of the 325-plus million Americans are 65 years or older. Just the 47 million residents aged 65 years and older would make the US one of the 30 most populous countries in the world, as populous as Spain, or as Canada and Cuba combined! However, the average US resident is much more health-conscious today than five years ago. S/he is more active, conscious of the food choices and portion sizes, and undergoes regular checkups. This shift has been enabled by various factors, such as the high cost of healthcare, consumer education and nutrition programs (such as Safeway's SimpleNutrition program), as well as the government's policies such as those requiring chain restaurants to display caloric content under the Healthcare Reform of 2010, etc. The number of physician visits by patients continues the steady upward trend observed since the 1990s. However, now the visits are different: the proportion of visits for preventive care (as opposed to corrective care) is significantly higher than any time in the past.

Stemming from the increased awareness among the general population and the policies that encourage preventive care, insurance companies, as well as Medicare/Medicaid, have started to reimburse increasingly for outcomes, not the treatment. Payers have been developing more sophisticated metrics to measure physician quality. The models for measuring outcomes are not perfect but are viewed as having the potential to improve the effectiveness-to-cost ratio of the US healthcare system, often considered to be among the worst among the developed nations.

Unfortunately, at the same time that the population has become more health-conscious, the US healthcare sector is also experiencing a shortage of certain healthcare workers. The nationwide shortage of pharmacists experienced since 2005 continues, primarily because of retirements of pharmacists and active pharmacists choosing to work only part-time. Nurses are also in short supply; staffing ratios in hospitals and clinics have lagged demand. Furthermore, with a large proportion of experienced nurses retiring from the workforce and their replacement coming from fresh graduates, the average tenure among nurses has dropped significantly. There is also an increasing trend of unionization among nurses. The Bureau of Labor Statistics reported that union membership in this group increased from 12.9% in 2000 to 14.8% in 2015. The unionization trend has primarily been observed in hospital settings. However, unlike in other professions, money has not been the primary driver behind the increase in nurse unionization: unionized nurses earned only 14.3% more than their nonunionized counterparts in 2009 (compared to the average of 27.9% union premium). Nurses use collective bargaining primarily to fight mandatory overtime and hiring freezes. The availability of primary care physicians has also kept on dwindling, as a result of their relatively lower-income and shortage of medical resident positions in teaching hospitals.

In the last five years, although computational and biological sciences have continued to make theoretical advances, the conversion of scientific discoveries into practicable technologies has been somewhat stagnant. Until 2011, this was primarily due to the weakness of the US economy. After a five-year hiatus until 2012, firms have slowly started investing in bio-information technologies, but the fruits of those investments haven't yet been realized in the market. The same has happened with electronic medical records (EMR). Hospitals have continued to struggle to remain profitable as healthcare is shifting from acute care to non-acute care settings, and have refrained from making capital investments in technology.

Driven by high-profile recalls of drugs (such as Sudafed, Tylenol, and Coumadin) in the past few years, a higher level of health-consciousness among the average citizens, and the sensitive nature of biopharmaceuticals, there is a heightened focus on the security, safety, and efficacy of medicines. The firms conveying the drugs to the ultimate patient have to ensure that their fidelity is not compromised in the supply chain. Different states have laws for tracking the pedigree of drugs in the supply chain from the manufacturer to the consumer. These pedigree regulations often differ by state. For instance, this variation is seen in the method of tracking pedigree (paper vs. electronic), level of serialization (tracking unit doses vs. boxes), the starting point of pedigree tracking (manufacturer vs. distributor), etc. Following the lead of the US Drug Enforcement Administration, all 50 states and the District of Columbia have now established Prescription Drug Monitoring Programs (PMP) to prevent illegitimate use of prescription drugs. These programs also vary by state: different states monitor different schedules of substances and allow different parties to access a patient's prescription drug utilization data. States have also taken it upon themselves to develop regulations regarding the climate control of biopharmaceuticals and other biotech products in the supply chain. This is a new category of medical treatments and different states have not yet converged on the best way to regulate the safety of these drugs.

The provisions of the Affordable Care Act of 2010, such as guaranteed insurance coverage, a cap on annual deductibles, increased transparency in pricing, subsidized coverage for low-income families are now fully in place. The Affordable Care Act has greatly increased access to healthcare and has brought insurance coverage to every one of the more than 325 million US residents. The consequent increase in the number of people using the health-care system, combined with the increased health-consciousness of the average citizen, has dramatically increased the volume of drugs sold in the US.

Society is also highly environmentally conscious. The turn-of-the-millennium environmental conservation movement was not a short-lived fad. Americans are much more likely than before to reduce, reuse, and recycle. Sensing this societal trend, companies also focus on making their operations "greener". This has led to an increase in the use of renewable sources of energy as well as more fuel efficient automobiles.

Exhibit 9.6: Medford Scenario "Hiber-Nation" (Circa 2010)

Hiber-Nation

Seven years since the global economic crisis, the US economy has still not rebounded to the health it enjoyed in 2006–07. The unemployment rate in the US hovers in the high single digits; the financial condition of those employed is not too rosy either. Over the last five years, per capita disposable income has grown by a meager 2% annually. The staunched supply of a family's income is exacerbated by the high cost of living, primarily led by high energy prices.

The socio-political turmoil in the African and Middle East nations that started in 2010 has created an environment of uncertainty not seen since the last oil crisis. This uncertainty fostered high oil prices globally; the US was no exception. The lukewarm US economy has shrunk the tax revenue of the Federal government. To respond to the rapidly burgeoning budget deficit under the shrinking tax revenues, Congress has resorted to aggressive spending cuts. Medicare and Medicaid budgets have been slashed. Wall Street does not see an optimistic future either; analysts are bearish on the growth of US companies.

In the past seven years, the healthcare sector has continued to experience consolidation within and across industries. In a very slow-growing economy, firms have used horizontal as well as vertical consolidation as a means for growing their revenues. Pharmaceutical companies, struggling to maintain revenues after the expiration of patents on their blockbuster drugs, bought fledgling biotech companies. National pharmacy chains have acquired independent and regional pharmacies, and further strengthened their foothold in the distribution of the drugs directly from manufacturers cutting out distributors. As retailers have encroached on their traditional territory, distributors have resorted to acquiring smaller distributors to maintain and grow their revenue. Very few small and regional distributors remain in the industry. This high level of consolidation in the US healthcare sector over the last decade has left fewer players in the healthcare supply chains. After consolidation, retail pharmacies and clinics shut down the "duplicate" retail outlets in the same geographic area. This has significantly reduced the number of retail pharmacies and clinics in both urban and rural areas, which has in turn reduced the network complexity of US healthcare supply chains. The weaker economy has forced retailers to simplify their supply chain structures and policies to reduce their product variety. They have standardized the assortment of products carried in various retail pharmacies. Pharmacy chains have also developed web-stores, which allow them to aggregate demand from a wide geographic area and reduce variability. All of this has helped to simplify the US healthcare supply chains.

The healthcare sector has witnessed extensive advances in information technology since 2010. Leading IT companies such as Google and Microsoft, as well as a plethora of small and start-up firms, have developed healthcare IT solutions to improve access to information about a patient's health, improve diagnosis accuracy, and simplify business processes. The 2014 National Ambulatory Medical Care Survey, the nation's foremost study of ambulatory care in physicians' offices conducted by the Centers for Disease Control and Prevention, shows that more than 80% of US physicians' offices now have a full or a partial electronic medical records (EMR) or electronic health records (EHR) system in place. This is a significant increase from 50% adoption in 2010 and was partly enabled by the incentives from the Medicare/Medicaid Electronic Health Records Incentive Programs in President Obama's 2009 American Recovery and Reinvestment Act. The adoption rates in the hospitals have been even higher. Software and technology firms have developed a large number of data analytics solutions to use this EMR/EHR data for making better diagnoses and disease prevention decisions for patients. Supplemented by the advances in computational power and cloud-based computing, healthcare informatics is one of the fastest-growing fields today, attracting some of the brightest minds to develop algorithms for faster and more accurate diagnoses using patient data.

The decrease in supply chain complexity achieved through network simplification and product standardization, and the increase in economies of scale enabled by consolidation have helped ease cost pressure in the healthcare sector from the enormously high levels experienced five years ago. Techno-logical advances have contributed significantly to reducing costs as well by simplifying business processes in hospitals, reducing frequency of medical errors, and by making physician and hospital quality visible to patients.

While the cost pressure in the healthcare sector has eased primarily from the actions of the private sector, the continued dismal performance of the economy and the burgeoning budget deficit has forced Congress to cut Medi-care and Medicaid budgets. This has forced many aging workers postpone their retirements and work part-time to get health benefits. Pharmacists are one such group. According to the Pharmacy Manpower Project, 90% of all licensed pharmacists are actively practicing pharmacy—a significant increase from 86% in 2004. This has created a large pool of knowledgeable and expe-rienced pharmacists working in the US healthcare sector. Additionally, there is no longer a shortage of nurses either. The number of first-time US-educated nurses has continued to grow at a little over 7% annually for the last 15 years since 2000. Because of this steady supply of US-educated nurses, more than 3 million registered nurses work in the US healthcare sector today.

The crowning glory of the second decade of this millennium has been innovations in biotechnology. Combined with the advances in related fields such as computational biology and genetics, biotechnology has produced a vast array of biopharmaceuticals that target the underlying targets—not mere symptoms—of many serious diseases. The fruits of mapping the human genome, completed more than ten years ago, are also beginning to pay off in the form of gene therapy products. Sensing the huge potential future market for biologic products, generics manufacturers are working to develop biosim-ilar pharmaceuticals. They are primarily aimed at chronic diseases like diabetes and are in the early stage of development.

Even though biopharmaceuticals have grown significantly in the last five years, the total volume of drugs in the market is still dominated by generics. This is not a surprise because pharmaceutical manufacturers did not have sufficient patent-protected drugs in the branded drug pipeline to replace the ones that lost patent in the last five years. The generic drugs are also more favored by the patients as well as the providers in the present weaker economy. Any fears about the quality or safety of the generic drugs were allayed by a deliberate effort by the Food and Drug Administration (FDA) to assure people that generic drugs are held to the same high standards and have the same performance as their brand-name equivalents.

The biologic products contain living organisms and need to be maintained in a controlled climate from the time they are manufactured until they enter a patient's body. The significant volume of advanced medical treatments in use, and the memory of the high profile drug recalls (such as Sudafed, Tylenol, Coumadin, etc.) have increased awareness and focus on the security and safety of drugs in the supply chain. Firms have to take greater care in ensuring that the pharmaceuticals released into the supply chain are safe for consumption. This means, preventing tampering of the legitimate drugs, maintaining legitimate drugs in the specified climate condition, and preventing the introduction of illegitimate drugs in the supply chain.

The government has taken a larger role in shaping the US healthcare sector. Provisions of the Affordable Care Act of 2010, such as guaranteed insurance coverage, a cap on annual deductibles, transparency in pricing, subsidized coverage for low-income families are now fully in place. Different states have laws for tracking pedigree of drugs in the supply chain from the manufacturer to the consumer to protect patients from contaminated or counterfeit drugs, as well as regulations about climate control in biotech supply chains. Different states have adopted laws that suit their interests best, creating a variety of pedigree laws across different states. This variation is seen in methods of tracking pedigree (paper vs. electronic), levels of serialization (tracking unit doses vs. boxes), the starting points of pedigree tracking (manufacturer vs. distributor), and so on. Following the lead of the US Drug Enforcement Administration, all 50 states and the District of Columbia now have established Prescription Drug Monitoring Programs (PMP) to prevent abuse of prescription drugs. The programs are not uniform across states either: different states monitor different schedules of substances and allow different parties to access a patient's prescription drug utilization data. Regulations about climate control in biotech supply chains also vary across states. As a result, healthcare firms often need to adopt different business processes in different states. Governments have also taken on the responsibility of ensuring drug safety in the supply chain, recognizing that in a weak economy, market forces may not push companies to spend money to ensure drug safety in the supply chain. The consolidation in the distribution sector had resulted in a few large distributors that were deemed too big to fail and essential to operating the country's pharmaceutical supply chains. Government agencies decided it was best in the interest of the public to set up checks to ensure that drugs remain secure. Distributors are no longer held accountable for drug safety.

As expected, the US population continues to age; the median age today is 37.5 years. About 15% of the 325-plus million Americans are 65 years or older. On its own the 47 million residents aged 65 years and older would make the US one of the 30 most populous countries in the world, as populous as Spain, or as Canada and Cuba combined! Furthermore, the Affordable Care Act of 2010 has brought insurance coverage to every one of the more than 325 million US residents. This increase in the number of people using the healthcare system has dramatically increased the volume of drugs sold in the US.

However, the health-consciousness of the average American is no greater than what it was a decade ago. Obesity continues to be a huge problem in the US. The prevalence of obesity among children tends to be even higher. Three-fourths of all US adults are either obese or overweight! Health economists argue that the continued weak US economy has "exacerbated the obesity epidemic" as people are tending to pressing short-term needs at the expense of their health in the long run. However, a small group of economists argues that the reason for the low health-consciousness is not the weak economy, but rather the moral hazard created by the universal insurance coverage provided by the Affordable Care Act: individuals are less careful and responsible for their health knowing that the public or private insurer will pay for any of their health needs. Home-based healthcare has failed to grow as it was expected to five years ago for the same reason. Regardless of the reason, the low health consciousness of the general public is a real and worrisome issue. The number of physician visits by the 15–64 years old has remained flat or slightly declined. Furthermore, when the patients see a doctor, the visits are primarily for treating an ailment, not preventing it. Doctors find this general lack of initiative for one's own health frustrating. Hospitals have less incentive to specialize; they have remained "general," offering low-end services to the cost-conscious public.

Payers (insurance companies and Medicare/Medicaid) continue to make payments for the treatments and services patients receive from the providers. The switch from paying for treatment to outcome has not materialized. The biggest reason for the continuation of this payment basis is the strong opposition from hospitals and pharmacies to switching to outcome-based payments. They argue that it is unfair to base payment for their services on the patients' health instead of the treatment itself when the patients are not very health-conscious and do not take the necessary initiative to maintain a healthy lifestyle.

Society is highly environmentally conscious. The turn-of-the-millennium environmental conservation movement was not a short-lived fad. Americans are much more likely to reduce, reuse, and recycle than before. Sensing this societal trend, companies also focus on making their operations "greener". This has led to an increase in the use of renewable sources of energy as well as more fuel-efficient automobiles.

Exhibit 9.7: Medford Scenario "Zen" (Circa 2010)

Zen

The world is more democratic and safer than it was five years ago. The social movements of 2010–11 in African and Middle Eastern nations have led to political reform there. The threat of terrorism has diminished significantly due to the targeted crackdown on terrorist networks facilitated by the treasure trove of information gathered from Osama bin Laden's compound. This has also lessened fears of a disruption in the oil supply and has resulted in lower oil prices.

The US economy has grown steadily since January 2012. This growth has primarily been fueled by innovations in the energy and biotech sectors, and the market analysts are still bullish on the growth of these two sectors. The US unemployment rate continued to drop as the economy grew; it reached below 5% in Fall 2013 and has remained there since.

The US healthcare supply chains are far less complex than they were in the first decade of the century. The high level of consolidation in the US healthcare sector over the last decade has left fewer players in the healthcare supply chains. After consolidation, retail pharmacies and clinics shut down the "duplicate" retail outlets in the same geographic area. This has significantly reduced the number of pharmacy stores and clinics in both urban and rural areas. US Pharmacy chains have also developed web-stores, which allow them to aggregate demand from a wide geographic area and reduce its variability. Initiatives by the federal and state governments to standardize various regulations (such as those related to pedigree tracking or drug diversion) across states allow companies to design their processes and information-gathering to comply with fewer standard sets of regulations. All of this has greatly simplified the healthcare supply chains in the US.

Consolidation in the healthcare sector, and the resulting decrease in the complexity of the supply chains, has indeed helped lower the cost of delivering healthcare in the US. This has reduced cost pressure from the enormously high levels experienced five years ago. This has helped pharmaceutical distributors change the nature of their competition from cut-throat price competition to service-based differentiation. The Big-3 distributors have managed to distinguish themselves from each other based on their portfolio of services. The rate of consolidation in the healthcare sector experienced over the last five years has also now significantly slowed. Firms prefer to compete as small niche players in emerging industries (such as biotech manufacturing, specialty clinics and pharmacies) because it affords them the agility to rapidly develop and market the products of their emerging technologies. Pharmaceutical companies have staunched their desire to buy small biotech companies, as they realize that the productivity of a biopharmaceutical manufacturer suffers when brought under the bureaucratic control of a large, old-technology pharmaceutical company. The rumor of an impending bitter divorce between Sanofi-Aventis and Genzyme, barely four years since their marriage, is one prominent example. Large hospital chains and warehouse pharmacies realized that they have a lot to learn before they can simply acquire the niche clinics and pharmacies specializing in gene therapies.

The advances in biological sciences have been complemented by advances in information technology. The National Ambulatory Medical Care Survey of 2014, the nation's foremost study of ambulatory care in physicians' offices conducted by the Centers for Disease Control and Prevention, shows that more than 80% of all US physicians' offices now have a full or a partial electronic medical records (EMR) or electronic health records (EHR) system in place. This is a significant improvement from 50% adoption in 2010. Adoption rates in hospitals have been even higher. Software and technology firms have developed a large number of data analytics tools to use this EMR/EHR data for making better diagnoses and disease prevention decisions for patients. Supplemented by the advances in computational power and cloud-based computing, healthcare informatics is one of the fastest-growing fields today.

Advances in information technology have also greatly increased the number of locations where healthcare is provided. Today, patients can get reliable medical advice for advanced diseases from the best doctors located in any part of the world. While the internet had provided the necessary information infrastructure more than a decade ago, the capability to connect patients and physicians in a way that is economically feasible and comfortable for physicians is provided by the business models of web-based firms like AmeriDoc or MedicalWeb. Patients can receive a diagnosis from the comfort of their home and from more than one doctor if desired. Doctors can access a patient's health record online and prescribe medicines electronically, which patients can order from online pharmacies. This has practically turned every computer and mobile phone into a healthcare setting.

While technology allows patients to seek medical advice from any physician of their choice, the availability of healthcare workers such as pharmacists and nurses is scarce. The main reason for this is retirements of pharmacists and a significant portion of active pharmacists choosing to work only part-time. Nurse staffing ratios in hospitals and clinics have lagged the demand. Furthermore, with a large proportion of experienced nurses retiring from the workforce and their replacement coming from fresh graduates, the average tenure among nurses has dropped significantly. There is also an increasing trend of unionization among nurses. The Bureau of Labor Statistics reported that union membership in this group increased from 12.9% in 2000 to 14.8% in 2015. The unionization trend has primarily been in hospital settings. However, unlike in other professions, money has not been the primary driver behind the increase in nurse unionization: unionized nurses earned only 14.3% more than their nonunionized counterparts in 2009 (compared to the average of 27.9% union premium). Nurses use collective bargaining primarily to fight mandatory overtime and hiring freezes. The availability of primary care physicians has also kept dwindling, as a result of their relatively lower income and shortage of medical resident positions in teaching hospitals.

The proportion of generic drugs in the total volume of prescription drugs in the US has not changed significantly in the last six years; generic drugs still constitute about three-fourths of all prescriptions filled in the country. While branded drug patents have expired, the drop in the volume of small-molecule branded pharmaceuticals has been replaced by an increase in the volume of branded biopharmaceuticals. Branded biologic drugs have experienced enormous growth in the last five years, compensating for the revenue lost following the expiration of the traditional branded drugs patents. Furthermore, a significant portion of biotech drugs can now be delivered without cold-chain transportation, thanks to technologies like the sugar-drying technology developed jointly by Nova Bio-Pharma and the University of Oxford for delivering vaccines in African nations that lack a reliable cold chain network. US biotech companies continue to spend research dollars on making all of their products amenable to technologies like sugar-drying storage and distribution. This has kept the volume of drugs requiring cold-chain transportation to a very small fraction of the total volume.

As expected, the US population continues to age; the median age today is 37.5 years. About 15% of the 325-plus million Americans are 65 years or older. On its own the 47 million residents aged 65 years and older would make the US one of the 30 most populous countries in the world, as populous as Spain, or as Canada and Cuba combined! The health consciousness of the average US resident today is about the same as it was five years ago. The focus is generally on fighting diseases with advanced treatments and seeking advice from the best doctors, and not so much on preventing diseases through healthier lifestyle choices. Obesity continues to be a huge problem in the US. The prevalence of obesity among children tends to be even higher. Three-fourths of all US adults are either obese or overweight! The number of physician visits by 15–64 years old has remained flat or slightly declined. Patients' visits to their doctors are primarily for treating an ailment, not preventing it. Doctors find this patients' general lack of initiative for their own health frustrating.

Insurance companies and Medicare/Medicaid have continued to make payments for the treatments and services patients received from the providers. The switch from paying for treatment to outcome has not materialized. The biggest reason for the continuation of this payment basis is the strong opposition from doctors, hospitals, and pharmacies to switching to outcome-based payments. They argue that it is unfair to base payment for their services on the patients' health instead of the treatment itself when the patients are not very health-conscious and do not take the necessary initiative to maintain a healthy lifestyle.

Approximately one in eight Americans are still uninsured, often as a personal choice. The volume of drugs delivered in the US has grown in proportion to the population only and has not seen an enormous increase, as the Affordable Care Act of 2010 got mired in court challenges in many states. The Supreme Court ruling of 2013 repealed one of its key provisions saying "fining individuals for failing to buy insurance is not within the scope of Congress's taxing powers". This was a big victory for the opponents of the Affordable Care Act who viewed it as the federal government overstepping the rights of states and individuals. However, the legal battles between the proponents and opponents of various provisions of the law are still going on, and the Act has not resulted in the sweeping changes in the US healthcare sector everyone expected (or feared). Protracted legal battles involving the healthcare reform have discouraged the federal and state governments from introducing new regulations in the healthcare sector. The regulations on climate control in storage and transportation have been relaxed, especially since a large majority of the biologic drugs can be delivered without a cold chain due to revolutionary technologies. Regulations on drug prices have also taken a back seat; drug prices are far more obscure to parties other than the transacting partners. A secondary effect of the legal battles is that the federal government and individual states have made efforts to make the existing regulations more uniform across states to create an environment that facilitates interstate commerce. For the pedigree regulations, this has greatly reduced the variation in the methods of tracking pedigree (paper vs. electronic), level of serialization (tracking unit doses vs. boxes), the point where pedigree tracking begins (manufacturer vs. distributor), etc. across different state laws. Similarly, following the lead of the US Drug Enforcement Administration, all 50 states and the District of Columbia now have established a uniform Prescription Drug Monitoring Program (PMP) to prevent illegitimate use of prescription drugs.

Even though the government's participation in the healthcare sector has been scaled back significantly, this, by no means, is a world where drug security and safety issues are ignored. High-profile recalls of medicines (such as Sudafed, Tylenol, and Coumadin) have put a spotlight on the security and safety of drugs in the supply chain. Firms have to take greater care in ensuring that the pharmaceuticals released into the supply chain are safe for consumption and that their fidelity is not compromised. The media campaign by the National Institute of Drug Abuse for the abuse of prescription drugs has created awareness of the problem among the youth and parents. Coordinated efforts by the federal and state prescription drug monitoring programs have helped staunch the supply of prescription drugs for nonmedical purposes.

Society is highly environmentally conscious. The turn-of-the-millennium environmental conservation movement was not a short-lived fad. Americans are much more likely to reduce, reuse, and recycle than before. Sensing this societal trend, companies also focus on making their operations "greener". This has led to an increase in the use of renewable sources of energy as well as more fuel-efficient automobiles.

Exhibit 9.8: Future Freight Flows Scenario "Global Marketplace" (Circa 2009)

This is a mercurial and hyper-competitive world. Trade takes place openly and vigorously among virtually all nations. Market-based approaches are used to face most contemporary challenges.

We are living in an exceptionally fast-paced, highly connected, and volatile world. The speed of every facet of life has been increasing year over year for the last several decades. Time is viewed as the scarcest commodity for people and businesses alike. In order to keep up with all of this rapid change, companies are constantly on the lookout across the globe to find the best talent, spot the newest trends, and identify new markets to serve and vendors to source from.

This, in turn, has led to a general consensus that the world is more connected than ever before. Imports and exports are both on the rise for most countries. In fact, global exports are three times higher than they were at the turn of the century; now representing over 60% of the global GDP. While there are still sporadic outbreaks of localized conflicts, the last 30 years have been relatively peaceful. This is due, in no small part, to the level and breadth of global trade.

Not only are physical products flowing freely between countries, but too are ideas, money, and, notably, people. Immigration has skyrocketed across the globe, resulting in a much greater exchange of cultures, languages, and customs. The percentage of US citizens fluent in two or more languages has tripled over the last 25 years. Large global or multinational firms have become melting pot for society at large. Two out of every three employees of Global Fortune 500 firms are working in a country other than that of their citizenship.

The interconnectedness and speed of this global market are not without negative effects, however. For example, the level of volatility in all aspects of business has increased dramatically. A labor strike in South Korea, say, can have huge ripple effects in a manufacturing plant in Brazil. This "butterfly effect" is exceptionally hard to detect ahead of time—so the frequency and magnitude of these disruptions continue to increase. As a result, firms are taking extensive precautions and steps to keep the flow of goods both smooth and secure.

There is also tremendous volatility in commodity prices. Trade barriers between countries are at an all-time low, which means that raw materials and commodities can be procured from all over the world. This increases the level of competition and reduces the ability of any local supplier to sustain a geographically based monopoly. In today's world, price—rather than accessibility—is the key criterion for choosing a commodity, product, or supplier.

The collaboration between firms across national boundaries has further expanded regional markets to the point where they have overlapped and blended into a single, global market. US firms have established and maintained intense collaboration with companies across the world. Affordable and seamless supply chains are encouraging companies to invest in global manufacturing capabilities, with most large firms using a mix of off-shore and nearshore plants to remain low-cost and flexible. Vertically integrated firms are more the exception than the rule. The cost of moving goods anywhere in the world is very reasonable, primarily due to new and cheaper energy sources and technologies, and non-obtrusive environmental regulations. Energy costs, although relatively low, remain extremely volatile because of the continual natural and man-made supply disruptions of oil-based fuels.

Because the world is a single market, countries succeed by exploiting their specific comparative advantage. Countries and regions tend to specialize in producing what they do best and rely on other countries—halfway across the world in some cases—for everything else they need. Traditional powerhouses such as Japan, Germany, and the United States no longer control the capabilities and resources needed to manufacture highly specialized, high-value products. Although developing countries are not at par with the advanced nations yet, they have found niches and are investing heavily in developing their industrial competencies.

Faced with so many choices, customers have become increasingly fickle in their tastes. Customers today expect to have an infinite SKU selection coupled with immediate delivery. This has had many consequences. For example, retail sales are predominantly conducted online, even for grocery and low-value consumer packaged goods items. With web-based storefronts, retail firms can be (and are) located virtually anywhere in the world. The individual or "eaches" size of these web-based purchases has increased the level of local parcel delivery. With a significant proportion of the US population living in large and dense cities, this individual delivery to residences is the cause of much of the congestion within urban areas. Last-minute postponement for final product customization is now common practice.

Even with the dominance of the market and industry, governments still play an active and vital role. Many citizens believe that one of the government's main jobs is to minimize those regulations that prohibit or hinder global commerce; to act as guard rails keeping firms on the right track rather than speed bumps slowing them down. This is reflected in the fact that the average number of regulations affecting a typical international business transaction has been cut in half over the last two decades. Intellectual property protection and enforcement of the Rule of Law are also on the rise globally.

This positive view is not universal, however. It is said by cynics that, in this brave new world, "the only regulation is that there are no regulations." Sizable segments of the population believe that too much of government policy is overly corporate directed with little protection for the environment, safety, health, or the poor and disadvantaged citizens. Many people feel disenfranchised and the level of income inequality has been stubbornly high for decades.

In this world, the private sector has taken the lead in addressing the pressing issues of the day. Any attempt by governments to get involved in regulating business is seen as an unwelcome intrusion. Citizens generally trust markets as the most efficient way to operate a market and they are more than willing to allow them to 'work their magic.' So far, their patience and confidence in the market forces have paid off. A case in point is the now routine hassle-free immigration across most nations and the dramatic increase in global food production.

Exhibit 9.9: Future Freight Flows Scenario "One World Order" (Circa 2009)

 Facing global scarcity of key resources, nations establish international rules to ensure their fair and sustainable use. Global trade thrives, but its course is shaped by the very visible hand of regulation, at times an iron fist in a velvet glove.

It has become clear that oil production has peaked. Renewable energy technologies have failed to live up to the heightened expectations of replacing coal and oil. The environmental crisis faced by the world's population has taken on an urgent dimension, as looming scarcity of resources increases social and political tensions both within and across nations. Policy avenues are aggressively pursued at a global level to ensure equitable access to clean air, drinkable water and healthy food for vast populations across the world, as well as access to the raw materials and energy required to sustain their communities.

Fearing conflicts and war over the growing scarcity of vital resources, the governments of the most powerful countries come together to create a supranational entity, the World Sustainable Trade Organization (WSTO), to regulate the use of resources and resolve disputes among nations. While many see the WSTO as a replacement for the World Trade Organization, it is in fact much stronger than the WTO ever was. The WSTO reaches far beyond trade and has been given real teeth for strict enforcement. Also, through monitoring and reporting, it dictates efficiency and penalizes waste, prioritizing usage according to global needs. All world powers and most other countries have signed the charter of the WSTO, and are working towards full compliance with its regulatory framework.

Paradoxically, and despite the forecasts of detractors, global trade has not only remained strong, but it has actually continued to thrive in this heavily regulated world. The regulation-based system of balancing availability and needs did not replace the traditional market-based system of balancing supply and demand. Instead, it has redefined the boundaries of the free market, therefore complementing it in unexpected ways. For example, grains are shipped from greener regions where they are produced in abundance to places where the land is not fertile. Metals are shipped in the opposite direction, from the arid yet mineral-rich countries towards the agricultural foci of the world. Technology and labor follow a similar pattern: less developed countries serve as providers of young labor for more technologically advanced countries, which in turn export their technology and knowledge back to developing countries in the form of finished goods and services. Many analysts describe the new system as one of "global optima" for the long run, where the objective is sustainable use, not just short-term corporate profits.

What gives shape to trade flows is not the invisible hand of the market, but a very visible body of regulations. These are seen by many as a 'green bureaucracy,' a necessary nuisance. At the end of the day, while individual firms still get to make - for the most part - their own decisions as to what to produce and where, it is in the how that the influence of the WSTO's global bureaucracy and its ever-growing tapestry of regulations play an influential role, sending the right signals to the market: how much water can be used, how much carbon diaoxide can be emitted, how discards should be recycled, etc. As a result, the speed of global trade - once mercurial and chaotic in the days of globalization - has slowed down into an optimized order, more entangled in regulations and quotas, yet less volatile and—in consequence—more predictable.

Forged by the struggle for survival of globalized markets, firms have adapted relatively quickly to the new demands of a regulated world. Tracking and offsetting greenhouse gases, even to the level of zero emissions, is now a prerequisite for doing business. Manufacturers with similar needs have grouped together to create large-scale facilities, known as production clusters, where they find relief in numbers. They have found it is more cost-effective to comply with tight regulations when the cost of required technology can be shared by many. Production clusters, coupled with ultra-efficient supply chains that make use of sensing and advanced computing, are emerging as the greenest solution.

Regulations for urban areas have also forced local governments to adapt. Through a series of stick-and-carrot regulations, the WSTO has sent municipalities a clear message: cities must clean up their act, too. Regulations promote more efficient use of energy and water in urban areas, a reduction in transportation emissions, and a more effective treatment of waste and sewage. The largest cities in the world now compete for subsidies and try to avoid penalties, on the basis of improving their performance against a series of sustainability indexes. As a result, large cities have continued to grow even bigger, even as they strive to make their environmental footprint smaller and easier to offset.

Regulators have become aware that online purchasing has a much higher carbon footprint than shopping in person. In order to offset the higher per-pound emissions of home delivery, most urban municipalities have mandated that parcel carriers charge customers a flat tax on all home deliveries. The effect of this tax is felt more on smaller, cheaper packages. Since for consumers it makes little sense to pay a $5 tax for the home delivery of a $10 book, most large cities have seen the appearance of consolidation centers, where goods from many retailers are consolidated and delivered to the final customer only when a certain amount of products have accumulated. This has radically changed the last-mile delivery of goods in metropolitan areas.

Exhibit 9.10: Future Freight Flows Scenario "Naftástique!" (Circa 2009)

Naftástique!

World trade shifts away from a single global market as a small number of large regional trading blocs emerge. China, Europe, and South America form their own economic clusters. The United States joins with Mexico and Canada to make North America a self-sufficient economic community.

A scarcity of critical natural resources, coupled with continued growth of the world's population, has restricted the ability of most nations to provide for their citizens. Basic commodities have become scarce and prices have risen accordingly. Relationships among world powers are strained by prolonged and intense competition for raw materials and energy sources. While there is persistent, and sometimes intense, political tension between many countries, direct military actions have been minimal. Inward facing policies designed to protect dwindling resources have served to reduce and fragment global trade. In response to this, a small number of very large regional trading blocs have emerged across the globe.

The trading blocs have been defined not by physical walls outlining their territory, but by the simultaneous presence of trade barriers hindering commerce across the blocs —such as high tariffs on imports, complicated customs procedures— and elimination of barriers to commercial activity among countries within a bloc. Such policies have naturally incentivized businesses to seek partners within their own bloc to meet their resource needs as much as possible. It is faster, easier, and cheaper to obtain goods and personnel from within one's own bloc.

China, for example, has forged a particularly intense alliance with countries in Africa. Many African nations, rich in natural resources and desperate for investments and new technology, found a natural partner in the resource-starved and over-populated China. Intense trade of materials, technology, and labor started taking place inside this Sino-African economic bloc, with the Yuan as the de facto currency.

Other regional blocs have emerged over the last 30 years. The European bloc, having survived the crisis of the "twenty-teens," has emerged stronger than ever. It has developed strong trading partnerships with both Russia and the Middle East to access natural resources. Powerhouse Brazil led the Mercosur bloc; Japan, Korea, and Southeast Asian nations have similarly formed a Pacific bloc. Smaller countries were forced to ally themselves with existing blocs to keep their economies alive. However, a few larger nations like India, Venezuela, and Australia decided to remain 'unaligned' to any particular bloc and trade with all clusters.

The United States formed its own bloc along with Canada and Mexico, called the North American Economic Community (NAMEC). Complementing each other in natural resources, technological capabilities, and workforce availability, NAMEC has emerged as a strong economic cluster. Commerce among NAMEC nations has increased tremendously. US borders with Canada and Mexico are essentially seamless for freight and passenger movements. Widespread use of the vast domestic reserves of natural gas and coal, and heavy investment in renewable sources, made the North American nations almost totally independent of foreign oil. While energy prices inside NAMEC tend to be higher than the historical averages, they are also significantly less volatile than in the past.

The United States undertook a re-domestication of manufacturing to NAMEC countries, with a clear emphasis on promoting processes that take advantage of local resources and talent. Unemployment in all member nations has fallen as more manufacturing and other jobs are re-patriated to North America. Advanced communication and manufacturing technologies enable more efficient production closer to the population centers..

Migration among NAMEC nations has become fluid. Cross-NAMEC work visas are issued for millions of young workers from the United States, Canada, Mexico, and other Latin American member countries. Millions of aging Americans retire to Mexico and Canada. This influx of retirees has made some parts of the Mexican coastline the "New Florida," creating new demand south of the border for higher-value goods and services. The mixing of the different member countries within NAMEC has led to a higher percentage of the United States population speaking more than one language. While a majority of US citizens still only speak English, a sizable (and growing) percentage is bilingual—primarily with Spanish as the second language.

Environmental concerns are driven from the bottom-up by the activism of the consumers inside the blocs and embodied into regulations that favor the energy sources used in that bloc. Previously disparate environmental regulations in Mexico, the United States, and Canada have been standardized into a stricter corpus of rules. However, environmental regulations vary greatly across different blocs, as the member countries of each bloc enact the regulations that protect the environment while allowing the bloc to remain self-sufficient to meet its energy demands. Rising temperatures have increased the agricultural output of countries located in higher latitudes. In North America, Canada's production of grains and other agricultural products has increased dramatically. So far, however, the global increase in temperatures has had a very limited impact on coastal cities and in the operation of maritime ports.

Fixed currency exchange rates are established within the blocs, which in turn has stabilized currency fluctuations across blocs. While the majority of global trade is conducted within regional trading blocs, there is still some trade between the blocs. This inter-bloc trade is, however, mostly limited to supplementing technologies and materials that are not available in member nations. Many are surprised that despite the lack of a truly global market the regional clusters manage to operate as self-contained trade systems. Inside each of these blocs, trade links have led to stronger political links and a sense of shared purpose. Member nations take pride in working together towards self-sufficiency.

Exhibit 9.11: Future Freight Flows Scenario "Millions of Markets" (Circa 2009)

Through advanced technological breakthroughs, the United States becomes highly self-reliant in terms of energy, agriculture, manufacturing, and other needs. There is increased migration towards smaller urban areas that are supported by nearby regional innovation hubs that can manufacture highly customized goods.

The last three decades have been witness to tremendous technological advances and social changes that have led to a high level of regional self-reliance in matters of energy, health, food production, and manufacturing. Not only has the United States as a whole become highly self-sufficient, but individual regions and cities have also become much more self-sustaining. The primary drivers of these changes were technical breakthroughs that are collectively referred to now as the "Three Pillars."

The first pillar is abundant and low-cost energy. Advances in drilling techniques and improved seismic testing enabled the economical location, capture, and production of tremendous quantities of natural gas from the massive shale formations across the United States. Renewable energy sources, such as solar and wind power, have also increased the total United States energy production. The net effect is some of the world's cheapest, safest, and most stable electricity production. The lower cost of producing electricity contributed to the almost universal adoption of first hybrid and then electronic vehicles.

The second pillar is the widespread use of intelligent manufacturing to include 3D printing, flexible robotics, and other advanced manufacturing techniques. These advances enabled the production of small to medium batches of a wide variety of products at reasonable costs. Essentially, the cost advantages of leveraging economies of scale that dominated manufacturing throughout the last several decades of the twentieth century were replaced for many products by the ability to cheaply produce a wide range of highly customized products. While manufacturing has not advanced to the stage of "home replicators" that local maker enthusiasts once envisioned, it has led to the development of regional manufacturing hubs across the country. These manufacturing facilities are close to consumption centers and are fueling the expectations of consumers for the rapid creation and delivery of highly personalized goods. A key innovation that transformed the manufacturing industry was the separation of digital design from the physical production process. This has in turn led to the creation of a new industry sector of pure digital design firms that develop and sell small-run or custom designs.

The third technological advancement was the widespread adoption and use of virtualization. Working and shopping from home—or from any other location—has become the standard rather than the exception for many people. Most households order products and services directly from the home and receive them there as well. Online shopping with prompt delivery to residences has largely replaced physical stores. People still go shopping in person—but the retail experience has evolved into an event rather than just a way to acquire physical products—similar to how movie theaters adapted when home entertainment systems were introduced. As goods and services have become more mobile than people, there is less physical commuting to work. Ironically, the level of travel for pleasure has increased since a large percentage of the workforce can work from any location.

A social change that has emerged over the last several decades is the increase in social interaction—both virtually and in person. It appears that while people can now work and live totally isolated from other humans, very few actually do. Instead, there has been a groundswell migration towards "livable cities" of a moderate size where people can enjoy the benefits of interacting with others in an urban setting without the overwhelming congestion and other drawbacks of an impersonal mega-city. As these mid-sized cities continue to grow, however, pockets of exceptionally high-density residential and commercial space are being created that mimic some of the problems and challenges faced by mega-cities—albeit at a smaller scale.

In this widely fragmented, yet highly connected, society, small and mid-sized cities are growing at a faster rate than the megacities. Local governments compete with each other to attract investments to create "innovation clusters" that feature a mix of technology, manufacturing, and distribution facilities.

Technological advancements and cheaper energy have ushered in a new age of affluence: average household income has increased, personal consumption has soared, and standards of living have improved. It is not a technology utopia, however. The income gap has widened between the traditional "blue-collar", "white-collar", and the newly established "no-collar" creative class. Many traditional jobs have been displaced and those workers struggle to find new vocations. This is especially true for older workers who are not as able to adapt to newer technologies. Government programs and regulations at the federal, and more commonly, state and local levels have been introduced to minimize this gap—with limited success.

Also, while new agricultural techniques, mainly genetically modified fruits, vegetables, fish, and livestock have significantly increased the quantity and variety of food products available to consumers, there has been a significant amount of resistance from some sectors of the population. Food considered "Absolutely Organic" is generally available, but at a much higher cost. There are also still lingering suspicions in some parts of society over the safety of hydraulic fracking for natural gas.

In this fast-paced environment, the optimal production site is closer to consumption centers. The affluent and savvy buyers of this world demand products customized to their needs and tastes. While American consumers prefer locally produced goods, they are not inherently against foreign products, provided they meet their high expectations of personalization and delivery speed.

Trade between countries is still active, but for the first time in history, the value of imported and exported services exceeds that of goods. The United States is a net exporting country when considering services, such as digital designs. Physical trade still occurs, but at a lower level and in different forms. For example, global trade of raw materials has increased while transportation of finished goods has decreased. Raw materials and components are transformed into goods when and where demanded by the final consumer. In addition, intellectual property that is used within most local manufacturing is traded freely across the globe, although there are some risks concerning theft of these "recipes" and instructions in certain areas of the world.

Exhibit 9.12: Graphic Presentation of Freight Infrastructure Segments Created by the MIT Team for the WSDOT Future Freight Flows Workshop

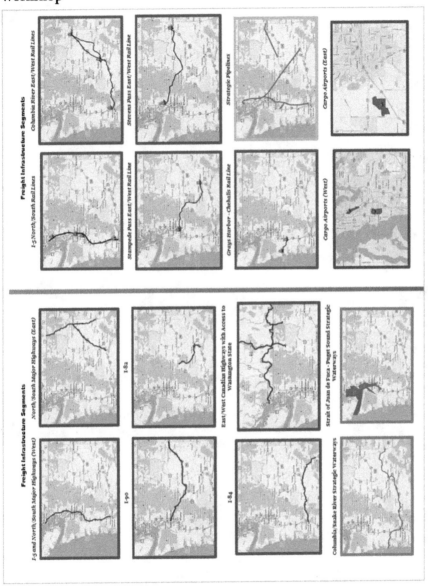

Index

© The Editor(s) (if applicable) and The Author(s), under exclusive
license to Springer Nature Switzerland AG 2022
S. S. Phadnis et al., *Strategic Planning for Dynamic Supply Chains*,
Palgrave Executive Essentials,
https://doi.org/10.1007/978-3-030-91810-1